TOO YOUNG THE HEROES

T0040465

TOO YOUNG THE HEROES

*A World War II Marine's Account
of Facing a Veteran Enemy
at Guadalcanal,
the Solomons and Okinawa*

George Lince

McFarland & Company, Inc., Publishers
Jefferson, North Carolina, and London

The present work is a reprint of Too Young the Heroes: A World War II Marine's Account of Facing a Veteran Enemy at Guadalcanal, the Solomons and Okinawa, *first published in softcover in 1997 by McFarland.*

Frontispiece: The author home from the war, Rome, New York, 1946

LIBRARY OF CONGRESS CATALOGUING-IN-PUBLICATION DATA

Lince, George, 1926 —
    Too young the heroes : a World War II marine's account of
facing a veteran enemy at Guadalcanal, the Solomons and Okinawa
/ by George Lince.
        p.   cm.
    Includes bibliographical references and index.

    ISBN 978-0-7864-7607-7
    softcover : acid free paper ∞

    1. Lince, George, 1926 —   2. World War, 1939–1945 —
Campaigns — Pacific Area.   3. World War, 1939–1945 — Personal
narratives, American.   4. United States. Marine Corps — Biography.
5. Marines — United States — Biography.   I. Title.
D767.9.L56   2013
940.54'26 — dc21   97-273

BRITISH LIBRARY CATALOGUING DATA ARE AVAILABLE

© 1997 George Lince. All rights reserved

*No part of this book may be reproduced or transmitted in any form
or by any means, electronic or mechanical, including photocopying
or recording, or by any information storage and retrieval system,
without permission in writing from the publisher.*

On the cover: The author at 18, already a combat veteran of Okinawa; seal of the United States Marine Corps

Manufactured in the United States of America

McFarland & Company, Inc., Publishers
    Box 611, Jefferson, North Carolina 28640
        www.mcfarlandpub.com

CONTENTS

I DEDICATE THIS BOOK to my mother and father, George Wayne Lince and Frieda Florence Lince, for life, love and success; my wife, Margaret Jean Lince, for faith, dedication, love and support; my brother, Gerald Kenneth Lince, for faith in me; my brothers-in-life, Robert Lince (deceased) and Raymond Lince, for companionship, love and happiness; my special son James George Lince, for happiness and a satisfaction of being a father; my daughter Catherine Marie Ledford, for being a faithful daughter and a model mother; my daughter Virginia Florence Colwell, for the motivation of writing; my daughter Marie Margaret (deceased), in remembrance of love; my daughter, Jeanne Ann, and my son, Timothy Wayne, for youthful memories; my grandson Lt. Mathew Lince (USN) for his support; my young grandchildren, Suzanne Marie Lince, Janet Margaret Lince, Curtis Elliott Ledford, and Travis Evan Ledford, who make being a grandfather a life-satisfying happy time; my adult grandchildren, Matt, Robert, Eric, Kristina, Jonathan, Bryan, Chris, Joey, and Danny, who gave me love and happiness in their youth; and my great grandchildren, Rebecca, Nicolas and Jennifer.

I also dedicate it to all United States Marines, living and dead, especially those who gave their young lives for our freedom on Okinawa; to Corp. Leo H. Dettor, USMC; Corp. Hugh E. Graham, Jr., USMC; PFC Richard P. Humenick, USMC; PFC Donald C. Jensen, USMC; Corp. John B. Martin, USMC; Corp. Calvin R. Mosher, USMC; 1st Lt. Robert Romo, USMC; Sgt. James A. Satterwhite, USMC; PFC Edward L. Smith, Jr., USMC; Pvt. Bruce Treatt, USMC; Pvt. Paul R. Timothy, USMC; Pvt. Walter G. Watrous, USMC; PHM3 Michael R. Nowakowski, USN; Norman C. Brown, US Army; Pvt. Jack A. Dunn, USMC; T/Sgt. Frank Janik, US Army; James Leslie Simms, US Army; and to all the young marines I knew by their face or their nickname only.

I dedicate it to a living memorial marine family, Major Michael Woodman, his wife, Michele, and their children, Shawna, Danielle, Kristen, and Kimberly.

I dedicate it to special marines James A. Cox, Walden Mahan, James C. Dorn, G.G. Martin, and Bill Siegfried.

I dedicate it to all my classmates and friends who gave their lives in World War II; and to all the people of Okinawa; and to my writing team support, Jo Anna Petropoulos and Donna Wenzel.

INTRODUCTION

My story is an attempt to both entertain and educate. By relating my experience, I hope to show the reader something about how teenagers react to war and the aftermath of face-to-face combat. In their normal youthful upbringing, few understand the responsibility of defending the freedom that they enjoy with their family and friends. When this responsibility is suddenly thrust upon them, the shock can produce mental disturbances and abnormal character changes. The uneducated American populace tends to respond to war with the repeated question, "What happened to Johnnie?" If Johnnie dies bodily, there are no questions to be answered. However, what happens to Johnnie when his youth dies mentally on the battlefield? For the young soldier, the question may never be answered.

For Johnnie, often labeled a victim of circumstance, those who benefit from his sacrifices never seem to express real appreciation. In my story I ask, why the indifference to deeds that should have a life lasting reward of appreciation and gratitude? Did the lack of bombs dropping on the main streets of America allow people to believe that war was an exercise in gallantry and splendor? Did our movies, historians, and the uniformed nonparticipant in front-line combat paint a picture of romantic interludes that distorted the truths about the horror of war?

My attempt is to express personal, youthful feelings that I believe were shared by my comrades, all of whom were heroes to the Nth degree, never abandoning their love of life. The love that was engraved into their spirit by the love expressed and maintained in the American home gave them the bravery that led them to victory. Heroes all! Cowards none!

1

THE BEGINNING

The Jap shells tore unmercifully and indiscriminately into dirt, metal, and flesh alike, hell-bent on destroying the youth of America. Thick, choking clouds of green smoke accompanied each explosion. A panicked cry, "Corpsman!" alerted all of us to the frightening reality that a marine had been hit by the deadly flying shrapnel.

We advanced over the hill, and, with the almost surrealistic magnifying vision that comes with the surges of adrenaline, I saw my first dead marine. My 18-year-old mind saw these horrors and registered them as the actual, inescapable results of the deadly game we were engaged in. I didn't want to play anymore; I wanted my marbles back, and I wanted to go home.

Where was the war I enlisted for? The one where John Wayne was rested and clean, and the girls were standing in line to kiss him? He was never dirty, lonely, and frightened, only filled with an incredible energy. John Wayne never begged for water or had the flesh hanging from his neck in raw strips. He never got bloody feet and never had to crawl through thick, black mud. John Wayne always managed a good night's sleep, and his head never drooped in exhaustion. Where were the marching bands, the flags, and the girls? Most of all, where were the cheers of the grateful population? That was all back at the movie theater. I had shown up for the wrong war.

In 1938, I was a junior high school student in Rome, New York. Dark clouds of war were spreading over Europe. The greedy, grasping tendrils reached out to engulf the rest of the world. Japan had been ravishing Asia systematically since 1932, and, in Europe, war had begun in earnest when Germany invaded Poland in September 1939. As Europe became more and more embroiled in war, Japan planned further expansion into the Pacific, the ultimate goal being global domination. America's full involvement in this conflict would not occur until the year 1941, when Japan would make the deadly and ultimately self-destructive error of attacking Pearl Harbor on December 7, 1941. This brutal show of overconfidence would prove to be their undoing. In 1942, the Japanese would taste defeat for the first time since 1932, at the hands of American marines. The marines would never lose a battle in World War II, where uncommon valor was a common virtue. The Rising Sun would begin to set. Never once did I foresee my part in Japan's widespread pursuit of political domination.

But the United States government was so anxious to avoid war that it accepted the "mistake" theory, together with an indemnity. When it did so, a sigh of relief passed over America. In a Gallup poll conducted during the second week of January 1938, 70 percent of the American voters who were interviewed and had an opinion on the subject favored a policy of complete withdrawal from China, including the Asiatic Fleet, marines, missionaries, medical missions, and all.

At the beginning, while the Axis powers were priming their youth for the killing, cruelty and devastation that comes with war, we confined our youthful activities to an enjoyable, happy, worry-free life. We cheerfully made full use of our personal rights of liberty and pursuit of happiness, blissfully unaware of the inescapable collision course between the two worlds. Neither the generals nor the stately leaders, with their weapons and careful military planning, would determine the results of this conflict. The outcome would be decided in large part by the actions and abilities of all of us innocent, unprepared, apple-pie-loving, girl-chasing "Mommy-boys" in the meeting between us and our counterparts overseas. Band leaders Benny Goodman and Glenn Miller were the heroes, the role models, of the day; not a thought was spared for the likes of General MacArthur and Admiral Nimitz. This lack of preparation would seem to spell easy victory for the opposing forces and their respective dictators. However, youth, strength, and love of country would prove a formidable opponent to the hatred and cruelty utilized by the enemy. The outcome of this war would validate the theory of "Right over might."

I remember starting my first drafting class in junior high school in 1938. We were all quiet and reserved on our entry into class. "Prof" Cardoff demanded the utmost in seriousness and discipline. There was no excuse for foolish behavior in his class, even though we were still children. I was still in knickers with garters holding up the long stockings. I could not wear long pants until I reached the age of 13. Christmas would provide me with my first pair of trousers and would mark the beginning of my teenage life.

Prof. Cardoff was from the "old school" where respect, integrity, excellence, discipline, and dignity were all combined into a singular, very wise personality. He was a strong character and would brave freezing, thirty-degree-below-zero weather with bald head defiantly uncovered, daring the cold to override the strict discipline he had over mind and body. His only mode of transportation, his feet, propelled him in long strides. His motto for continued health and dexterity was "Keep your feet dry and your head bare." This prescription for life was unchallenged; he never missed a beat in his responsibilities. He was much more than just a teacher of scholastic subjects. He brought his own unique vision and personality into his classroom, where some of it was transferred to his young students. Being late to his class was equal to committing the original sin. The rattle of loose glass in the door being closed by a trembling hand, invading his concentration, would bring an instant icy stare. Failure, in any form, was a stranger to Prof Cardoff, and he expected it to be that way for students also. Untidy dress and unkempt hair were unheard of. Such sloppiness in appearance could only lead to a correspondingly slovenly attitude. Climbing the old, worn steps in the school, where so many had gone before, gave a feeling of security and stability and knowledge that this was right, this was where you belonged. Dropping out was unimaginable. Prof Cardoff, as much a part of that school as those well-worn stairways, was instrumental in giving countless youths purpose and pride in life.

The very first thought of war was brought into our minds in one short statement made by Prof Cardoff: "All you young boys will become involved in the greatest war the world has ever known." We were momentarily subdued, and there was no discussion after class. Maybe we all knew, in some primitive corner of our minds, that this was the horrible truth, and there was no escaping from it. However, we recovered quickly (as young ones do) from this serious forecast, and by the end of the day, we no longer gave it any thought. It was a prophecy not to be fulfilled until many years later.

Historian Samuel E. Morison begins his examination of the war in the Pacific with the words of St. James:

> *From whence come wars and fightings among you? Come*
> *they not hence, even of your lusts that war in your members?*
> *Ye lust, and have not: ye kill, and desire to have, and cannot*
> *obtain: ye fight and war, yet ye have not...*
> *James 4:1–2*

Saint James may not have been the brightest of the Twelve Apostles, but in these trenchant words he announced a fundamental cause of all war that is particularly applicable to World War II. Two nations which regarded themselves as "have nots" fought and made war to obtain what they wanted and, owing to the weakness or shortsightedness of their immediate neighbors, won a series of astounding victories. But their own cruelty and oppression aroused the rest of the world against them, and in the end they had less than nothing.

No historian, however, may assume the complete righteousness of his nation, or the inevitability of a war. He must ask himself whether a wiser statesmanship might not have averted, or at least postponed, a conflict which brought so much misery to the world, burdened his own country with responsibilities it never wished to assume, and opened up a dark prospect for the future civilization.

The Japanese and American peoples had very different sets of values, each derived from a long past; yet their interests did not clash and their formal relations remained generally cordial for more than fifty years. Through numerous writings and personal contacts, Americans had learned to appreciate the peculiar virtues of the Japanese and they in turn regarded the United States as their best friend in the outside world. The work of Commodore Perry and Townsend Harris in bringing Japan out of a precarious isolation into the comity of nations, even saving her perhaps from dismemberment by European powers, was generously appreciated in Japan and often acknowledged. In the Russo-Japanese War American opinion was uniformly anti–Russian, and the mediation of President Theodore Roosevelt probably saved Japan from defeat. The United States and Japan were associates in World War I and, although acute differences between them developed at the peace conference, both countries made concessions. Japan gave up Shantung and the United States placed the Philippines on the road to independence. The naval limitation treaties, with their nonfortification clauses, seemed to postpone indefinitely all causes of conflict. Economic relations between the two countries were mutually profitable; each produced raw materials and manufactures that the other wanted. No American group or set of interests wanted war with Japan; on the contrary, aversion to such a war was so strong that only a long series of provocations, culminating in the treacherous attack on Pearl Harbor, made war possible.

Why, then, did Japan attack America? The immediate occasion, as we well know, was the Far Eastern policy of the United States, seeking first by persuasive diplomacy and finally by economic sanctions to restore peace and union to distracted China, as against a Japanese policy that aimed to conquer and control that immense country.

Japan was the only important nation in the world in the twentieth century that combined modern industrial power and a first-class military establishment with religious and social ideas inherited from the primitive ages of mankind, which exalted the military profession and regarded war and conquest as the highest good. True, the country possessed an intellectual élite who had accepted the Christian ethic if not the Christian religion, and attempted to guide the Japanese nation into the ways of peace; but those Western ideals vaguely comprehended under the term "democracy" had made so little dent on the people at large that they were swept away by a self-conscious and active group of military extremists.

The crucial decade was that of the 1920's, and the field of conflict was Japan itself. Japanese militarists, seeing their traditional primacy undermined by civilian elements, and their dreams of conquest vanishing, deliberately provoked the "Manchuria Incident" to reestablish their power. When *Hakko Ichiu*—"bringing the eight corners of the world under one roof," [the goal of] the probably mythical Emperor Jimmu around the year 600 B.C.— was resurrected in 1931 as a slogan of national policy, it was signal that the old Japan had won.

Thus the long-run effect of these well-meant efforts by the Anglo-American powers to prevent an armaments race merely turned Japanese opinion against them, and provoked reactionary, militarist elements in Japan to desperate measures, in order to create a state of national emergency which would overwhelm the civilian and liberal elements of the nation.

An ideological movement deliberately promoted to prepare the way for an overthrow of liberalism and representative government was already under way.

The Kodo-Ha and the "Manchuria Incident" were very important in developing the attitude of Japan. This was an Oriental version of National Socialism, sometimes called the "Showa Restoration," sometimes *Kodo-Ha* or "the Way of the Emperor," and by other names as well. Essentially a lower middle class and junior officer movement, its basic motives were hatred of the rich who were getting richer, hatred of the white man and his industrial civilization, an ardent desire to restore military supremacy at home and to make conquests abroad. Numerous secret societies, of which the Black Dragon was the most notorious although not the most powerful, furthered the movement. Ikki Kita's *Reconstruction Program for Japan*, which came out in 1920, was the Japanese *Mein Kampf*. He proposed the abolition of the Diet, a distribution of private property, nationalization of important industries, suppression of all political criticism, a reconstruction of the government so that there would be no barriers between "the nation" (i.e., the Army) and the Emperor, the "freeing" of 700,000,000 "brethren" in India, China, the Philippines and European Asiatic colonies, and a Japanese hegemony of the Far East which in turn would lead to *Hakko Ichiu*, the hegemony of the world. The government tried to suppress Kita's book as a troublemaker, but it circulated widely and had a tremendous influence in the Army and among the people. Naval limitation and the American Immigration Act fanned the movement white-hot.

The militarists planned a *coup d'etat* in 1923. The Tokyo earthquake prevented this, and their next opportunity came in 1931, General Hayashi, a Kodo man who commanded the Japanese armed forces in Korea, moved his Kwantung Army into Manchuria without the permission of his government. Neither the Foreign Office nor the War Department knew anything about the "incident" until after it had occurred. The Foreign Minister had to accept the accomplished fact and explain it as best he could to the world. A state of war with China followed, and this gave the military a legal and constitutional control over the Japanese government.

Mr. Henry L. Stimson, Secretary of State in the Hoover Administration, promptly protested against the Japanese invasion of Manchuria; the League of Nations invoked the Kellogg-Briand Pact and appointed the Lytton Commission to study the situation and report. On 7 January 1932 Secretary Stimson announced what is known as the "nonrecognition policy." The United States would not recognize any "situation, treaty or agreement" brought about by the use of force. And, in an open letter of 23 February 1932, Mr. Stimson invited the nations of the world to follow suit. Tokyo replied by formally recognizing the independence of "Manchukuo," and setting up a puppet Manchu emperor. China countered with an anti–Japanese boycott; Japan landed sailors and soldiers in Shanghai, drove Chinese forces thence with a maximum of savagery and destruction, and having saved her "honor," withdrew at the end of May. The Lytton Commission reported at the end of September, condemning the Japanese action in Manchuria. Japan replied by withdrawing from the

League of Nations. In the meantime, the militarists had consolidated their power by the simple means of getting rid of inconvenient persons; during the first half of 1932 the Minister of Finance, the chief manager of the Mitsui interests, and the seventy-five-year-old Prime Minister were assassinated. It was even planned to kill United States Ambassador Joseph Grew and Charlie Chaplin (then visiting Tokyo), in the hope of provoking a war with the United States and thus riveting military control on the government.

Throughout the discussions that preceded the war, the Japanese government and press so continually harped on their desire for "peace" that many well-meaning Americans, who chose to shut their eyes to actual events, were deceived. Even the Imperial Edict of 8 December 1941, announcing the opening of war to the Japanese people, threw the blame on Great Britain and the United States for placing obstacles "in the way of peaceful commercial endeavors of the Empire," and declared the objective of the war to be "everlasting peace in East Asia." This was not hypocrisy. The Japanese simply put a different meaning on "peace" from that of any Western power. To them it meant complete control—military, political and economic—of all Oriental countries by a Japanese ruling class, a control imposed by force and terror if not abjectly accepted by other orientals. It meant exactly what Ikki Kita wrote, "A feudal peace obtained by the emergence of the strongest country, which will dominate all others of the world." It meant *Hakko Ichiu*.[1]

Like any young boy of my era, I spent many hours in the library looking at books with large photos of the fighting in World War I. I would stare into space, picturing myself reacting to similar circumstances. Would I be a hero or a coward? Death was a concept still as foreign to me as it was to any youngster. It never crossed my mind. My only concern was whether I would be brave and courageous, or whether I would be frightened into an embarrassing and cowardly act. These thoughts flickered through my mind on a daily basis but were unanswerable until the actual day I would face that choice and my own instinctive reaction. However deeply buried, Prof Cardoff's prophetic remark had left an everlasting impression. But even as our compatriots across the sea were preparing for our meeting, our juvenile minds were not overly concerned. Girl-chasing, not war preparation, filled our days.

Time would march on in step with the unchecked marching of barbaric feet, sounding a deafening explosion of death and devastation in Europe and Asia. Meanwhile, the youth of America was in step with teenage fun and games. War and our future participation were separated not only by actual oceans but also by oceans of thought. War preparations were ignored to listen to music and laughing girls, both of which would silence the sound of marching feet.

My noontime lunch at home with family was dominated by a radio commentator replacing our love of life with realistic fear of the future and its aftermath. Life was so good I wondered why should it ever change. I had no thirst for power or domination of people. Love was so good. What was the reasoning for not loving other human beings? But the marching feet could be heard when the music stopped, and girls were not laughing.

The marching feet began to be heard in our classrooms, at our dinner table, in our movies, in our music, at our parties and with our goodbyes. Young men were leaving their homes to go to an unwanted war.

Now we had parties. Not of fun and games, but parties of goodbyes. At my father's camp, we all said goodbye to Henesey from Booneville and Oper from Ava, two farm boys in their early twenties. Their lives had prepared them for love, not war. The death marches in Bataan and Africa would be the last time they heard marching feet.

Though our drafting class now carved solid wood models of aircraft for the Battle of Britain; though our engineering futures were placed on hold; still my main concern was to make it home on my bicycle in time to listen to Glenn Miller in our living room each weekday night. With the large console radio in our living room six inches from my best listening ear, I would listen, and wonder why this life should have to change. Why erase these everlasting moments of enjoyment?

This very radio would change my life drastically. One day, after a 15-cent movie with my friend Al, I was once again in front of this beautiful console radio, with magic push buttons and programmable off-and-on settings. But now, instead of music, I heard the marching feet in my living room. The Japanese had bombed Pearl Harbor, killing more than 2,000 Americans. There was no one else in the house. I was alone and frightened. I sat there in silent despair. All I could hear was marching feet.

The next day at school, saddened conversation about our beginning involvement in an unwanted war was dimming our hopes for a happy future. Soon, one by one, my 17- and 18-year-old friends began volunteering for the service. Spirited, red-blooded teenagers did not hesitate to fulfill their responsibility and their dedication to country and family. Now, our very talented and winning football team received a wartime setback. Our highly respected and gifted coach volunteered to become an army air corps pilot. Another coach took his place on the field, but never replaced him in our hearts. The new coach had something missing, mostly between his ears. He would never volunteer or be drafted for any kind of winning effort. Our team reflected all of his abilities for losing. Football suddenly lost all of its glamour and glory. One by one, the team became younger, less talented, and less attractive to all.

Another change was that there began to be more girls than boys. At 16, I had no competition. Soon the young ladies were singing, "They're either too young or too old."

Life began to be boring and empty. Almost all the young energy and excitement was away from home. My writing career began by writing to my many friends now in the service.

A desperate attempt to join my friends and their efforts was foiled when my lie about my age didn't pass muster. Two friends and I went to New York City to join the Merchant Marine. My friends, both 17 already, were accepted. For me, however, my real desire — to be a marine — held me back. Though I had been a seaman on the Great Lakes that summer, the Merchant Marine did not excite me. Consequently, I showed little persistence in persuading the recruiter to accept me at 16, and I was turned down.

On the train ride back home, I decided to stop off in Albany to see a girl-friend at the State Teachers College. She consoled me in my emptiness and loneliness.

In 1942, the marines had defeated and stopped the Japanese on Guadal-canal for the first time since their barbaric devastation had begun. I had to join these heroes of our time. These young men were the fruit of life. I had to be with them. I must be a marine. Prof Cardoff's prophecy was coming true.

My "sweet sixteen" year was becoming my miserable sixteen year. Con-fused and uncertain about my future, I lost interest in school sports. I dropped out of school to help my father in our family service station. Twelve-hour work days, six days a week, made life uninteresting. I wanted to grow older faster than time allowed. Age 17 would not come soon enough to satisfy my unquenchable thirst.

At last I was 17, ready to join the marines. What could stop me now? So many people I loved were in the marines. Now it was my turn.

The war drew closer and closer, and a fever pitch of patriotism was reached. Nobody was immune. By the time I was a young teenage boy, with the idealism and natural energy of that bloom, America was fully immersed in the war. I thought it was time to do my part and enlist. I was ready to become a hero and I rushed to join the marines. But I was rejected each and every time because of my poor eyesight. I took trains to Albany, Syracuse, Rochester, and Utica, hoping to slip in somehow, somewhere. I tried to enlist on at least ten separate occasions. Finally, I spotted a possible weakness; I would sign up for the draft! I was only 17 years old, but most of my friends were making the listing, and the fever to wear the gold marine emblem was burning in my soul.

I dragged a friend along to the draft board (for backup) and told them that I had turned eighteen "just yesterday." Luck was with me; no one asked for my birth certificate or any other proof of age. I was one step closer to the coveted emblem! I was even give a stern lecture by the woman at the draft board. Head at angle, she shook her finger in my face as I was forced to listen to her: "Many boys, not eighteen yet, are signing up." Heart pounding, I could not look her in the eyes, but agreed with her, mumbling, "Oh, how terrible!"

In a week, I received my notice to report to the armory in Utica, New York. I was one of a thousand or more young men, all grinning from ear to ear, strutting like peacocks, chests puffed out beyond recognition — all naked! We endured the time-honored physical, the fingers in our crotch ("Cough!"), and the other indignities involved in determining our fitness for the upcoming ordeal. This was of no concern to any of us and in no way diminished our enthusiasm. We were prodded and poked, and suddenly we were in the U.S. Navy, naked and innocent as jaybirds but filled with boundless energy and pride.

I was in a pool of about 200 navy personnel standing at attention in a drafty room when, suddenly, three smartly dressed marines marched in and stood before us. They lined up expertly, immaculate in their uniforms, and in perfect unison, barked, "Is there anyone here who wants to be a marine?" One hand crept up. Out of 200, only one weak, young hand showed itself! It was almost high enough to see. One of them did notice and roared, "Front and center!" The body followed the hand through the last civilian door. No one was near him; everybody had quietly backed away, unnoticed, not wanting to be mistaken for that hand. I looked down and found my legs carrying me to the front. I was alone and terrified but at the same time proud to have had the guts to stand up and be counted. Step three accomplished! The marine emblem kept inching closer.

I paid attention as the eye charts were being read; this was the crucial test. Normally, my vision being 20/200 in both eyes, I could never pass this test. In preparation for this ordeal, I had drunk gallons of carrot juice and performed eye exercises outlined in the book *Sight Without Glasses*. It didn't help. As I watched, though, I noticed that they only checked to see what you were reading if you hesitated. Suddenly, it was my turn. With glasses hidden in my pocket, I rattled off a burst of letters, any at all. If you can't dazzle 'em with brilliance, baffle 'em with bullshit. It worked! According to the examiner, and for the first and last time in my life, I had perfect vision. The boy was "reading letters rapidly and without hesitation."

Before my head stopped spinning, I was in Albany, New York, being sworn in as a marine. I had passed the critical test! Now, there was no way out, and I was about to burst with happiness and pride. No matter that I was blind as a bat without my glasses! I was a marine.

The telegram to my Mother read, "In marines, on my way to Parris Island." I am sure that there must have been tears of shock. I'm sure she also wondered how I had accomplished this feat.

2

THE MAKING OF A MARINE

I stayed overnight at a hotel in Albany, New York, and boarded a train in the morning, starting my journey to South Carolina. I met five marine recruits on the train from the local area who were on their way to Parris Island. A soldier, shaking his head, hinted about what we were letting ourselves in for, saying "Just wait until the train stops and you get off and meet the welcoming committee!" We asked him what he meant by that curious remark, but he just shook his head and grinned.

After two days of travel, the train finally stopped in Yemassee, South Carolina, where we were to start the last leg of our journey. Excited with the whole adventure, we stepped quickly down from the train and came suddenly face to face with the "Welcome Committee." This was in the shape of one tall, sharp, hard-looking marine, who immediately roared, "Drop your butts and line up over here!" He did not smile, he did not offer a cheerful greeting, and he did not move. It was like running full-tilt into a rock wall. Our first instinct was to retreat, to back up into the train, but this wall had a voice and there was no denying that order. This tall marine bellowed powerfully and with absolute confidence. I did not smoke, but I would have in order to satisfy his command. Every order was shouted with utmost authority. There would be no talking, no laughing, and no socializing. This marked the end of civilization as we knew it and the beginning of military life. We lost all individual identity on entering this new world; our names were changed to "shitbird" then and there. The old soldier's words haunted us from that moment on. All romantic thoughts about the marine emblem fled from our minds.

Quiet and pale, shaken by this first encounter, we were loaded like cattle onto a bus that created an unimaginable amount of noise. No one could have heard us if we had all shouted at once. It didn't matter; talking was out of the question. At that point, we were too scared to even make eye contact with each other. By stepping off the train to those first commands, the "mommy's boys" had started their assimilation into the military lifestyle. I am sure that I wasn't the only one who was silently questioning his own sanity in making the decision to join the marines.

We rattled down the road on our way to the marine boot camp on Parris Island. As the old bus approached, I saw there were no fences. It didn't need any. It was a small island surrounded by deep swamps, with alligators and poisonous snakes providing more than enough deterrent for anyone even thinking about escaping. The entrances and exits were patrolled by very efficient-looking, unsmiling marines. Guards! My stomach did a sick flip-flop. Then, before my mind could really accept what my eyes were seeing, our transport was through the gates, and we had stopped in front of an expanse of flawlessly manicured lawns, richly decorated with beautiful flower beds. Handsome brick buildings stood just beyond. I relaxed a little and sighed with relief; this was more like it!

But that comfortable thought was shattered almost as quickly as it had formed. This was a temporary stop, for identification and registration purposes only. After this brief chore, we grabbed our civilian suitcases and started the two-mile hike to what would be our home for the next three months. Civilian shoes provided no comfort on this long trek. We passed row upon row of barracks and saw the immense asphalt-paved drill fields. Adding, even more, to the sense of pending doom that had been instilled in us by our experiences so far were the shouts, "You'll be sorry!" echoing between the two-storied, yellow, barracks buildings. Our barracks were soon upon us. Suddenly, we were ordered to "Halt!" and we were directed into the barracks, a yellow, H-shaped, two-story building. Our sleeping sacks were top and bottom iron bunk beds with thin, striped, sawdust-stuffed mattresses. They were close enough together to house all 74 recruits in one room. This arrangement left only about three feet between our faces. The footlockers that were to hold our personal belongings were only about as large as trunk-sized luggage cases. We moved forward to choose our places; the bottom sack being the preferred choice. Those who were not lucky or fast enough to get the bottom sack were left with the top sack and soon learned to be very, very careful when "falling out." As a high-pitched scream would prove, it was too easy to jump to the floor leaving the family jewels in the sack in your haste. A new term, "Fart-sack," the marine word for bedding, was introduced. I found out quickly that it was an all-too-accurate description; this is where you farted all night, muffled between the blankets and the sheets. The preference for the bottom sack became clear. Being below afforded a certain disgusting advantage, because the rising gases always managed to interrupt the sweetest dreams of the buddy trapped above. The few windows provided for the exit of these deadly gases seemed rather inadequate, and I am glad that nobody had the nerve or inclination to light a match.

The wooden floors were ours to be scrubbed spotlessly clean using a very nasty-smelling soap, lots of elbow grease, and our toothbrushes. We discovered that cleaning floors with such small implements was an almost impossible task. But, however comical it seems now, or however physically exhaustive it was then, the fact remains that we did this many, many times for the dreaded white glove inspections which occurred at regular intervals. Each ordeal started with the inspecting officer dramatically pulling on his white gloves at the door, while glaring at his surroundings. Then he would start his inspection, running his gloved fingers along all surfaces meticulously checking each and every crack, nook, or cranny. He missed nothing. Pulling back a smudged finger would immediately bring on a volcanic eruption of wrath. There were no excuses for this lack of perfection, and cruel penance was executed in harsh tones and harsher language.

Then, there was Sgt. Smith "greeting" us with a stern and loud lecture. He used language never before heard by our innocent ears and, among the other rules and regulations laid down in that severe voice, proceeded to tell us in no uncertain terms that we would "never smile again!" Then, suddenly he stopped talking and started walking in my direction. I was scared shitless! I lost any confidence I had been feeling even up to this point, and almost lost my bowels. My arms and legs went numb, and I froze in place, unmoving eyes to the front. He passed me. Before I could even let out the breath I had been holding, I heard a *pow* as he hit a young boy near me, knocking him out cold. The boy had to be dragged into the showers and doused with cold water to bring him back around. Evidently, the young recruit could not hold back his enthusiasm, and Sgt. Smith quite efficiently enforced his "no smiling" discipline on all of us by that simple, yet effective, action. Sgt. Smith was very, very serious.

I remember that sometime shortly thereafter, Sgt. Smith announced that he had received his orders to ship overseas. The platoon "passed the hat" and everybody who could gave a dollar. A dollar was about the only thing of value a "shitbird" had, and donating it was the only gesture capable of expressing our concern for him. He had made an impression on us, and I don't think anybody wanted to see him die in battle, so far away from home. Giving him the money was all we could do to show our feelings. It was very interesting that Sgt. Smith was still at Parris Island when I finally graduated and left. Had we been taken in for a good laugh? Or had his orders just been canceled? Only Sgt. Smith knew the true story.

The experiences that would transform us into fully automated adult killers, the end product, would not occur here but waited somewhere far away from American soil.

The next day, this procedure started in earnest. We became "shitbirds, first class" and were marched unceremoniously to the de-lousing chamber. Entrance into that room began the process of changing civilian mommy-boys into "shitbirds." We could not wear the marine emblem in this mode. The emblem was only for those who survived the 10-week ordeal as shitbirds. First came the stylish haircut that left a quarter-inch or less hair on our heads. Then we stripped ourselves of all civilian clothing, placing it in our suitcases to be shipped home. We moved as fast as we could, dropping coins out of our pockets onto the floor with our nervous fumbling. No one dared pick them up. Next was a nude dash to be dusted head to toe with a strong chemical powder that killed any insects, bugs or other life forms that might be hiding in any number of bodily crevices. Then another naked rush, this time to the quartermaster counter in the next room, yelling out our sizes, hoping to catch the correct clothing and shoes thrown in every direction. The embarrassment of full naked exposure prompted rapid dressing, regardless of how the clothing actually fit. A sudden roar, "Fall out!" led to an immediate panic-filled, half dressed response of all 74 shitbirds.

Three of the sharpest marines I had seen yet stepped to the front of this disorganized group of totally frightened, pale boys. The drill instructors stood tall and straight, legs slightly apart, hands clasped behind their backs, and announced loudly, "We will be Platoon 80!" Other encouraging remarks included, "You are the sorriest group of shitbirds I have seen in my life!" "You people" or "You shitbirds" preceded every command. In our innocence and youth, we imagined nothing less than fire coming out of their mouths with each remark, like terrifying dragons. Weeks later, though, those who survived would learn to love and respect these exceptional individuals for the rest of their lives.

Our permanently assigned drill instructors (D.I.s) were the pride of the Marine Corps. Pfc. Seets was as sharp as the razor-edged pleats in his tailor-made trousers and shirts. His shrewd, dark eyes seemed chipped from granite and missed nothing. The "piss-cover" cap, seated at a confident angle on his immaculately groomed pitch-black hair, was always in place. His 135-pound body possessed a voice that could penetrate the thickest skull and almost total deafness of the most dense mommy-boy like a drill. His rhythmic marine cadence for marching commands gave confidence to even the most inhibited shitbird. There was no chance to defy his commands. They were delivered in a way that prompted automatic and instant response. The sing-song sound of "Woon reep, woon toot threep, woon reep, woon toot threep" rang out clear and strong. Nowhere else in the military world could this particular sound be heard.

Corporal Brown was a much larger marine. Some of his bulk might have been attributable to his dedication to the "slop Shoot," the marine beer saloon, and its offerings of 10-cent mugs of beer. He, like the rest, never quite managed the immaculate sharpness of Pfc. Seets, but his bellowed commands received the same instant reactions. He was a stern, uncompromising combination of instructor and leader.

Sgt. Winslow, an "old-time" marine, had more of a fatherly appearance, with the nature to match. His voice was not as strong as the other drill instructors' and his marine cadence was almost without rhythm. That was very unusual for a marine. But the commands became only incidental after we learned to march, so his non-rhythmic cadence didn't matter anyway. He was not the typical hard marine. His own individual experience had tempered his personality with an emotion that might have been sympathy. The speech he gave at our graduation was close to tearful. As an experienced veteran, he had seen the realities of combat and feared that most of us would not see our next birthday.

This group of dedicated marines had the impossible job of sharpening us weak, young shitbirds into a physical and mental force that the fighting units of other nations had a lifetime to prepare. And these D.I.s had only 10 weeks to accomplish this miracle.

The first morning at boot camp, as all mornings from then on, started at 4:00 A.M. The bellows of "Drop your cocks and grab your socks!" and "hit the deck!" interrupted many a beautiful dream of the pretty girls back home. These roared commands became our alarm clock for the rest of our stay and proved quite effective. From then on, we "hit the deck," our feet already running before they even touched the floor.

Never again would we wake up to a refreshing, leisurely shower. The open stall area had only eight shower heads, and any lingering person caused a dangerous flurry of irritation from the waiting hoards. Piling three deep at the fourteen sinks, we had only 10 minutes to shave off the youthful face fuzz and perform the rest of the morning wash-up ritual. This was all we really needed; the true stubble, the tough whiskers that would bring complaints of reddened faces from girlfriends to be, were still somewhere in the future.

We had even less time to make our sacks, which had to be made tightly enough to bounce a coin. The flurry at a Macey's half-price sale would never compare with the maneuvers performed by these 74 adolescent boys, straining to make their bunks in the allotted time, creating a virtual whirlwind of bony elbows and knees. The only motivating force was the absolute terror of the D.I.'s stare; but it was enough! To our young imaginations, he was like a prehistoric monster, fangs bared and dripping with the gore of the few unfortunate enough to meet that stare eye to eye. Any infraction, of any rule, would bring that stare to bear on the unlucky violator, and the shit would really hit the fan. Nose to nose, no more than two inches apart, the D.I. would stare down his hapless victim, delivering a verbal blast of questions, including "Do you love me?" Every answer was wrong.

Among the many seemingly super-human traits of our drill instructors, one of the first we discovered, was their uncanny hearing capabilities. Conversation was forbidden, especially after taps. It didn't matter how soft and low the attempt, the whisper always carried to the D.I., somehow transmitted miraculously through walls and doors. This inevitably led to a midnight "fall-out" command and moonlight exercises on the drill field, when we should have been sacked out on our thin beds, dreaming sweet dreams and giving our bodies enough rest to get through the next day. It took only two of these unpleasant interruptions to enforce that rule.

Civilian veneer was discarded quickly in this manufacturing process. Mind and body started to rapidly gain strength, elevated to the level of confidence and courage required to sustain the weight of responsibility that came with the marine emblem. Some of us would lose as much as 45 pounds to reach this plateau of fitness.

At first, even though we did have a marine emblem on our jacket, we definitely looked like shitbirds. We marched, ran, and marched some more. Between all the physical activities were the venereal disease (VD) movies. These informational reels, shown for our health benefit, scared the young virgin boys into thinking that sex wasn't worth the gamble! Sweets, in any form, were not allowed at boot camp. Even candy bars, know as "Pogey Bait," were taboo. Even so, one Sunday "off," another shitbird and I sneaked over to the PX for some ice cream. Sneaking back with our prize, we were caught by the D.I. returning to the barracks and ordered to stand at attention in the hot sun with the two-quart buckets on our heads. Not allowed to lick any of the sweet sticky mess as it ran down our faces and past our mouths, we stood stone still as the ice cream melted down to our toes.

Then, our combined efforts slowly bringing everything together, the confidence started to build within us. The marching feet in cadence became a beautiful song. The physical workouts, as exhausting as ever, became exhilarating. Even though there was still no smiling, the pride and confidence was starting to show; we were becoming marines. Our eyes started to reflect the confidence and pride in ourselves, replacing the fear. We stood straighter and walked taller. We were being shaped and sharpened into an unstoppable, lethal unit, just as the steel of a sword is molded and honed into a deadly fighting weapon. The cast and molding were almost complete; the final honing of the killing edge would follow in future experiences.

Discipline was taught in unusual and severe ways. Dressed in winter woolens and enclosed in the stifling barracks, we were given two minutes to make up our sacks. Even though it was 85 degrees outside, all windows were closed and the steam radiators turned on. It was too hot for even the D.I. to stay in the squad room; he waited outside for this drill. After practicing this exercise for an hour, the two-minute time allotment was reached then cut to a minute. We never succeeded, but the point had been driven home. Do it right and do it quick, under any circumstances. Another exercise was to extend

A proud marine boot named Jim.

our rifle out in front of and perpendicular to your body. The 9½ pounds of rifle was enough to numb the arms and shoulders in seconds. We couldn't move for anything, even to swat at the aggravating gnats. Just one time a young boy interrupted his pose in order to wave away a particularly irritating gnat that was dining on his neck. The slap was noticed by the D.I., and the boy was instructed to scratch his own neck with intensity. The blood ran freely, and again, the point was driven home to all of us. Follow orders, to the letter, no exceptions! The Burma Road March was another example of torture. We duck-waddled to marching commands, in full gear, and then pounded the pavement until our fists bled. Discipline didn't rest and took no vacations.

I received great news that Bob, whom I called my "brother in life," had joined the marines. My other "brother in life," Ray, was already in the Corps. Ray and Bob were special. Although they were my father's brothers, when their mother died, they came to live with us. I always considered them my brothers, for we were the same age and grew up together.

About two weeks later, I was able to find Bob and visit him. We were two proud American boys now united in a common cause. Our meeting was a happy time. Posing for pictures, we dramatized our newfound adventure by flexing our muscles with fixed bayonets in an attempt to frighten the whole Japanese army into an immediate unconditional surrender. How naive we were to the awaiting horrors of death and destruction.

But this was a time to enjoy life. That evening, we went to an open-air theater to watch another of Hollywood's romantic depictions of war. This romance could never be reality. These beautiful tales of fantasy would keep us marching toward the real war even though the romantic war never existed. These movies, as innocent as they were, could be creating a false concept of war. However, the means, justified in its cruel form of killing, would bring happiness unchallenged for a lifetime.

At the open-air theater, we made sand mounds for pillows to complete our temporary pleasures. Bob was with me for now. Nothing else seemed very important. Moments of happiness last for a lifetime.

After surviving this physical transformation, we were ready for the rifle range, a one-hour march (with full gear, of course) from the barracks. Barren and dismal, the rifle range had no trees, grass, or flowers. Only sandy dunes covered the landscape. There, we were housed in half-moon shaped quonset huts. Dark and dingy, they had metal roofs, few windows, and only one door. A nightly fire watch was necessary; an errant spark from the pot-bellied coal-burning stove would have burned the place down in few seconds. There was room for about fifteen single sacks in each little hut.

Some mornings started even earlier at the rifle range. Beginning at 3:00 A.M., the first order of business, accompanied by much grunting and groaning,

"Brothers-in-life" and marines Ray Lince (left, marine air corps), Bob Lince (center, a seagoing marine), and George Lince (right, marine infantry).

was to prove our success at moving our bowels on command by proudly displaying the evidence clinging to the toilet paper. Those not successful remained indefinitely seated in despair. Only the next activity requiring their presence would come to the rescue of the "No-Shit" brigade.

The latrines, along with the showers, were in a large, garage-type building. The commode was nothing but a long narrow trough, through which water ran continuously. Rough wooden boards, with round holes to accommodate the shitbirds' asses, were laid on top of this trough. The dropping of a lighted wad of paper into the rushing water entry point would cause hairy asses to pop up instantly, like leaping dominoes. The jokester had plenty of time to vanish before the first potential marine felt the flames.

This was the place where we would become excellent marksmen, the world's best. We were taught by the most skilled riflemen in the world. These incredible men stood at our sides instructing us to "Hold your breath and squeeze the trigger!" This soon became an automatic reflex, like breathing. The marines' ability with the rifle was unmatched by any other military organization in the world. We learned sniper-like marksmanship in order to accurately hit a nine-inch circle at 500 yards. Eight shots, all fired within seconds, left a hole the size and pattern of a dollar bill. There would never be any wounded enemy, just dead enemy. Our rifle was our greatest asset, our most potent weapon. To call your rifle a "gun" was a mortal sin. Referring to a rifle as a "gun" brought on one of the most humiliating lessons yet. The shitbird would have to run up and down the company streets holding the rifle high with one hand and holding his personal gun pulled out of unzipped trousers with his other hand, shouting, "This is my gun, this is my rifle!" This exercise, executed with loud authority, was to identify each object for once and for all. The one to go through this particular training and the viewer of this spectacular sight would never, never make that mistake in identification again. Also, any act of dropping your rifle, or otherwise treating it with disrespect, was quickly corrected by another original lesson. Being ordered to sleep with several rifles for many nights formed the appropriate attachment, love, and respect.

Marching back from the rifle range, we arrived at the barracks and KP. KP was the most rotten duty of all. The endless mound of potatoes infiltrated our dreams at night, rudely pushing aside the sweet dreams of girls and glory. KP meant 14 boring and humiliating hours of dishing out food, killing flies, scrubbing pots and pans, washing floors, and emptying garbage. Another nasty task, second only to KP, was guard duty from 2:00 A.M. to 4:00 A.M. Exhausted by the strenuous exercises of the day, we would literally fall asleep while walking, waking only as we toppled into the ditch by the side of the road.

One of the first and last exercises at boot camp included engaging in

Parris Island, 1944: United States Marine Corps Drum and Bugle Corps, in which the author served before his transfer to the infantry.

physical combat with other platoons. Every outgoing platoon was victorious; the incoming "shitbird" didn't have a chance. These physical contests sealed our new confidence. The weeks of grueling work had paid off. Then, suddenly, our glory day was upon us. Our trials and tribulations over with the completion of boot camp, we could now wear our marine emblem with all the confidence and pride of new, young heroes. We were marines! Our pictures were taken, our backs pounded, a parade was given (for us!), and each of us received a 10-day furlough. We were cocky! The bands played, the red carpets rolled out, and the girls flocked to us like moths to a flame. The power of the marine emblem was incredible!

The 10-day furlough was spent in our home towns and became a blur, filled with girls and fights. All the families and friends threw parties for their favorite "heroes." We hopped the trains from Savannah and Charleston to our home towns for a never-ending daze of drunken festivities. The reputation of the young servicemen as being wild and destructive had prompted many businesses to put up "No Dogs or Servicemen Allowed!" signs. That made no difference to the marines on furlough. They just slept on park benches and on the carpeted floors of hotel lobbies. Marine life was a party, filled with girls and booze, and we thought it would last forever. There was no idea yet of the weight of responsibility that came with the marine emblem. Right now, being a marine meant having a wild and glorious time.

After furlough, I was quickly brought back down to earth as I discovered that the glory of the marine emblem still might not be for me. I had lied about my sight, but it was too late to boot me out because my poor vision wasn't discovered until after I was sworn in. I was medically labeled: "Recommendations and considerations make this man acceptable for duty." My grand and

Author at Field Music School, Parris Island, S.C., 1944.

glorious dream of being in the Marine air corps was rudely shattered and swept away as I was sent to the drum and bugle corps. Along with the rigorous calisthenics and military exercises, I had to learn 96 bugle calls and 20 drum movements while trying to stay awake in the stifling hot classrooms. There were good times, though, rubbing shoulders with some of the greatest men of all times. I became buddies with the some of the Glenn Miller, Benny Goodman, and Hal McIntire band members. In fact, Hal McIntire's drummer was a very close friend of mine. There were some good "jam" sessions at the barracks music room.

After my boot camp furlough, some lovely ladies, magnetized to my uniform and the act of bravery by being a marine, became devoted pen pals with promises of love forever. Meaning, of course, until the next serviceman came home on furlough. One love became so passionate and so dedicated to her hot burning letters, she married the next sailor who came home on leave, but my life as a mail-order Don Juan went on.

My new assignment to the Field Music School on Parris Island was boring but gave daily satisfaction that I was a marine and a proud American.

Each day began with calisthenics at 4:30 A.M. Then, skipping a lousy breakfast, we began polishing and shining in earnest. We were probably some of the sharpest 17- and 18-year-olds in the world. At about 7:30 A.M., we marched off to the Main Station, nice comfortable brick buildings to raise our flag with all the glory and pomp we could provide. At precisely 8:00 A.M., all movement froze, both human and mechanical. The trumpets hit a high note, the drums rolled, the music began, and the flag started its rapid ascent to its highest position. All eyes were on our flag and salutes were frozen in dedicated splendor. We marched away with tears, shed with great personal satisfaction. Marching down a side street, we stopped each day in front of the hospital. The band played a morning mini-concert to the pleased ears of the patients. Then, off we went for our boring day of playing drums and bugles in unharmonized repetitive sounds of practicing for future buglers of the United States Marine Corps. Young fidgety minds and bodies seemed to be tortured in the hot stifling classrooms, with no fans or air conditioning to soothe us. We were restless to find the means for the destruction of the Japanese disease that caused these unhappy conditions. Although we had liberty, letters from home, a dedication to the sense of duty, life seemed to offer no hope for a future.

I received a letter from my mother saying my brothers in life were coming home for a weekend. Ray, in the Marine air corps, and Bob, a sea-going marine on the USS *Duluth*, would be home together. I had to find a way to be there.

I went to my corporal in charge and asked how I could get a 5-day pass. The next morning I was standing before our commanding officer petitioning his kindness and consideration. When he gave his approval, I almost shouted, "Whoopee!" But the disciplined marine that I had become would not allow this display of instant happiness. I thanked my corporal and dashed off to the barracks to begin my packing.

Author (left) with "brother-in-life" Ray Lince.

The next day, I went to Yemassee, South Carolina, to board the "Champion" train to New York. Every service person in the world was waiting to board the Champion. No reservations! First come, first serve. When the train stopped it appeared full already. These were anxious moments, with pushing and shoving, almost in a panic, toward the awaiting train. This was the only way to take us all toward our destination. It was impossible for all of us to satisfy our instant dream of going home. I believed I was too far back in the crowd to ever have a chance to be selected as a next passenger on the Champion, but somehow, with a little wiggling and pushing, I was face to face with the conductor. My mouth dropped open as I awaited his shout of, "That is all." But instead I saw a smile of kindness, and an arm pushing out a commanding hand toward me as he spoke: "One more." Wow! What a fantastic, thoughtful man he was. Had I not made this train, I would have had to go back to the base because there would not be enough time in my five-day allotment. I would have only two important days at home, spending most of my time on the only fast train available.

I was so excited, I was speechless. Only my eyes could say thank you. I bounded onto the train, walking from car to car, but I found no empty seat. So, in between cars I made a seat on my bag and was there all night long. I was so excited at the thought of being with my brothers in life, maybe for the last time. The train and a five-day pass would bring us together again.

Our two-day blur of fun and family ended too soon, and soon we were all back at our duty stations. All of our futures were unknown and certainly not controlled or determined by our personal desires.

My boring days would begin with no real sense of purpose in relationship to this unwanted war and its pending aftermath. I enjoyed playing with the band, and the quality of my buddies made the situation very tolerable.

Johnny Burns, from Charleston, South Carolina, became a very close buddy. At night, when we were out of the rays of the daytime torturous sun, we ran our mileage around the drill field. Johnny Burns was strong and very athletic. His strength and kindness would be demonstrated on the next weekend liberty. Johnny and I, with another marine, hitchhiked a ride into Charleston. While in the back seat, I dozed off for a few minutes. When we were dropped off short of our destination, we started walking along the highway. Suddenly, without warning, the marine that accompanied us started cussing at me unmercifully. He was quite disturbed about me falling asleep. He did not let up with his verbal attack.

Finally, I had enough of his nonsense. I stepped in front of him, looked at him eyeball to eyeball, cocked my right arm and aimed my closed fist toward his mouthy head. *Pow!* I hit the intended target. And the intended energy sent him flying across the ditch. He bounded back up, toward me, and I was ready

Author (right) with marine buddy Johnny.

to hit him again. But suddenly Johnny, with his vise-grip arms, was holding back my arms so I could not protect myself. The gutless, mouthy hero hit me on the side of my head, and I was really upset at this point. I was now ready to annihilate the guy. But Johnny was my best friend at that moment, so I tried to cool off. In silence we all started walking toward Charleston. Johnny and I went together toward his house, while the mouthy hero left our unfriendly company.

At Johnny's house, we got his car for an evening of fun. A car with rationed gasoline and our marine uniforms were all we needed to attract southern belles with eyes of invitation to personal pleasures. After our catch of selected beauties, we parked overlooking the bay, creating a romantic environment. These reputable belles had to be taken home to answer to their father's curfew time. Young virgin marines were still alive and well regardless of the war-time environment. This was still not a time to abandon morality. At Johnny's home, he made some phone calls to find a room for me for the night. Southern hospitality was still available to this Yankee far from home.

So there I was, in the middle of a hot night, in a hospitable stranger's house with all the comforts of home. The next day I awoke refreshed and thankful to Johnny and his friends. I had made friends that night with people I would never see again. I went back to the base feeling proud of being an American. The experience was another reason why I was a marine, and it strengthened my willingness to give up my life so that this way of living would withstand the Japanese barbaric attempt to destroy it.

However, I knew that the drum and bugle corps was not for me. I needed to pull another magic trick out of my hat, preferably the same one that had gotten me into the marines in the first place. Finally, it hit me. I had old scars on my lips from a past car accident. Petitioning the drum and bugle corps board for a transfer, I cited those scars as the reason I couldn't blow the bugle anymore. I was subsequently transferred to the Marine Infantry, Camp Lejeune, North Carolina. Finally! Here was the chance to be a real marine.

3

ON TO THE MARINE INFANTRY

We left Parris Island at 3:00 A.M., leaving the barracks without saying goodbye. The train ride was very slow; we stopped every hour, it seemed, to avoid hitting the cows that stood in the middle of the track. The short trip seemed to take hours, and we arrived at Camp Lejeune late at night. The trip from the train to the tent area seemed to take forever. Even the calisthenics at Parris Island did not prepare us for this trek. Our seabags weighed a ton, and we discovered quickly how out of shape we really were! The next morning, our records had not arrived yet. Everybody not given furlough after boot camp could sign up for a ten-day leave, and I saw my chance to gamble again! Many others were tempted to gamble also and obtain another ten days of fun, fun, fun; however, the penalty for receiving an additional ten-day furlough meant spending time in the brig, a place to avoid at all costs. The brig was hell. Men in the brig had their heads shaven and were treated worse than animals, even beaten. Even so, I took a chance, signed up, and received another ten days to go home and have a good time with the girls and spend time with my family. Now it was time to say goodbye. It was a time to kiss my mother and give handshakes to my father and brother. My childhood sweetheart stood by watching nervously. She was wearing a pale pink dress with a flower in her hair. I began kissing my childhood sweetheart with tearful, wordless embraces. Was this our last time together? Would faith end our love by sacrificing my young life in exchange for world peace? At the moment, our fear of what could happen did not seem to be a fair exchange. Love seemed to be too good to have anything interrupt its longevity. I was anxious to leave quickly with no lingering agony of saying goodbye. The night before, my sweetheart and I had acted as though it might be our last night together. She gave me a good reason to get the war over quickly. I found out how pretty girls were even without a pretty dress on. In fact, they were even prettier than I believed. But now, our back-seat adventure and exploration had to be placed on hold. Life was so unfair at that moment. I hated the old people who started this war.

I held on to her hand as long as I could then turned quickly away to somehow freeze my memory of her youthful and sweet beauty. She was a reason to win a war and come home safe and sound.

I bounded out of the house to my waiting sailor buddy's car. He said,

"It's tough to say goodbye." I replied despondently, "Especially now because I know where I am going."

I arrived at the train station in plenty of time. My sailor buddy drove me there, and now he would say goodbye. Little did I realize that this was our last goodbye. His life would end in the Pacific only a few miles from my land combat. He would have been a good, lifetime friend always willing to help me. After the war, life would have to be content with memories of a real friendship on my last ten-day furlough. I believed ten days' extra furlough was a fair trade for time in the brig. But, my magic was still with me, and I was never caught. These days of such super enjoyment came around only once in a lifetime. Now, I was mentally ready for my future as a marine. We were being prepared for the job ahead, made ready for entering into the dangerous world where we would wipe out the deadly, cancerous disease gnawing at our doorsteps, having to leave our safe and loving homes in order to accomplish this task. And all of us knew, no matter what happened, we would return as changed men. With a sad finality, brave young men lovingly and gently kissed mothers and girlfriends good-bye. Their love would be taken overseas, kept in our hearts and souls, and would be the source for the unflinching courage that would sustain us in the ordeals ahead. Our strength ultimately came from that part of our souls, not from our bodies or minds. We were fully prepared to sacrifice our young lives to preserve the beautiful home life that we all enjoyed. The corner drugstore teenager was on his way.

Camp Lejeune is a large base, proudly called the world's most complete amphibious training base, at more than 111,000 acres. Approximately 85,000 of that is land; the remainder is under water. "We can conduct most of our training here at Lejeune. We are, of course, running out of space because of new weapons systems and new deployment techniques. And we're attempting to do something about that," the commanding general said. "One hundred eleven thousand acres sounds like a lot of land but when you take out all of the things that we have to take out of that, like inhabited areas, endangered species areas, water and marshy areas not suitable for 'good' training, it cuts down a good bit of maneuver room."

The Training and Support section of Headquarters Battalion is one of the largest in the Corps and provides support for the head quarters command at Lejeune. Marines attached to the battalion fulfill many tasks to support the quad command's extensive training schedule.

Camp Lejeune was a continuous sea of tents among the tall southern pines, with long wooden sidewalks running throughout. We were housed in the tents, and the elite marines and administrators at the main station were housed in beautiful brick buildings, surrounded by perfectly groomed lawns and flowers. The tents were not heated, and the cold night air penetrated our bodies to the bone; there were never enough blankets and clothing to go around. Sunrise was a welcome sight. The calisthenics and the two-mile morning run soon warming our chilled bodies. The bright sun, though, never entered the dark and dingy mess halls where we waited in long lines. Amid the tents, there was a small area where marines were housed in little black metal huts. I ran into a hometown friend staying in one of these. Bill had married a girl from Australia while he was with the 1st Marine Division. Bill had combat experience on Guadalcanal. He told me it was risky going into battle with eyeglasses on. I wished Bill good luck and thanked him for his honest answer.

Time at Camp Lejeune was another step in the formation of this tremendous fighting force with most of the time spent in developing our bodies. There was little concern for the mind at this point. The marines from Parris Island started their transformation into confident and strong marines. We were going overseas to fight the cruelest soldiers on earth, yet not one hour was spent in mentally preparing us for the real test of facing this enemy. Perhaps the realism of what we were still to face was too horrible and complicated a matter to discuss. Maybe the experienced marines felt that the true facts would frighten many of us into going AWOL. So many hours of film were shown regarding the dangers of VD that we almost thought the war was about that disease!

Camp Lejeune made us all wish that we were back at Boot Camp. The night patrols kept us so exhausted, that even simple conversation was almost impossible. The thunder made by our marching feet broke the silence of the night and dispelled all remaining childish dreams and activities. Like knights from some medieval time, we put on our shiny helmets, slung the rifles over our backs, and marched off into the North Carolina woods, leaving only the stench of a totally inadequate insect repellent in our wake. Walter Winchell, the renowned radio commentator, criticized the U.S. Marine Corp. for the lives lost during the many amphibious landing practices on Onslow Beach, citing unnecessary cruelty and disregard for marine lives. However, as dangerous and treacherous as that beach was, it did not compare to what we were to face in the Pacific.

Our short and grueling time at Camp Lejeune over, we received orders to ship out to Camp Pendleton, Oceanside, California. We were packed like cattle into an ancient World War I train. The bunks must have been at least eight high. It was fortunate that our bodies had been trained into such leanness! A marine with just one extra pound of weight on him would never have gotten into, or out of, one of those bunks. We arrived at the rolling hills of Camp Pendleton, where we would go through even more vigorous maneuvers.

After a few weeks of intense training exercises at Camp Pendleton, we were granted liberty. I spent this time in preparation for the trip overseas. I felt no compulsion to go on liberty. Maybe I was too excited with the upcoming reality of actually traveling to the Pacific and being part of the effort in driving the Japs off the face of the earth. I spent the weekend doing laundry, shining shoes and having my picture taken to send home to my family.

Then we were off to San Diego, on a bus this time, to board a ship and start our voyage into the unknown. The time was filled with nervous anticipation and still more nervous preparation. We did not know what was in store for us. Many wondered if we were on our way to "soft" duty in that most exotic location, Hawaii. Reality soon proved us wrong. Our final destination would begin a drama in our lives that could never be forgotten. And the silent heroes would sacrifice their young lives in their final quest for freedom.

At San Diego, we boarded the USS *Wharton*, a cruise-line ship converted to a troopship for military use. Most of us had never been this far away from home before. We all stood on deck watching the receding horizon and wondering if we would ever see our families and loved ones again. For many of us, this was the first real view of the ocean, but the excitement was diminished by the seriousness of the situation. How many of us would never see home again?

Saying a silent good-bye to America, five thousand marines started the 17-day journey. During the whole trip, not a word was said about the war and what we were being sent to accomplish in the Pacific. Strangely, no other ships traveled with us for protection; our only defense against enemy ships and submarines was to sail on a zig-zag course.

We spent most of our time on deck. Only at sunrise and sunset were we required to go below deck. We quickly headed below decks when the general quarters alarm sounded. The hatchways were sealed and secured by a Marine with a loaded rifle, providing effective therapy for anyone who might be inclined to suffer from claustrophobia. At these times, the ship became a silhouette on the horizon, making an easy target for enemy submarines.

The sleeping quarters were large, badly lighted and poorly ventilated rooms, filled with row upon row of stacked bunks no more than three feet apart. It was kind of a cross between boot camp and the old WW I train, so we were already used to living very close together and being treated like so many head of cattle. The mess hall was a compacted area of picnic-type tables. Men were shoved so close together, the only way to eat was with elbows awkwardly clamped to your sides. A few marines had food literally jammed down their throats when some unthinking marine raised his hand (and elbow) to scratch his nose. Raising a foot was just as dangerous. Two feet raised simultaneously at each end of the seating bench would activate a pin release and cause the supporting bar in the middle to disengage. Unsuspecting marines were unceremoniously dumped to the floor, chins striking the table with dull thuds on the way down. Keeping the feet flat on the floor prevented this from happening, but nobody ever seemed to remember this. There were at least a dozen of these "interruptions" at every meal, and what started out as a funny consequence to a perfectly casual and normal action quickly lost its humor.

Everybody had certain duties aboard ship, and a couple of buddies and I had a most exciting one. We would dash back and forth between the tables at chow time, balancing pitchers like seasoned waiters, filling up drink containers. This was actually to our advantage, because we were able to obtain extra food. And besides, what else was there to do on this crowded, boring trip?

All the water the ship carried was needed for drinking and cooking, leaving little available for showers. With so many young men in close quarters, breathing was almost unbearable. We were able to spend most of our time topside, though, and the ocean breezes were without a doubt much more pleasant than the odors trapped in the stale air below. Once, I was even lucky enough to find a shower dripping cold water. In the middle of the night, while everyone was asleep, hoping I would not be caught, I quickly stripped and spent the next four hours with a cake of soap underneath that steady dribble. After that, I was able to live with myself a while longer.

The USS *Wharton* was actually an army ship manned by the navy, and the food was excellent. Thanksgiving time was upon us and the galley was piled high with turkeys. Three of us decided we could not wait and set up a plan to relieve the kitchen of one of those juicy birds. Silently, we maneuvered into position, casually forming sort of an assembly line. One man snatched the bird off the table, wrapped it in a towel, then passed the bundle into the hallway where the second man waited. Another touchdown pass to the third man waiting further down the hallway, and then the mad dash through a maze of nearly 5,000 marines, to the victorious collaborators' bunks. The maneuver was executed brilliantly, going off without a hitch, and the accomplished thieves gathered together secretly for a satisfying pre–Thanksgiving feast.

As we passed over the equatorial line, we were all initiated into the exclusive "Equator Club." Young men who had never crossed the equator before were "polliwogs." Men who had been over this invisible line were known as "frogs." During a special ceremony, just like a fraternity, the polliwogs formed a line and, one by one, were paddled on their bare wet bottoms by the frogs. With that ritual, all polliwogs were turned into frogs. We had been initiated into a select brotherhood, the "benefits" becoming all too quickly apparent in the tropical heat and humidity.

The seas are generally very calm near the equator and, after general quarters at night, I would go back up and head for my special spot. From my place under the five-inch gun at the bow of the ship, I gazed at the starry skies. The calm, gentle movement of the sparkling, moonlit waves and the brief twinkling flash of the flying fish as they leaped above the water gave a wonderful sense of peace. Even that hard deck seemed comfortable as I relaxed into peaceful dreams. It was easy to forget about the storms of war and of the havoc wreaked by those black clouds; war was not a reality for us yet. I never took part in the 24-hour, high-stakes poker games going on below decks. Too often food, drink, and sleep became secondary priorities for the players, and I preferred my beautiful dreams and a comfortably full belly. I was rarely interrupted; conversations were few. Everyone seemed preoccupied with their own thoughts. The fact that we were headed toward an unknown destiny robbed us of any enthusiasm for the trip and had a tendency to silence the most outspoken marine.

4

PELELIU TO PAVUVU

Our course on the *Wharton* was determined by a series of events and policy changes dating from the late summer of 1944. A United States Marine Corps history, *The Assault on Peleliu*, summarizes the situation at the time: with the Marianas won and the great Japanese naval base at Truk now cut off from support, the American strategists turned their attention to the last remaining obstacles in the westward drive. The Palau Islands in the western Carolines, 1,000 miles west of Truk and only 500 miles east of Mindanao, lay on the flank of any advance on the Philippines. Should they be invaded? In a high-level Navy conference on the question, the leading dissenter was Admiral Halsey. Arguing that the conquest of the Palaus would prove too costly, and fearing a repeat of Tarawa, he proposed bypassing the Palaus and striking directly at the Philippines. Nimitz, on the other hand, felt that the islands were too great a threat to ignore — and Nimitz was Halsey's superior.

Accordingly, plans were laid; the 1st Marine Division was to storm ashore on Peleliu Island, site of the largest air base in the Palaus, on September 15. Major General William Rupertus, the division commander, felt optimistic about the invasion. Addressing his officers after a landing rehearsal at Guadalcanal, Rupertus said: "We're going to have some casualties, but let me assure you this is going to be a short one, a quickie. Rough but fast. We'll be through in three days. It might take only two." But Stalemate II, as the operation was known, bore an all-too-prophetic name. The struggle for Peleliu would drag on for weeks, to rank with Tarawa as one of the bloodiest battles of the Pacific war....

> The battle of Peleliu claimed the lives of 1,252 Marines and 277 soldiers; another 5,274 Marines and 1,008 soldiers were wounded in the fighting. Ten thousand Japanese soldiers and civilians perished. So well protected had been the Japanese by their caves and tunnels that it took an average of 1,589 rounds of heavy and light ammunition to kill each of Nakagawa's men.
>
> "It seemed to us," one Marine officer said later, "that somebody forgot to give the order to call off Peleliu. That's one place nobody wants to remember." And the battle went largely unnoticed back in the States. While Marines and soldiers were still locked in a tragic struggle with the enemy, another event in the Pacific had drawn the world's attention. MacArthur, with attendant fanfare, had returned to the Philippines.[2]

Our ship's original course was to the Palau Group of Islands, specifically Peleliu, where the 1st Marine division was engaged in a blitz. Casualties were extremely heavy and the marines on board our ship were to be the replacements for the fallen marines. Our 5,000 were not enough to fill the void, but another ship, carrying another 5,000 marines, was on its way. That ship traveled on the same course and was a couple of days ahead of us.

The first day on Peleliu, known as D-Day, was a nightmare of death and destruction. In the first few hours, while storming the beach, almost a 1,000 marines had died on the white virgin sands, turning them bright red with American blood. The Japs had a network of mortar patterns for every marine position. Even had it been possible, retreat was a word not known to those brave marines. The survivors of the beach slaughter moved ahead as rapidly as possible to eradicate the enemy. The Japs, in their positions of advantage, were wiped out along the way. Digging out, blowing up, and burning out were the only methods available to the marines for the killing of these vicious Japanese. Despite all odds, these courageous men advanced relentlessly, giving no quarter. Many different areas became so bloody they were named "Bloody Nose Ridge." The coral surrounding the caves that protected the Japs was stronger than concrete and made their bunkers that much harder to penetrate. Even the 16-inch shells from the battleships and 500-pound bombs delivered by the aircraft were not able to break through these fortresses.

In the first 197½ hours the 1st Marine Regiment were in combat they suffered 1672 casualties. Expressed in percentages by battalions, the 1st Battalion — 76%, the 2nd Battalion — 51%, the 3rd Battalion — 55%. The fighting was extremely intense.

This fierce battle ended as suddenly as it had begun. There were no prisoners; 1,500 marines were dead, thousands of others wounded. It had taken 31 days to prove to the Japs that their boasting was in vain. They had believed that even a million marines couldn't have taken Peleliu. During this living hell, 20,000 marines proved the Japs wrong. All these young heroes willingly sacrificed their lives for a useless piece of real estate. The island was left vacant, useless as a military advantage. What a horrible price for glory. And who would reap the rewards of this folly? The medaled generals and admirals were the winners, watching the bloodshed through their binoculars, restless from the indigestion caused by seven-course meals served by uniformed, disciplined waiters.

The blitz at Peleliu had ended in victory, the marines expressing their glory once again. But their youth had turned frightened captive and was finally destroyed, dissipating like rainbows escaping from a ravaging hell. Trumpets sounded in muted silence.

On the USS *Wharton*, we had been headed for Pelileu. No longer needed there, we were diverted to Pavuvu, in the Russell Islands. We were on our way to fill the sacks left vacant by the marines who had fallen on Peleliu. The plans for the next blitz, and more training of the untried new marines, began in earnest.

Our destination was the South Pacific, past Hawaii and close to New Guinea. Our journey would end on a tiny land mass known as Pavuvu, an island that is in the Russell Islands group located just below another, larger group, called the Solomon Islands. Like Guadalcanal, these islands had already been secured by the Allies. There was no need for anything but routine patrols, and the islands were used mostly for training new marines.

The ship finally anchored, and 5,000 marines moved quickly off the ship onto the dock area. Our trip had been boring and cramped, and we were ready to set our feet upon land again, however foreign the soil. Everybody grabbed their seabags, which were already lined up on the wharf. I looked for mine, but it wasn't there! The clothes that I had spent my weekend of liberty washing and ironing in preparation for the trip had been swiped by a "buddy," one who had spent his liberty thoroughly enjoying himself at the many farewell parties. We had become good friends during the long trip, talking about high school, girls, and our families. I was proud of my state of readiness, and excited about finally being a part of the greatest effort on earth. We were going to destroy the disease that was threatening our world! In some casual conversation with this so-called buddy, I had mentioned my efforts in getting my gear ready. And he repaid me by stealing everything I had. I spent the next week of my spare time searching through the clothing of dead marines, looking for some clothes that would fit me. This was very gruesome, and it was a step in the development of the necessary emotional numbness that was essential for survival. This numbness would eventually become part of all our "Asiatic" attitudes.

Leaving the docking area and walking down the sandy clay roads toward our camp, I saw tents in every direction. Suntans and shorts were the uniform of the day. Our destination was about two miles down this road. There, I would join the A-1-7 (A for company, 1 for 1st battalion, 7 for the 7th Marine regiment) of the 1st Marine Division. I was ecstatic! My dream was coming true. I was going to be part of one of the best fighting machines in the whole world. Filled with silent pride, I marched forward to begin living this dream.

Pavuvu was actually an immense palm tree plantation, owned by the Palmolive Peet Corp. Here was the source of the famous Palmolive oils. The palm trees stood in stately rows, about 25-five feet apart. It was not uncommon to see a marine flat on his back, knocked unconscious by a falling coconut. This was to be our home away from home, with its vegetative hazards and large population of land crabs and rats. Though thrilling in its own way, a land crab

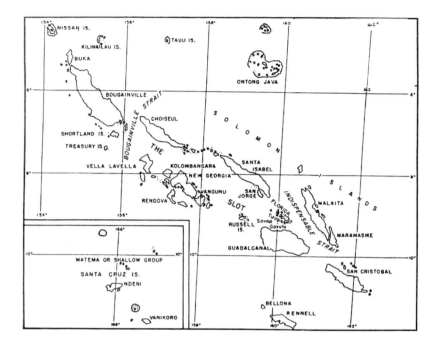

Solomon Islands, with inset showing Santa Cruz. (United States Marine Corps map.)

was no substitute for the girls I dreamed about! After every morning call, we spent at least 15 minutes clubbing to death the land crabs and rats that hid under and in everything.

This island also introduced us to our first tropical climate. It was necessary to dig miniature moats around our tents for the water run-off after the many sudden tropical storms. Wearing underwear, or any other constrictive clothing, was impossible because the heat and humidity worked together to create a bad case of jungle rot in any area that was constantly rubbed by cloth or straps. Some cases were so severe, the men had to be sent back to the States. I found that daily iodine treatments kept the fungus at bay; still, it never completely went away and the itching was embarrassing, irritating, and often bloody.

Soon, we reached the A company area and the sergeant proceeded to call out the particular platoons to which we were assigned. I was to go to 3rd platoon, 1st squad. Approaching my assigned tent, I got my first look at some of the best fighting men the world had to offer. Speedy Dorn, Walden, Hampton, and Jackson were to be my sackmates. Beaming with pride, I introduced myself and shook their young, strong hands. "That's your sack," said Speedy, pointing to the one next to his, the gesture crossing his muscular left arm over our right hands still clasped in a strong welcome. And then I made my first big mistake. "I'm from New York!" I said enthusiastically, neglecting to specify which New York. Even though I was from upstate, and the word got around that I was from New York City, the phrase "New York" conveyed the same reaction then as it does now. I was immediately tagged a "city boy," and a weak one at that, because I wore glasses.

Little did I realize the impact these few young men would have on my life. I had no fear, no anxiety, even though there was the very real possibility that my life could end here in the Pacific. I was eager, young, proud, and felt welcome here. I went to my sack, rolled up the mosquito net, and stowed my gear. All the comforts of home, surrounding all of us on the same mission: Kill those Japanese!

The next day started with roll call, the half-dressed marines scrambling to line up. The men, half-awake and still stretching the kinks out of their backs, greeted each other with huge yawns and sleepy stares. Our makeshift uniforms of unlaced shoes (no socks), and shorts (no underwear) would have sent any stateside, or other "by-the-book" officer into instant cardiac arrest. Casual dress in the extreme, including floppy hats and unbuttoned, loose shirts, was our uniform. However, our snap to attention belied our bedraggled appearance. Our movements, crisp and sharp, heads held high, chests out and chins in, announced us as the pride of America, the U.S. marines. The platoon lieutenant eyeballed us all with satisfaction and executed a brilliant 180° foot command movement to face the 1st sergeant, who stood about 50 feet from the rest of the men. Then came the "sound off" command to the 1st sergeant. "Headquarters Platoon, all present and accounted for!" "1st Platoon, all present and accounted for!" "2nd Platoon, all present and accounted for!" "3rd Platoon, all present and accounted for!" "4th Platoon, all present and accounted for!" The jungles of the South Pacific rang, and probably still echo today, with those dedicated words of honor, love, loyalty, and devotion to country. The 1st sergeant, swinging his right leg and foot in front of him, spun around another 180° to face the A Company commanding officer, 1st Lt. Blinco. Lt. Blinco was obviously in full charge of the company. He had the dark good looks and dense musculature of his Italian heritage, and, although not very tall, he had the bearing and presence of a strong leader. He walked proud, looked sharp, and always put his men's needs in front of his own. I am sure he treated his beautiful wife and four children, who were waiting for him at home in California, with the same respect.

Saluting the C.O., the 1st sergeant shouted, A Company, all present and accounted for!" This spinning foot movement of his was unique, and not found in the marine, or any, military manual. Twenty-plus years of marine

[39]

life had created this "salty" non-military maneuver, which was admired by all. A Company drew on this individual flourish in developing its own personal and unquenchable *esprit de corps*. "All present and accounted for!" had an everlasting meaning to all those united in the same cause, the fight for freedom.

The command "Dismissed!" began our first task of the day: clubbing to death the land crabs and rats that had overstayed their welcome. They came out of the jungles at night in such numbers we could hear their claws scrabbling across the road on their way into the tent area. Our day had begun, and the tropical heat bore relentlessly upon us. Before we had even begun to move, the 90-degree temperatures and humidity had already, instantly, soaked every shirt, sticking them uncomfortably to our skins. Day and night, the temperature was a steady hot, hot, hot! There were no cooling breezes or mild, gentle evenings. Only the daily, afternoon showers would bring a short respite from the oppressive heat. First business of the day accomplished, we started our routine training.

I was overwhelmed by the comradeship that started to develop between us during these days. It was like nothing I had ever experienced stateside. Friendships forged here were permanent and serious. Even though we were destined to kill, and had the tools and knowledge to kill, we never harmed one another in any way. We were a team. This was borne out by the fact that our area did not have a brig; it was not necessary, we had no criminals. We spent the days together as a close unit, learning to survive. Selfishness was a luxury we could not afford.

For evening entertainment, we grabbed our homemade stools, our bottles of warm coke or beer, stuck a cigar between our teeth, and off we went to the movies. The evening temperature still hovered around a muggy 80°, and evening dress consisted of the same shorts, sockless open shoes, and a silly little floppy hat of the day.

There were no tropical breezes to cool the evenings. Come to think of it, the Russell Islands never had refreshing tropical breezes; there wasn't even enough air movement to wave the ocean water to the beaches. The only things that caused the air to move were marines chasing the land crabs every morning or tearing after "Jack the Ripper" every night. It was a tropical climate designed and perfected for disease and discomfort.

The coral-based floor at the amphitheater was neither comfortable nor clean. The makeshift stools, with their low backs, would serve to keep our backsides out of the dirt and were comfortable enough seats for our 17-year-old bodies. We made our stools and desks from discarded crates taken from the dump. To complete our ingeniously made "study," we needed light. That came in the form of empty coke bottles, refilled with gasoline, with a rope stuck in for a wick. Accompanied by thick, black smoke, they still provided enough light to see. What time was not spent in training or at the movies was spent in writing home.

December 2, 1944

Pvt. G. Lince 83441
1st Bn. Co. A Plt 3
7th Marines
% Fleet Post Office
San Francisco, CA

Dear Mom & Dad:

I have arrived here and everything is fine. We crossed the equator and we were initiated. Everybody that hasn't gone across the equator gets initiated. And they really initiate you. We also crossed the international date line which made me gain a day.

I had two Thanksgivings. One aboard ship and one on the island here. I can't say where. It's in the Southwest Pacific though. We had plenty to eat both times.

We take pills for Malaria and it turns the fellows yellow. I am going to get quite a tan here I can see.

There are plenty of coconuts and of course palm trees. There are natives here and we call them "gooks." They work very hard and are really black.

There are big crabs that crawl into sacks at night. They are all over the place. They range from six to ten inches large.

The island was occupied by Japs once. There is plenty of jungle.

You can send package if you care to. The papers too. Did you get those pictures? Send me a small one. I'll tell you who to send the rest to. What do you think of them? Don't forget to have your picture taken. Three of you together. Mom, Dad, & Jerry and send it to me. Not too large of a picture.

Everything is better than I thought it would be. We have plenty of recreation. I have seen some good movies.

I haven't Puffles and Gene's address. I wish you would send them. I lost my pen aboard ship. Could you send me one. The quickest way possible.

I have received one letter dated October 27th is all. I am where I said I thought I was going. Remember Marie Iandermills old boyfriend?

So Fred has gone over. Do you know where? They don't censor incoming mail so you can write most anything. I will send something which will be self-explanatory. I am sure you will understand it.

We have nice swimming here. The coral cuts your feet though. It's first time I have swam in salt water.

I sent some birthday cards. I finally found some. Dad better get a deer

this year. I wished I could go with you Dad, but I have to get a little prac-
tice over here first. I certainly had fun when we went hunting on my fur-
lough.

Your loving son,
George

My own makeshift desk sported a large picture of a girlfriend, her dress hiked up high over smooth, lovely, long legs. It was great to hear the inspecting officers' eyeballs click as they passed by. I never failed an inspection while she was on display. Eventually, though, the picture ended up floating to the bottom of the sea, along with my seabag. My interest in the girl soon followed. In a fit of passion and total misjudgment, those pretty legs, accompanied by the rest of her, married a sailor.

After the movies, we had more cigars, warm beer, and warm coke with our buddies. There was no popcorn or other snack foods, not even a radio to provide soothing music for lonely minds. After a "refreshing" helmet shower, it was a nude dash to reach the sack underneath the mosquito netting before the land crabs did. Clothes were laid out underneath the thin mattress, providing a sort of compression "ironing board," then it was on to sleep. Most of us were just young teenagers, not knowing when or how we would get home, dreaming dreams that might never be. Then, after just a few hours, the brutal sound of the bugle shocked everyone awake, shattering the dreams of home, love, and girls. Finally, even the dreams turned cruel, the good endings vanishing in the stagnant air with the harsh sounds of the bugle. And it was again time to face reality. It took just one second to get one day closer to death and destruction.

One of my sackmates was already an old veteran marine, one of the noncommissioned officers (NCO) assigned to train us. Speedy Dorn had participated in the Cape Glouster Blitz and had fought at Peleliu, where he had been wounded. He was a very handsome boy from Utah, and even though he was only nineteen years old, his hair was already beginning to gray. Speedy's lanky six-foot body obediently followed the long strides of his casual walk. Although his soft tones did not convey an outwardly negative attitude, conversations with him were brief and to the point. Speedy did not waste time with idle chatter. I do remember him telling us about some of the fighting on Cape Glouster after somebody mentioned that particular blitz. In that quiet voice, he talked about the battle. Cape Glouster was a battle more against the elements than the Japs, a total opposite of what he had faced on the Peleliu blitz. Cape Glouster had few passable roads, and most of the danger lay in getting stuck in the knee-deep, black mire. Everybody, the marines and the enemy, had to fight their way through the thick, dark muck and the incredibly dense tropical jungles. There, the storms lasted for days, and the men were miserably wet 24 hours a day. The blitz was successful, though, the marines effectively cutting off the Jap supply line with few casualties. The Japs offered little resistance, and most escaped into the thick vegetation without much of a fight. There, the Japs starved to death, hiding from the marines who had them surrounded. Speedy recounted these facts with a total lack of emotion and facial expression. He was the perfect example of being "Asiatic." Being Asiatic meant not caring for anything or anybody in any way, and showing no outward emotion. Speedy was a fully programmed adult marine killer. There was no room in his mind for anything else. Life for him was filled with nothing but hate for, and killing of, the Jap.

Jackson was also from Utah. He didn't relate much with the rest of us. He was more distant than quiet. Jackson, too, constantly wrote letters home and, unlike most of us, he was married to a loving and faithful wife. Jackson was not one to mix with us peons. He spent his time "socializing" with the NCOs. Jackson was the typical drafted marine, his enthusiasm was not great and what there was of it was directed toward finding a way home.

Walden, another sackmate and combat veteran, had seen 31 days of hell on Peleliu. He was a Texan, a real American, a strong, upright marine. Like Speedy, Walden had gray hair at the age of twenty. This was the man more responsible for saving my life than anyone else, even though I had no way of knowing it then. Beating him in a casual boxing match had gained me his respect, and we became close friends. I had been minding my own business, cleaning my rifle, when Hampton started harassing me. Hampton wanted me to put on some boxing gloves and go a round with him. He was from Arkansas and wanted to beat the hell out of a guy from New York. He knew I couldn't fight. My face was too pretty, and my having to wear glasses convinced Hampton I was weak. After a while, though, I got tired of the pestering and gave in to him, putting on the gloves. The fight was over in a few short minutes. Hampton lay on the ground, dazed and amazed. Walden, who had been watching with the others, went up to him and said, "Give me those gloves!" Even though I was a little winded from my bout with Hampton, Walden was soon on his back too. From that day on, Walden and I were greatest of friends. When he saw me taking verbal garbage the other marines handed out, he would tell me "go ahead, pound him! Show him what you can do!" My boxing ability, and the fact that I was writing letters to different girl friends back home, inspired Walden to give me a nickname "Dude Boy."

Letters from my mother were newsworthy and a moral builder. She never wrote of worry, negative thoughts or expressed concern about my safety. She gave me confidence by believing in me, and that I would do my best regardless of the situation.

Shirley from Teaneck, New Jersey, uplifted the whole group with her wit. Her letters were welcomed by everybody, especially Walden. Mary Frances, Elinor, another Shirley, Betty Lou, Gloria, and all the others gave me many reasons to survive.

My father wrote me approximately five times in three years. He just did not want to believe what I was doing.

Today would be a great day. A regimental parade at the dock landing in the best uniform available in the South Pacific. No tie, with khaki shirt and trousers pressed in stylish form between our mattress and cot while we had sweet dreams of home. Shirts and trousers were placed in exacted positions to receive the ultimate in pressed pleats. Somehow, the many untouched wrinkles gave away the secret of a non-professional effort. The appearance of clothing slept in for a fortnight would be more of the undisguised truth.

However, with the pride of the marines testing our shirt buttons, wrinkled clothing was not noticed.

Without the legendary shiny mirrored shoes, we marched to the docks in our "Boondock" type rough shoes. Moving in unison at the dock landing, all 3,600 of us solidified into an organized unit.

The call for "attention" was shouted. The proper salutes and roll calls were given. Then the band began to play. Goose bumps ran up and down my back and neck. I could see the American Flag and our regimental flag proudly carried high by young men who were far, far from home. When the band played "Waltzing Matilda," our regimental song, shoulder to shoulder, one behind the other, we marched and we marched. Our marching feet could be heard around the world. We were the marines. Japs take notice: the marines are marching.

Humphrey and I would team up as BAR Man and Assistant BAR Man. I was the Assistant, as usual carrying the extra ammunition for the Bar, and I had an M1 rifle for my personal firepower. Speedy Dorn was our Fireteam Leader and Corporal.

Off we went to Cowshit Island to do some daily maneuvers in the jungle. Speedy deployed us with hand signals. Our movements were swift, taking advantage of all the jungle cover. The body feeling was like popcorn in a hot oven. No time to relax and think. Just move, move, and move. The need for fast movement and covering each other with our personal firepower was becoming a natural habit. Like aggressive, fast-moving, live machines of destruction, we started to become the integral living part of the mode of our tactics called "Blitz."

Not everything was peaches and cream. My feeling of daily accomplishment disappeared when Speedy, without warning, burst my bubble of satisfaction. Speedy yelled, "Lince, you train like a damn German." My heart fell to my feet as quickly as an elevator with a severed cable. Not being able to reply, I never challenged Speedy and his comment. Maybe the real meaning was never known to me. Maybe Speedy gave me a compliment, and I did not realize it. Speedy and I became very close buddies in the remaining days we had together.

The day was Sunday and even in the Pacific theater of war Sunday was a special day. Three veterans of the Peleliu blitz and I combined our thoughts and ambition to make a trip down to the bay. Today, I would receive a sudden unwelcome awareness that I was in a war where someone was going to try and kill me. "The Jap would wait all night with nerves of steel if he knew he could kill you five minutes before dawn," Red said to me as a warning father or brother. He looked at me straight in the eye and added "Don't ever forget this!" I gave a deep sigh breathing again as my heart had stopped because my brain had exploded in dramatic amazement.

For the first time, someone had told me what my enemy was like. I suddenly learned he not only had slanted eyes and yellow skin, he had a determined mind to kill someone. No one, but no one, ever attempted to inflame my anger to kill. All of my commands had been forward march, attention, at ease, fall out, halt and etc. The killing or dying topic seemed to be ignored.

But now my experienced combat buddies gave me valuable insight to the real war and what I could expect. At 18 years old, this man's folly was difficult to comprehend. With no buses, trains, or airplanes available to make a quick exit, my thoughts shifted focus to the beautiful blue waters we were approaching. Silence seemed to capture us after "Red" had awakened me to the real war. A cloud of despair seemed to hang over all of us. Maybe the others realized our controlled destiny. Unknown to us that day that only one of us would survive the blitz. Could it be that the very concern of my experienced combat buddies made it possible that one of us would survive.

I went into the blue water with my shoes on because the many coral formations could cut feet to shredded, bloody skin in seconds. The colorful fish swam serenely in this natural aquarium of beautiful splendor. The thoughts of war vanished in the middle of this tropical paradise. Only the thought of "why was it necessary to go to war when all this beauty is given to man freely by God." What more could man want?

We all joined together for our trip back to our tent area. "Grabassing" (pushing and shoving each other) was our mood towards each other. It was difficult to imagine that on a later day we would be killing and dying together.

At first, I was assigned as assistant Browning Automatic Rifle (BAR) man (boy) with Speedy's fire team, with the red-bearded teenager from Arkansas, Hampton, as my BAR buddy. Lying in his sack, Speedy would watch me write to my girlfriends. Although he didn't show it, I thought that he seemed to enjoy

First Marine Division bivouac area on the island of Pavuvu. (United States Marine Corps photo.)

the smell of the perfume from the many letters I received in return. "In a very short time," Speedy told me, "you won't be writing those letters any more." He hadn't written his own parents in over two years. Speedy believed the writing effort futile because we were in the middle of a controlled destiny that had a very high percentage rate of sudden endings. According to Speedy, there was no need to plan for a future that would never happen, a future that could include love and girls. Our only goal and purpose in life was to hate and kill the Jap disease.

But there were never any complaints from Speedy. He performed his duty to the fullest. He was an unsung hero, and the beneficiaries of his efforts will never know or realize the agonizing pain that was extracted from him, from his youth. At that point in time, neither did I.

Now it was time to go to the rifle range. I was with Speedy Dorn's Fire Team carrying an M1 as an assistant BAR man. We marched to the rifle range in a forced march to flex our muscles. It was about three miles away, so the march was rather easy.

My first weapon practice was with a Thompson Sub-Machine Gun. The main purpose of the practice was to hold the weapon on the target while the rapid fire pulled the barrel up and to the right. Soon I was hitting with deadly accuracy. Next, I used the BAR, lying down in a prone position. The purpose was the same as the sub-machine gun. Hold the weapon on the target while the rapid fire pulled the barrel up and to the right. Soon perfection was accomplished.

Now the fun began. We had a contest for a fifth of whiskey for the best shot in the company. M1's were the chosen weapon. The first group laid down prone, ready to fire. In front of us was the saltiest marine I ever saw. He looked like he had at least 20 years in the Corps and his dungarees, turned-up hat, and face of hard leather expressed his years of dedication. He yelled "ready on the left, ready on the right, watch your target!" He paused, then said, "Target!" With that command, he dove for cover, then all hell broke loose. M1's fired eight shots in seconds. Then the scores were counted. I had fired a perfect score. Then the old Sarge got up again. We were now in different positions. He yelled his salty commands and dove for cover. The firing began. The scores were counted, and I shot a perfect score. One more time, the Sarge yelled his commands, dove for cover and the firing began. Counting the scores, I was leading the company with a perfect score. Then, without warning, a disaster happened. As I lay prone ready for the second to last firing, a tropical rainstorm started with its buckets of rain. I was soaked in seconds, and my eyeglasses had no windshield wipers. I had to remove them and wipe them off. The salty Sarge held up the firing for me until I wiped off my glasses. I fired and still was leading everybody with a perfect score. Still raining buckets, it came time for our final round. But I was not so lucky this time. The Sarge was not patient this time and I was given zero on my final round. My perfect score with a zero round score took me out of the race. However, not all was lost. Dutt, my buddy, was the winner, and he shared the booze with me. So Dutt and I felt independently wealthy and strolled back to our bivouac area alone. However, our innocence did not pay dividends, and ten hours extra police duty (EPD) was our reward. We stayed with the company from then on, regardless of our nervous emotions. We later learned that our forced march to the rifle range was faster than the record-holding 81 Mortar Group. The entire group was American Indians, and to beat them was an unbelievable accomplishment. So Dutt and I did our EPD, digging holes and filling them with rocks for nice new urinal troughs. Somebody had to do it. Why shouldn't we?

Along with the discomfort caused by the tropical hazards of the island, I discovered the most demoralizing of all was the enemies' constant harassment. One of the few Japanese left on the island at this time became famous for his actions. We named him "Jack the Ripper."

One night, my first experience with him, I was jolted out of a restless sleep by shouts of "Walden, Walden, is that you?" I could hear Hampton at the opposite side of our tent, nervously trying to strike a match. He kept asking, "Who the hell is standing at the head of my sack?!" Is that you Walden?" I quickly came fully awake and, heart pounding, gripped my knife and started to move cautiously to the opposite side of the tent to see what had startled him. I was about halfway there, moving in a crouching position, ready to leap at whatever it was, when I heard our makeshift bridge, the board over our "moat," squeak as if someone had stepped on it while making a quick getaway. In the pitch dark, no one had gotten a good look at the intruder, however we did see a human-like outline. We knew that it must have been one of the Japs that had been left on the island, and that he was hiding in the jungle.

Night after night, this maniac would creep out of his daylight hiding place and proceed to terrorize the whole division. He would steal into the area noiselessly, stand motionless at the head of a sack, and suddenly start swinging his machete around wildly, violently slashing the protective mosquito netting around the sleeping marine. His attacks caused chaos throughout the whole area and tested our nerves. Night after night, the darkness was split by the warlike yells and screams of the frightened young marines. If we had had ammunition, we would have shot up the whole area in our panic! As it was, all we could do was post sentries at each end of the company street, armed with rifles, hoping to catch this silently approaching shadow. There was no ammunition, but the rifles were fixed with deadly bayonets. For a group of young inexperienced marines, this was a nightmare. Even the veterans preferred the front lines and an enemy they could see to this elusive ghost.

We had no electricity, and the Jap madman used this to his advantage. He got by us every time, and although he caused no one any actual physical damage, his insane tactics were successful in totally unsettling our minds.

After many weeks of this horror, the attacks stopped, ending just as suddenly as they had begun. Maybe he had just grown tired of it all, or maybe he had finally been killed during one of the routine patrols. We were never to know what happened to him. We were left only with the shredded remains of what had once been our peace of mind.

Strange incidents, such as these, would stick to my memory like glue and were never in short supply. Shortly after, another one would be added to this quickly expanding niche in my mind.

I had special guard duty one night and was completely puzzled as to why. I didn't really mind the hour. The special time of 2:00 A.M. to 4:00 A.M. seemed to be hours of enchantment for me. It was too early to be awake and too late to go to sleep. On the way to the corporal of the guard to receive my assignment, I mumbled under my breath, "What a horrible way to spend two hours of my life!" The corporal of the guard was located in very small area. It consisted only of an open tent, with a cot for the bugler and an improvised desk strewn with instruction papers and orders. Upon arrival, the mystery began in earnest. I was given a loaded 45 pistol and my orders were to shoot to kill first and then holler "Halt." This sounded backwards, and my mind at 2:00 A.M. started spinning. This was not a fun assignment. I was to kill first, whoever it was, and then give them a chance to halt? How could this be? I would be killing unfairly, at the very least, and certainly without cause.

I aligned my 160-pound body, complete with reeling brain, behind the corporal of the guard, and we proceeded to go relieve the marine sentry, who was still waiting for his "kill first, then warn" target. He welcomed our presence and, looking like he couldn't wait to get out of there, happily and quickly reported that he had not had a chance to carry out his insane and unusual orders. I hoped it wouldn't happen on my watch, either!

My post was right outside the 1st sergeant's tent. The flaps were up, and I could see where his sack was. However, I couldn't see anyone sleeping in the sack. All I saw was a lighted cigarette glowing in the dark, at face level, indicating that no one was sleeping in that cot. If it was the 1st sergeant, he was also on guard, looking for the person whom I was ordered to shoot without warning. Whoever this mystery person was, he was sure keeping the 1st sergeant on his toes, awake and fearing for his safety. After a few weeks of 2:00 A.M. to 4:00 A.M. duty, the mystery duty was finally partially revealed to me through the ever-active marine grapevine (scuttlebutt).

It seems the 1st sergeant, in keeping with the present prejudice that exists for the American Indian, had dealt unfairly with one of our American Indian marines. The marine Indian, already familiar with the dirty "deals" that Americans dish out, responded in a definitely unhappy manner. Apparently, he decided that he had quite enough of this prejudice. A simply worded note, describing the Indian's displeasure and consequent resolve, had very effectively created the many sleepless nights and days of fear for the 1st sergeant. Even though he was a 1st sergeant, with at least 20 years of experience, he was no match for an irritated American Indian trained as a marine. At least, he had the presence of mind to realize the seriousness of the situation, that his life was in danger, and to post the guard.

The cigarette glow I saw every night that I stood on guard attested to the fact that even the extra protection was not sufficient to encourage the sergeant to get some sleep. I guess he wasn't ready to be scalped. Time passed, however, and the lack of activity seemed to lessen the 1st sergeant's anxiety. As each day passed, he became more relaxed. The actual offense the 1st sergeant committed was never divulged, and the Indian involved was not known by the marines who protected the sergeant during this time. We never found out why the subject was avoided. Was it embarrassing? Disgusting? Personal? Hopefully, somewhere beyond the scuttlebutt, they had finally smoked a "peace pipe," forgiving and forgetting past wrongs. After all, there were more important matters to attend to during that time and other avenues in which to direct any kind of explosive anger.

As the weeks went on and on, we learned how to get drunk on Aqua

Velva shaving lotion, drink warm beer in tomato juice, and become buddies for life. Steel bonds that were forged between the comrades at arms would literally save lives. Our teenage life started to dissipate, washed away slowly, with each tropical shower. This was the island that gave us our first lessons on the realities of war and the grief it would bring. Boyhood pranks and innocent smiles were quickly becoming a thing of the past.

On the way to the mess hall one day, I met up with a stateside buddy, G.G. Olson. Rolling his black eyes, he said, "What the hell are you doing here?!" He was a machine gunner in C Company. Together, we headed to the mess hall, a long, tented, screened building, complete with packed dirt floor. There was no electricity to shed light on the dismal, unrecognizable, flavorless "food," all taste and texture having been removed by the dehydration process. There were picnic-like tables to eat on, but most of the time we took the food back to our tents. We used our own mess gear, two halves of an aluminum 4" × 6" × 1" deep pan, washing them ourselves by dipping them first into boiling, soapy water, then rinsing them in clear boiling water. This was our own unique sterilizing process. A corpsman stood at the end of this line, popping an anti-malaria pill into each mouth. This pill turned our skin and urine a distinct yellow. All we needed was slanted, squinty eyes, and we would look exactly like the Japs.

"Double-G" just laughed about the whole situation. He was always upbeat, and being around him could lift anybody's spirits. We would talk about the buddies we both knew, and he would say "That S.O.B.!" and laugh.

Later that week, Double-G introduced me to a friend of his from Rome, New York. Billy Siegal was his name, and due to that prominent feature sticking out of his face, he quickly acquired the nickname "Bazooka Nose." Bazooka Nose was a veteran-hero, having been wounded on Peleliu. Both Double-G and Bazooka Nose were the best of marines, excellent role models for the youth of America. Both had the hell scared out of them by Jack the Ripper. Double-G's net had been slashed to ribbons. We didn't see each other often because we were all assigned to different companies, but we would pass each other during maneuvers. Double-G would shake his head at me, roll those black eyes of his, and say, "How the hell did we get here?!"

I soon left Speedy's fire team to become a flame thrower, bazooka, and demolition specialist. When we received our rations of beer and Coke, I would go and trade my beer for Speedy's Coke. It was my only chance to see him. He never had many words to say, but there was always a sort of friendship apparent in his eyes. He had an outward calm appearance. His adult killer instincts were normally hidden and unseen, only to erupt like a raging volcano at the sight of the enemy. His effort, no matter how measured, was a significant straw in breaking the back of the Jap Empire. He would remain unnoticed by the world; his only reward would come from an all-knowing God.

At my new assignment, I met my Sergeant Rizzo, a 6'1" redhead from Pennsylvania, who looked more like a clerk than a marine. He acted like a clerk, too, keeping to himself most of the time. Rizzo had the unique ability to disappear at the first sign of trouble. Even though he had good muscles on a well-built body, he seldom put them to use. If Sgt. Rizzo had any wisdom to give to young marines, he failed miserably his responsibility to instruct and lead. He kept these useful items securely locked away in that little mind of his. Rizzo often walked with a strange sort of insect-like scuttle, very different from the usual strong marine stride.

I soon discovered that pains in the ass came in several forms and ranks. As if dealing with Sergeant Rizzo wasn't enough, I had a newly acquired commanding corporal. "Hey, Lince, report to Paterson for extra duty!" "Hey, Lince, the lieutenant needs a job done!" "Hey, Lince, they need help in the mess hall!" "Lince, report to the docks for duty!" Corporal Powell, one of the most memorable marines I would ever meet, yelled these orders from the neighboring tent, not bothering to raise his carcass to look me in the eye. He constantly picked me for the nastiest, dirtiest duties. Powell had a ball expressing his dictatorial powers in the only way he could by picking on a subordinate. Powell was my slavemaster corporal, not because of his ability as a leader, but because he had survived a blitz. Promotion to corporal was not necessarily due to leadership ability. Rather it was given as a reward for survival, to fill the vacancies left by the fallen marines. Powell did not have an ounce of leadership skills. He wanted to pick on one particular individual and drive him like a slave, thereby expressing his meanness, ugliness, and stupidity. His rich, aristocratic, unsmiling features contrasted sharply with his over-sized, ill-fitting clothes and warped mind, giving him an exceptional, almost ridiculous, appearance. It was difficult to picture him as ever being youthful. Somewhere at Cape Glouster, Peleliu, or Guadalcanal, his mind had become twisted, bent like a pretzel.

Sgt. Rizzo assigned Snyder and me, with our combined selfless efforts, as a flame-thrower team. Snyder was a curly, red-headed, strong, handsome boy from South Carolina. He was a star football player, and I could see the girls lined up waiting for him to come home. Snyder had an unselfish gentleness that contrasted oddly with his muscular build, and I especially valued the time we spent together, talking about our loved ones and girlfriends.

Our first job detail together really stank. I mean, literally, really stank. Our assignment was to take out the garbage. We went down to the docks and stepped aboard a flat metal platform-like "boat" equipped with an outboard motor. Our cargo, the garbage, was already on board in 50 gallon drums. We spent at least two hours on the "boat," with no protection whatsoever from the blazing sun. Our cargo, garbage barrels filled with decaying scraps of food, a haven for maggots and flies, was destined for the ocean. The stench was almost unbearable. We had no water, and no sun-tan oil, and by the time we reached the place we were to dump the garbage, we were as red as lobsters.

When we returned to the docks, we were in severe pain, being both dangerously dehydrated and just as dangerously scorched by the sun. We tried to obtain a measure of relief by spreading shaving cream over each other's backs, but it didn't quite do the job. We couldn't go to sick bay, because getting "government property" exposed to enough sun to cause a painful and restrictive condition was a court-martial offense.

After the war was over, the *Saturday Evening Post* would report that these kind of events were being planned on a daily basis, in order to keep us fighting mad. We had volunteered to fight a war, not to accept this type of treatment from our own people. But these daily irritating incidents served their purpose. We blamed the Japanese for them, and we wanted to kill him for forcing us into these horrible situations. We were becoming killing machines, expendable government property, and situations like these were planned to keep us that way.

A few days after this ordeal, Sgt. Rizzo came around with an exceptional opportunity. There was a desperate need for dock workers to load ships with ammunition, food, and water for the next blitz. This meant hard, extremely exhausting, backbreaking labor, 24 hours a day. There would be little time for sleep or rest. But, whoever volunteered for this effort would not have to participate in the next blitz. This was life insurance paying dividends of life instead of money. Snyder talked to me at some length about his feelings, describing a strange and powerful premonition. Premonitions were never taken lightly overseas. They became true too often for coincidence. Snyder believed he would die during the next blitz. This wasn't surprising, because flame-thrower, bazooka, and demolition teams had an especially high casualty rate. The projection was that at least half of our group of twenty were going to be killed, and at least half of the survivors would be seriously wounded. Snyder, therefore, grabbed the opportunity. He had very powerful ties to his family, and his greatest nightmare was of his mother receiving a KIA (killed in action) telegram. Such a telegram could kill her. He needed to get home, wounded or not, to take care of his mother. Working on the docks would spare her the horror of his death, and he would still be part of one of the most important efforts in the blitz. And boy, did Snyder work! He worked days and nights, back to back, with little or no sleep. The only chance I had to talk with him was when the rest of us had to go down to the docks in the middle of the night to help load the ships. Because this happened only occasionally, I hardly ever saw him again.

Snyder, now having been assigned to the docks, Rizzo buddied me with Rotolo. Rotolo was from New York City and had somehow managed to carry some of his teenage behavior into the Marine Corps. His darkly tanned face sported a permanent smirk, and he was street-wise and tricky, always scheming, his arrogant black eyes flashing with mockery. Rotolo was a typical tough-acting, know-it-all, bossy, smart ass from New York City. He was a seasoned veteran, having been a front-line marine on Peleliu. I was just an inexperienced combat Marine, and as far as I was concerned, Rotolo could practically walk on water. My false illusion of Rotolo would vanish, though, as time exposed his true nature.

Lamotta was probably the only marine from New York City who commanded and received respect. He was much, much older in appearance for his age. Thirty-one days on Peleliu was enough hell to give him gray hair and remove his smile forever. I cannot recall seeing Lamotta smile. He was quiet and confused. His attitude reflected a possibility that he did not care for life anymore. He somehow knew his destiny and waited apathetically for his time to come. He had no expectations for a long life or any reason to believe that he would ever return to his brief teenage life of excitement and pleasure.

He never discussed home, his past, his relatives, or anyone who may be living a life that was so remote it was not real. His dungarees fit like a glove. He held his head high anytime, anywhere. He seemed never to be any part of any verbal communication.

He was a young marine, old before his time with visible scars of spending too much time in hell. He was a very smooth operating, killing machine. Never blinking to change his view or his direction. A marine robot if there ever was one.

Our initial training over, we were now ready for the intensified activity that would introduce us to actual war-like conditions. We boarded the LSTs (landing ships tanks) and headed out to Guadalcanal. We were on our way to becoming a closely knit unit of adult killers, never again to return to a normal teenage life.

5

GUADALCANAL

From the United States Marine Corps history *Victory and Occupation:*

Guadalcanal was the primer of ocean and jungle war. It was everything the United States could do at that moment against everything the Japanese could manage at that place. From this the Americans learned that they could beat the enemy, and they never stopped doing it. The headlines from Guadalcanal did more for homefront morale than did the fast carrier raids of 1942's winter and early spring, for the last Americans had come to grips with the enemy; and the outcome of this fighting added in the bargain a boost to the spirit of the Pacific fighting man. The benefits from official and unofficial circulation of lessons learned there by the Army, Navy, and Marines were many and far-reaching.

Veterans of all ranks from all branches of the service came home to teach and spread the word, while many more stayed on to temper the replacements coming out to the war. Barracks bull sessions and bivouac yarns added color and not a little weight to the formal periods of instruction. Thus was the myth that the Japanese were supermen shattered, and the bits of combat lore or the legendary tall tales and true which begin, "Now, on the 'Canal..." still have not entirely disappeared from the Marine repertoire.

General Vandegrift summed it up in a special introduction to The Guadalcanal Campaign, the historical monograph that contains the Marine Corps' first study of the operation:

We struck at Guadalcanal to halt the advance of the Japanese. We did not know how strong he was, nor did we know his plans. We knew only that he was moving down the island chain and that he had to be stopped.

We were as well trained and as well armed as time and our peacetime experience allowed us to be. We needed combat to tell us how effective our training, our doctrines, and our weapons had been.

We tested them against the enemy, and we found that they worked. From that moment in 1942, the tide turned, and the Japanese never again advanced.

Likewise, Guadalcanal was more than just another battle for the Japanese, but the lesson they learned there was a bitter one. The occupation that they started almost on a whim had ended in disaster, and from this they never quite recovered. Captain Ohmae summed it up:

... when the war started, it was not planned to take the Solomons. However, the early actions were so easy that it was decided to increase the perimeter defense line and to gain a position which would control

American traffic to Australia. Expansion into the Solomons from Rabaul was then carried out. Unfortunately, we also carried out the expansion at the same time instead of consolidating our holdings in that area. After you captured Guadalcanal, we still thought that we would be able to retake it and use it as an outpost for the defense of the empire. This effort was very costly, both at the time and in later operations, because we were never able to recover from the ship and pilot losses received in that area.

Unfortunately for the Japanese, there were very few lessons from Guadalcanal that they could put to effective use. In a sense this was phase one of their final examination, the beginning of a series of tests for the military force that had conquered the Oriental side of the Pacific and they failed it. After this there was neither time nor means for another semester of study and preparation. Admiral Tanaka had this to say about the operation and its significance:

Operations to reinforce Guadalcanal extended over a period of more than five months. They amounted to a losing war of attrition in which Japan suffered heavily in and around that island... There is no question that Japan's doom was sealed with the closing of the struggle for Guadalcanal. Just as it betokened the military character and strength of her opponent, so it presaged Japan's weakness and lack of planning that would spell her defeat.

The Allies entered this first lesson with sound textbooks. In the field of amphibious warfare, Marine doctrine hammered out in the peacetime laboratory now could be polished and improved in practice and supported by a rapidly mobilizing industrial front at home. Modern equipment that everybody knew was needed began to flow out to the test of combat. There it took on refinements and practical modifications, as doctrines and techniques improved. New models continued to arrive and were quickly put to use in the hands of now-skilled fighting men.

For example, landing craft, which went into mass production, aided the tactical aspects of amphibious assaults and also lessened the logistical problems at the beachhead. Improved communications equipment made it possible for the Marine Corps to improve and make more effective many of the special organizations and operational techniques that previously had been little more than carefully sketched theory. Air and naval gunfire liaison parties that were tested on Guadalcanal later became the efficient tools of integrated warfare that Marines had been confident they could become.

This strength of new equipment and ability enabled the Allies to take command of the strategy and a contest began. The psychology of total war found expression for the front-line Marine in his observation that "the only good Jap is a dead one." But an even better Jap was the one bypassed and left to ineffective existence on an island in the rear areas: he cost the Allies less. Strength gave the Allies this capability to by pass many garrisons.

Likewise, Guadalcanal proved that often it was cheaper and easier to build a new airfield than to capture and then improve one the Japanese had built or were building. This coincided well with the basic amphibious doctrine long agreed upon: never hit a defended beach if the objective can be reached by traveling over an undefended one. Together these principles sometimes made it possible for the Allies to land on an enemy island and build an airfield some distance from the hostile garrison. This the Marines did in November 1943, at Bougainville. A perimeter was established around the airfield, and there defenders sat waiting for the Japanese to do the hard work of marching over difficult terrain to present themselves for a battle. It was a premeditated repeat of the Guadalcanal tactic, and when the Japanese obliged by so accepting it, they were defeated.

All services, units, and men in the Pacific, or slated to go there, were eager to learn the valuable lessons of early combat and to put them into practice. For the Marine Corps, an important factor in the continuing success of the advance across the pacific was the delineation of command responsibilities between the naval task force commander and the amphibious troop commander.

Late in the first offensive, General Vandegrift was able to initiate an important change in naval thinking concerning the command of amphibious operations. The General and Admiral Turner had often disagreed on the conduct of activities ashore on Guadalcanal, and Vandegrift had maintained that the commander trained for ground operations should not be a subordinate of the local naval amphibious force commander. His theory prevailed, and in the future the amphibious troops commander, once established ashore, would be on the same command level as the naval task force commander. Both of them would be responsible to a common superior.[3]

The cost of Guadalcanal was not as great as that of some later operations. The number of men and officers killed was 1,598, and the number wounded was 4,709. Defeat for the Japanese was more costly. Approximately 14,800 of their forces were killed or missing, while 9,000 died of wounds and diseases. But nothing could take from Guadalcanal its unique spot in history. The first step, however short and faltering, is always the most important.

Now, the combat veteran marines and the replacement marines sailed to Guadalcanal to begin forging a unit of an invincible fighting force. As the ship approached, I saw the island. It was majestic and forbidding, larger than I had imagined. The misty jungle and darkly beautiful mountains gave no hint that this would be the place to transform innocent, unsuspecting boys into warriors, to be filled with an all-consuming rage as dark and overwhelming as its mountains. The beaches were some of the most beautiful in the world, and it was difficult to believe that these white sands had witnessed such human devastation and suffering. The mountains had echoed the cries of horror and pain, while the gentle rolling hills had watched helplessly as the horrible drama had unfolded.

GUADALCANAL

The 1st Marine Division on Guadalcanal had driven the Japs back to sea and eliminated their existence as a fighting unit, at a loss of 37 American lives. Shortly after this victory, another 3,000+ Japs had landed on the beaches in an attempt to correct this situation. The Japs became lost for more than two weeks, wandering around the island trying to find the American marines. The marines found this exhausted, disoriented group and killed 2,200 of them, sacrificing 84 marines in the process. Except for a few remaining Jap survivors sneaking around in the jungles, the island was secure.

The original veterans of Guadalcanal, the remnants of the valiant fighting force that had secured the island, now teamed up with the young replacements of the wounded and dead to drive out the remaining Japs that hid in the thick jungles. The relentless search for the stragglers, combined with the teaching by experienced veterans, would serve as our combat training. The intensity was the same as actual warfare and was a continuation of our introduction to "real" war. Weeks of coordinated efforts would strip us of our youth and innocence, molding us into a tightly knit team of efficient killers. The enemy would never again be able to produce panic in the minds of these men. Each teenage mind had been kindled with a hot, bright fire — a fire that was ready to rage across the land and wipe the Jap disease off the face of the earth.

Our bivouac area was located in the center of a sea of black mud, at the edge of a dark, forbidding jungle. Beyond the jungle, there were high craggy mountains and rolling hills, filled with dense vegetation. This is where the enemy hid. Those that remained from the marine victories that had let the Japanese know that we were serious about winning this war. Each day, we would fight our way into the jungles, through the entrapping vegetation, not knowing what lay in wait for us. It was impossible to know what was out there in the thick mist, and each time was a harrowing experience. The jungle was as hot as an oven, and the air was positively stagnant. Even the birds and other animals were subdued. The trees created the skyline high above. The foliage was incredibly close, ensnaring one's limbs with every movement. It was incredible to think of anyone being able to move in this foliage.

The tropical ulcers on our feet, the jungle rot in every crease of our bodies, and the helmet straps creating the sore, raw patches on our necks piled irritation upon irritation. Within, the savage killing instinct bided its time, knowing it would soon be set free. There was no escape from the hunger, thirst, loneliness, and fear. Even the lowly mosquito turned malicious, giving me a case of malaria that would bring no less than six attacks in my lifetime. Our youth was pulled from our bodies, along with the heat and the jungle pulling from every pore.

Soon after we had arrived, the ship bringing our food rations had been sunk, adding a very real threat of starvation to the already unbearable situation. All we had to eat was old, World War I canned rations and very little of that.

One day, we found a Seabee outfit down the road from our camp. Thinking we could finally get a good meal, we got in their chow line. They started to refuse us, but, recognizing our marine emblems, they grudgingly let us through. Apparently, the Seabee cooks were already irritated about having to stay up late at night, baking doughnuts for the Red Cross, who would later sell them to the dirty and exhausted young marines. The Seabee's resented the overtime they had to put in to get the work done.

The comparison between our lifestyle and the Seabees' was demoralizing, to say the least. They were only across the road from us, but they slept in clean white sheets in tents above ground on wooden decks, covered with mosquito netting. They had two different types of cold drinks, and food! They had clean laundry and water to bathe in. It was hard to believe that anybody could be unhappy, surrounded by all this luxury. We slept in our unwashed clothes, used an ineffective smelly liquid as an insect repellent, showered in the rain, slept on the ground, and were forced to eat garbage. We could see no reason for the difference. Were we being punished? The answer was a resounding *yes*! This forced style of living inevitably brings out the beast in all men; the beast that can kill, kill, kill. As we passed other young men on the road, we could see the same feeling reflected in their eyes and on their faces. We were being primed and prepared to drive a menacing force off the face of the earth. The hatred was being fed and bottled up inside us, ready to be released at the right moment. No enemy could survive these miniature atom bombs when they finally exploded.

At first, something inside me seemed to reject this transformation. I instinctively rejected the hatred trying to take over my mind. I wanted such foreign matter to stay out. I would try to fill my head with pictures of pretty girls with smiling faces and beautiful fragrances, with remembered laughter and warm touches of love. Trying to blot out the reality of the jungle rot on my neck, I pictured girls running fingers through my hair. I brought up memories of the sweet smell of perfume, hoping that would get rid of the rotten odor of unwashed bodies. I wanted to fill my stomach with my mother's vegetable soup or spaghetti, not the swill that did nothing for the hunger pains and brought on terrible sickness. I needed to hear, and talk with friendly tones, and see someone smile and hear someone's laughter. I yearned for a real meal, a long cool drink of water, a good night's sleep between sweet-smelling sheets, and a bath. I wanted out!

Finally, one night in desperation, I ran to the edge of the jungle, holding my K bar, a six-inch Marine knife, close to my face. I hoped I would "accidentally" fall on the knife. I was willing to give up an eye in order to hold on to my escaping youth, a small price to pay. I stumbled and fell many times, but the knife point missed my eye each time. Finally, the temporary insanity loosened its hold on me, leaving me lying where I had fallen, completely exhausted and spent. The night was long as I sat alone at the edge of the jungle, watching the silent marines around the fire. There was no laughter, and there were no jokes. They had already surrendered their smiling youth, just as I would surrender mine at dawn. They had already made the transformation to adult killers, with no chance of knowing again what it would be like to be a teenager. Those that survive will go home and people will say "the war changed him," but they will never know why. Like the marines around that fire, I would leave my youth on Guadalcanal.

The next day, I stayed at our bivouac area while the others went into the jungle looking for the Japs. This exercise was maneuvers for the next blitz, but I was too exhausted and ill to join them. The sergeant had a hammock strung between two trees, and this was my chance to get some rest. As I climbed into the hammock, it spun and flipped me and the sergeant's gear into the black mud. This seemed typical of the whole situation.

I could never understand why Sergeant Rizzo had a hammock, and the rest of us had to sleep on the ground. But he wasn't the typical marine sergeant; the war had changed him in its own way. He seemed to exist only in body, with his mind kept perpetually, perhaps purposely, dull and absent. He never made any effort to lead us. He did not teach us the survival skills we needed, nor how to kill our enemy. Most other sergeants that I had known would have made Sergeant Stinker (John Wayne in "Iwo Jima") hang his head in shame. They were the true superheroes, always ready and willing to teach you ways to save your life. However, our Sergeant Rizzo was completely devoid of these virtues. He was taller than most at 6'1", and had a cap of red hair that really stood out in a crowd. His head was full of marine statistics, but any other wisdom he had was securely locked away in his mind, never to be shared. He seemed numbed in spirit and consciousness. He came from Pennsylvania, and he had been one of the first marines to fight the Japanese on Guadalcanal. Youth, if it ever had a chance to exist, had been most efficiently removed from his mind and body.

Sunday was still a special day, even in this hostile environment. We were free to do whatever we wanted that day, and I sought out my stateside friends in the 11th Marine Artillery. Somehow I found them and we spent the day in friendship. The main topic of conversation at the time was "how the hell did we get here and why." Many came in answer to the idealistic calling of "protecting our country," "Wipe out Fascism," and "Uncle Sam Wants You!" Everyone had seen the John Wayne movies, telling of war as necessary for eradicating fascism, and depicting the soldiers, sailors, and marines as noble, upbeat, and wonderfully patriotic. Everybody wanted to be the hero John Wayne portrayed. Some had been drafted with no other choice but to try and survive. We were too young to know why and too young to die.

Toward evening, my buddy marine and I started back to our areas. As we started down the long dirt road, we noticed the dark heavy clouds coming over the mountains. We stole two ponchos from a clothesline, hoping it would protect us from the rain. Suddenly, the sky split open. It quickly became dark as night, and the deep ditches on each side of the road were rapidly filling with water. Our ponchos made no difference, and we quickly became soaked to the bone. As we continued forward, we heard a bubbling sound coming from the rain-filled ditch. We ran to the ditch and pulled a marine from the water-filled trench, saving him from a drunken, watery death. As we pulled him from the water, we realized he must have been six feet plus and at least 200 pounds. He had to be a cook, to be that healthy. McCabe and I, weighing about 145 and 160 pounds, respectively, had our work cut out for us to carry this giant down the road. We propped him up between us and dragged him until our energy was exhausted. Then we would rest, releasing him from our grip. Like a felled redwood, he would slowly fall into the mud, splashing the black, sticky goop everywhere. He was too numb from "jungle juice" to even realize what was going on. He kept muttering that he had had enough of those Japanese, and he wanted to go home.

After about a mile, which seemed like twenty, we finally sighted McCabe's tent area. Totally spent, we dropped the giant on the ground and found the Corporal of the Guard, telling him of our find. The marine never knew who saved his life that day, nor did we ever find out his identity. But, we did hope that his wish would come true, and that he would go home alive, with some of his humanity left. It was the same wish most of us had.

After we had dropped our "friend" off, I continued down the road, now totally exhausted and alone. About an hour down the road, I had another sudden surprise and a chance to test my wit. Nerves of steel would have to be my greatest asset. I was walking along the right side of the road when, suddenly, a Jap came out of the tall Kunai grass. He turned to his right and started walking in my direction on the left side of the road. He glanced at me, just as I saw him, and our eyes met and locked for a long second in a fiery stare. His hair was coal black. His dark eyes didn't flinch or move in any direction.

I did not see any visible weapons, but that did not mean he didn't have a pistol on his right hip. He wore no hat. I did not look below his neckline, because I was watching his eyes for any head movement. There was none. He seemed to be looking right through me, his eyes directed down the road. He seemed to be ignoring my presence. I had no weapons other than my body with which to kill this Jap straggler.

However, I quickly realized that he was not hostile. He was not coming at me; he was going down the road past me in the opposite direction. He was as young as I was, and he posed no threat to my existence. Did he know who I was? Did he know what I was? What I was thinking? Where I was going? What I wanted? And did he even care? All these thoughts traveled with lightning speed through my mind as we passed each other. Neither of us flinched, moved away, or changed direction. Somehow, that seemed to relieve our anxieties. We walked past each other, no more than ten feet apart. And looking with a view from God's sanction above, I thought that this should be the way war should be fought, each soldier respecting the other's movements, the other's presence, the other's desire for life and freedom to live. Neither one damaging the other's direction or presence in life. I did not look back or feel the urge to run. I had no fear. I had a battle with the enemy, and we both had won. There was no suffering; there was no pain. We would both live for another day, possibly to fall in a future battle but not today. I felt good that day, because I had the chance to cause someone pain and suffering and I chose not to. I was still human and thanked God for that day.

I came back to my area and collapsed under a tree. Many of my buddy marines took one look at me asked "Where the hell have you been?" I could guess that my eyes were still wide in amazement. They all wondered what had happened. I was severely criticized for not carrying a weapon with me. In the marines, not carrying a weapon at all times is a cardinal sin. However, if I had been carrying a weapon, that passing moment on the road would have left only one survivor. I believed there was a reason I did not carry my weapon that day. I leaned back, feeling good about being human.

Over the next few days, we would go into the jungle, over the hills, looking for Japs. We rode up and down dirt roads in trucks, searching for the elusive targets. Bouncing around on the uncushioned seats, with the hot dust driven into our unprotected faces by the trucks, gave us a physical beating that made us all wish we were walking those unending miles. We became even more dirty, exhausted, and hungry. The programming, which was changing us into adult killers, was proceeding on schedule. *Where are you, you rotten Japs! I want to kill you for the shortsighted ambitions that created this unforgiving madness!*

I could see Hinton out of the corner of my eye, braced against the side of the vehicle, his head held high and directly into the choking dust flung up by the trucks. He looked like a Roman gladiator, a blond giant of a man, very Nordic. He was the Hollywood portrayal of the perfect marine. He looked and acted like a hero from one of John Wayne's war movies. Hinton was classically handsome, a good-natured, curly-headed blond from Texas. He had fought on Peleliu and had a scar on his back to prove it. I envied his calmness, strength, and serenity.

Day after day, we hoped the trucks would run out of gas or develop some kind of mechanical failure, anything to get us away from the torturous pounding. That day finally came, and we started walking the patrols. We went in and out of the jungles, day after endless day. It began to take a toll on us. We passed other marines on the roads, going in the other direction, and saw mirror images of our own gaunt, haunted faces, a chain gang without visible chains. The smell, the empty stares, the dragging feet, the hollowed cheeks demoralized us even more.

After these few weeks of learning how to become adult killers, we ended up at the beach. There we were picked up by a landing ship infantry (LSI). I walked through the water, up the special steps on the side of the ship, and went straight to the bow, where I collapsed in isolation. We started back toward Pavuvu. The sea that day had a very slow, rolling motion, and I had the dry heaves for hours. I thought I was going to die. It was embarrassing. I could see the ship's captain and crew watching my agony. They offered no sympathy and may have thought, "Just another dirty young marine so foolish to have left his nice peaceful home."

The *Saturday Evening Post* would further this reputation, in an article written in 1946. Eleanor Roosevelt, the president's wife, believed that all marines should wear special white arm bands to alert civilization of our presence. She also suggested that all marines spend two years on an island for deprogramming, in order to be able to return to civilization. In a way, this idea to transform fully programmed killers from the Pacific theater of war to "civilization" slowly and carefully had merit. Abrupt changes can only bring about abrupt actions, usually catastrophic in nature. Luckily, most of us had the chance to return to civilization gradually.

I wondered what had happened to the war John Wayne was in. That was the war I had enlisted for. How did I ever get here? I lifted my head and looked back at Guadalcanal. The stately mountains, rolling hills, and the beautiful white sand beaches did not express the ugliness that was now within me.

6

Looking Back at Tenaru River

As I tried to recover from my immediate trauma, I imagined I could hear the echoes of one of the most important land battles of the Pacific War. It was in August 1942, at the Tenaru River on Guadalcanal, that the Japs had tasted bitter, humiliating defeat for the first time. The road to victory toward Tokyo had been entered. There was no turning back. The Marines had landed, and the situation was well in hand.

Years later, a Marine corporal would record the following history:

> On Guadalcanal, August 21, 1942, it must have sent Lt. General Jyaku-take into a rage when he first got word that those raggedy-ass Marines from the First Marine Division had landed on the beaches of Guadalcanal. Mind you, those were impudent upstarts, who did they think they were trying to oppose the son's of the Rising Sun. Without a moment to spare, Jyakutake reached out for one of his units to oppose the Marines, but his famous Sendai Division was tied up in Java, his 38th Division was in Bor-neo, and some of his anti-tank and artillery battalions were as far away as Manchuria. The closest outfit to Guadalcanal was Colonel Ichiki's shock detachment at Guam. They were given top priority, and had to reach Truk Island by August 15, 1942, with a fast ride down the slot, in six of Japan's newest transports. On the night of August 18, they landed just west of the Malimbu River on the Canal. Colonel Ichiki landed with orders from Lt. General Jyakutake to land and consolidate his position, but this was not to be the case with the over-anxious Col Ichiki. Without waiting for the rest of his detachment to arrive from Truk, he sent out patrols on the night of August 21 in the direction of the Tenaru River to probe the Marines' positions. And probe he did.
>
> A-1-1 was in a bivouac area west of the Tenaru River that night when the Battle of the Tenaru River took place. On August 20, after a rugged day of patrolling, they came back to their bivouac area totally exhausted. Everyone was busy digging in for the night with their bayonets or entrenching tools and eating whatever cold C-Rations they had or could find. As usual, most Marines would look for a close friend or a guy from their home town to talk with, because after the sun went down, it was complete silence. Two Marines just laid in their holes and talked till dark-ness closed in. Just a few feet away from them was a platoon leader Lieu-tenant. Marines were dug in, just at the end of a coconut grove next to the Tenaru River. Marines tried to catch a few winks of sleep that night, but the land crabs that inhabited the coconut groves were as vicious as ever that night, and sleep was impossible. Around midnight, Marines

heard some shots being fired up around the mouth of the river where the 2nd Battalion, 1st Marines were dug in. Just in front of Co. "G" 2nd Battalion. There was a sand spit, formed by the river and ocean tides, and this was the spot that Colonel Ichiki's detachment decided to strike the Marines. Prior to their strike, a native came through our lines badly bayoneted by a Jap officer. He was taken to the [Command Post], where he told them of a large Jap detachment that was headed for the bans of the Tenaru. As these events were occurring, the Captain company commander got orders to move out. In the pitch darkness of the night, it was madness trying to shape up and move out, but move out the Marines did, with the roaring commands of a Captain in their ears. About a week before, the Marines had sunk two alligator tanks in a stream that was at the head waters of the Tenaru River and built a bridge over these two tanks. [The] Japs had never suspected and never even knew what was there. This little bridge gave the 1st Battalion access to the Japs' rear flanks. As the Marines hustled over this bridge and through some jungle that night, all they could hear was the clanking of rifles, canteens, and equipment. No man said a word. As dawn was breaking on August 21, the Marines had one brief rest period. One Marine took off his 240-round belt of B.A.R. ammo to adjust his trousers and as he dropped his pants he could feel blood running down both hips. The B.A.R. belt of ammo had rubbed them raw, but he moved, until, with other Marines, they were right behind the Japs in a nutcracker movement. The 1st Battalion was pushing the Japs right into the jaws of the 2nd Battalion at the mouth of the Tenaru. The Marines made their first contact as they moved out of the jungle into a coconut grove. It was really something to see, all these young spunky Marines firing at a live target for the first time in their lives. They thought they were at a turkey shoot, until they started to see some of their own men shot down dead. Then they started to calm down to the grim business of fighting. From the edge of the jungle, through the coconut grove, to the ocean, it was about 500 yards. As soon as the Japs saw us, a squad of them broke off from the main body and started running up the beach in an easterly direction, trying to elude the Marines. But under the strict coaching of their Captain's commands of "line 'em up, and squeeze 'em off," the Japs never made more than 50 feet before they were wiped out. Then the Company turned westward to attack the main body of Colonel Ichiki's detachment. As the Marines moved forward, Colonel Ichiki was all over the place. It was a matter of darting from one coconut tree to another, without getting hit, as the Marines came to a slight depression in the coconut grove terrain, and found two Japs playing dead. As we saw their bodies, our Colonel gave orders to use bayonets and one of the Marines went over to do the job. One of the Japs rolled over with a pistol in his hand and shot this Marine in the face, just above the right eye. After seeing that, a Marine opened up full automatic with his B.A.R. and that put a finish to that. As the Marines kept moving forward, a young Polish Marine from Detroit, who we all called Ski, kept looking back and smiling every time he squeezed one off and got a Jap, until one time, as he started to smile, his stare just froze, as his thumb was sheared off by a Jap bullet, just as clean as if a sharp razor was used. The most frustrating thing to the Marines in the Battle of the Tenaru was the double-action 25-caliber shells that the Japs were using. It was possible to hear them when they were fired straight ahead, but when they hit the coconut trees behind, it made the Marines think they were being attacked from the rear. ... [The Marines learned, too, that the Japanese rifles were .31 caliber. This meant that Jap rifles could fire the marines' .30 caliber ammunition, but Jap ammo was too large for marine rifles.] It was very frustrating thing. It was certainly good thinking on the part of the Japanese War Lords. The heat of the day was now building up, as the fighting went on and thirst became a very serious problem. The gunny kept yelling, "Don't drink in gulps from your canteens, just wet your lips." As the Marines approached a pile of Jap bodies, up jumped three Japs. Two were in good shape, but the third was wounded and they were carrying him as though they wanted to surrender. Just as they got near, the gunny jumped out in front of them and yelled "Cut 'em down, Cut 'em down" and with that, the two unwounded Japs reached in their shirts for grenades, but they never got to use them. All over the battlefield in this coconut grove could be found Jap backpacks and knapsacks. Upon opening some of them, the Marines discovered a little packet about the size of a Schick injector razor blade case, with three vials in it; one vial was dark red, one was pink, and one was green, plus a large syringe for injections. This was why some of these Japs fought so vigorously. Also found were locks of hair and pictures of Oriental women, plus some contraceptives and lots of grenades. There was talk that Colonel Ichiki's regiment was involved in the rape of Manila. As the Marines moved forward, the machine gun fire from the 7.7 Hotchkiss Manubus grew very intense. As they started to dart from a position of safety behind one of the coconut trees, the Manubu caught a Marine flat footed. The Marine didn't know whether to run forward to the next coconut tree or not, so he just sunk down in front of the tree. He had just left, and the Manubu went to work on that tree trying to cut him down. As his heart kept pounding, the bark from the coconut tree just kept falling down on his helmet. He thought his time was up. If that Jap machine gunner could have traversed his barrel down a little lower, that would have been curtains for the Marine. "Push, push, push" was the order of the day, until the Marines came to a depression in the coconut grove, which was covered with lime bushes. Little did the Marines know that inside these bushes were well over a hundred Japs, but they held fire until the Marines came right up on them. Then, as they moved, all hell broke loose, and both sides started firing at the same time. When the action was over the Marines suffered some killed and wounded. One Marine in particular, from New Jersey, upon seeing his best pal killed, went completely berserk and started picking up Jap 31-caliber rifles and smashing them against coconut trees as though they were straws in the breeze. Eventually he was subdued. Without any forewarning, the Colonel called in the 75-mm Pack Howitzer outfit for support. As they opened up and started to drop in the coconut grove ahead, they came so close you could smell the burnt cordite after the shell exploded. By the early afternoon, many Marines were out of water and some men's lips started to swell from lack of moisture.

The nutcracker was now slowly closing and the Marines could see the opposite banks of the Tenaru River in the distance. All of a sudden, two light tanks went across the sand spit at the mouth of the Tenaru. As they became embroiled in the mass of machine guns and human flesh, everything cut loose. One of the tanks became disabled when a Jap stuck a grenade in its tracks, but the other tank stood by the disabled one and they both fired in unison. The Japs were mowed down like flies, even though some tried to swarm aboard the tanks. It was now around 1330, eight and one half hours since the Marines first made contact with the Japs. The closer the Marines pushed the Japs to the Tenaru, the more they tried to escape by running along the ocean, but to no avail. Back and forth along the beach in a Gruman Wildcat plane was a Marine pilot who just mowed them down. By now, the sun was starting to sink and by dusk, it was all over. As the Marines trudged across that sand spit of the Tenaru River that night, they were a hungry and thirsty bunch of raggedy-ass boys. The Marines had lost 34 and had 75 wounded, but such is the price of war. Colonel Ichiki was one of the 700 dead Japs that still lay out there on the battlefield. In frustration, he burned his regimental colors and shot himself through the head. He and his detachment were annihilated. That night the weary Marines ate in the coconut groves. The Colonel told the men they were now real men and good Marines and that they were going to kick the Japs' asses all the way back to Tokyo. After a hot meal of red beans and beef stew, the Marines crawled into their fox holes for a little rest. Many of the Marines had no stomach for food that night, even though they hadn't eaten all day. The adjustment to real combat would take some time. This was the first major battle fought against the Japanese during the Second World War in the Pacific. It should be noted that much credit must go to men of the 2nd Battalion, 1st Marines who so gallantly held their ground on the banks of the Tenaru against the savage onslaught of Colonel Ichiki's suicide squad.[4]

Another, more formal history summarizes naval activity following this battle:

If seesaw naval battles raged off Guadalcanal for most of the remainder of 1942, this was only a six-month interval before the industrial strength of the United States weighed fully into the balance. New American airplanes, fresh crews, fleets of warships including aircraft carriers, escort carriers, battleships, cruisers, and destroyers, packs of submarines, and hundreds of support vessels soon appeared in the Pacific. The Americans continued their drive up the Solomon Islands chain to New Georgia and Bougainville in summer and fall 1943, closing in on the Japanese and annihilate the Japanese forces on that island. On land and sea, under the sea, and over it, Allied forces held the strategic initiative, and this gave them the tactical advantage around almost the entire arc of the Japanese "defensive perimeter." They were soon able to concentrate their forces and main base at Rabaul. American and Australian forces soon went on the offensive in New Guinea, too, and from the summer of 1943 on began to chop up and annihilate the Japanese forces on that island. On land and sea, under the sea, and over it, Allied forces held the strategic initiative, and this gave them the tactical advantage around almost the entire arc of the Japanese "defensive perimeter." They were soon able to concentrate their forces and strike with overwhelming, largely unanswerable strength, wherever and whenever they chose.

The notion of "perimeters" and "front lines" proved largely a fiction in the broad Pacific reaches, as American submarines hunted freely to the very coastline of Japan itself. With the Imperial Navy largely driven from the seas or forced into making high-speed shuttle runs under cover of darkness, and with Japan unable to support its overextended garrisons, the Allies took on the task of the piecemeal elimination of Japan's land forces. The numbers of troops actually engaged in fighting on either side at any moment were relatively small, but the length of the supply lines for both sides was unprecedented. It was in this logistics war that Japan's war machine was exposed for the hollow shell it was. Without supplies, food, ammunition, medicine, reinforcements, or information, no modern military can maintain even a semblance of capability for very long. Japan's military position disintegrated precipitately, and with it the prospect that Japan could secure a settlement on favorable terms — which seems to have been Japan's initial definition of "winning the war."

The war went from "victory" to defeat so quickly and with such decisiveness that the Japanese high command seems never to have fully come to grips with its altered strategic situation. Having launched the war on a logistical shoestring to acquire supplies, and having achieved a success that must have been beyond its own most optimistic expectations, Japan's military greatly overreached its ability to protect and support forces in the newly conquered possessions. A few figures tell the disastrous story of the consequences of American domination of the sea routes between Japan's Southeast Asian possessions and Japan itself: in 1942, 40 percent of all the production of the captured oil fields reached Japan; in 1943, 15 percent; in 1944, 5 percent; and in 1945, none at all. Looked at another way, Japan's crude-oil output, which had stood at 24 million barrels in 1940 (22 million barrels imported and 2 million produced domestically), was reduced in 1941 — largely by the Allied embargo — to only about 5 million barrels (3.1 million imported) and achieved a wartime peak of only 11.6 million barrels in 1943 (9.8 million imported, 1.8 domestic), less than half of pre–1941 levels. Japan's domestic petroleum production declined during the war years, falling to just 809,000 barrels in the first half of 1945. The most frantic efforts to produce synthetic and alternate fuels, including stripping hillsides of trees to make pine-root oil, could do little to produce the fuel needed to keep Japan's planes flying.

The strategic decision to scatter men and planes throughout the conquered regions left garrisons isolated when the Americans chose to penetrate the vaunted "defense lines" in the Pacific. There were almost no strategic decisions available to the high command that could have altered

[67]

the course of the war as it seemed to bear in on them. In fact, the Japanese high command was torn between irreconcilable strategic alternatives. Withdrawal from overextended positions, while theoretically possible, was exceptionally difficult to execute in the face of Allied power.[5]

The mountains had watched, majestically echoing the cries of horror and pain, not believing that time could erase this madness. The rolling hills were made for picturesque pleasure, not for bayonet dances of a living hell, too horrible for the fun-loving Americans to survive, even as standing victors.

Guadalcanal had ignored all of its tropical beauty for a moment and accepted into its bosom the heroes far from home who had sacrificed their lives, so that the island once again would be the paradise that God intended it to be. I imagined the fallen young marines somehow smiling, knowing that Guadalcanal was not a paradise lost.

* * *

(Special recognition and memory to PFC Edward L. Smith, Jr., USMC from Rome, New York, who sacrificed his life while helping to secure this victory. He was awarded the Navy Cross [the second highest medal] for his gallantry and heroisn. He is survived by his wife, Thelma, and a child.)

* * *

It was on this beautiful island that my buddies and I had begun our transformation to a unit of killers. Following our first training exercise there, we returned to Guadalcanal to make three more practice landings. The shredded remains of our humanity were to be fully destroyed by the end of this learning period; we were now ready for the action that awaited us.

BACK TO PAVUVU

We spent the last few days on Pavuvu in preparation for the next blitz, our bodies and minds ready to face the greatest challenge our young lives would ever know. We were confident. We were strong. We were determined.

The name and location of the island were not given to us, but rumor had it there was a large mountain at one end. The scuttlebutt was that if our courageous and undaunted heroics carried us to the top of that fortified peak, those who survived would be rewarded with a one-way ticket home. What a glorious fantasy! All of us truly wanted to believe in this fairy tale.

Our briefing room had a ceiling of blue skies and white clouds, and the invisible walls were decorated splendidly with gently singing palm trees. These invisible walls offered no acoustics for the soft-spoken briefing officer, so attentive ears leaned forward, straining to hear. Idle conversation was put aside.

The briefing officer outlined our responsibilities and goals. We had seven days to reach the opposite sea shore from our landing beach. The first wave would be the amphibious tanks. A Company, our company, would be the second wave on what was called Blue Beach 2. We were to get off the beach the first day and capture Kadena Airfield within four days. Although it was fairly close to the beach, we were expected to meet heavy resistance on the way to the airfield. The colored geographical map the briefing officer used was only about the size of a black board and showed nothing but the section we were to cross.

Looking directly at me and noticing my glasses, the briefing officer said "Marine, you look more like a college student than a Jap-killer." He was trying to lighten the mood of the group. Smiling, I chose to take this as a compliment. I was proud to be a part of this brave bunch of boys. Answering smiles of agreement reflected their pride in me also.

Turning his attention back to the briefing, the officer continued with some serious and startling news. The Japs had two chemical warfare battalions on the island. All marines would be issued the cumbersome, five-pound gas masks along with the rest of their equipment. All of us having had previous gas mask training, instructions were not necessary.

The next step in our preparations consisted of filling five-gallon cans with water, to be distributed during combat. Where did they find all these five-gallon cans? This seemed to be an endless and boring task.

We then went to the docks to load the ships with ammunition, food, and water. We also loaded white cross grave markers, a very demoralizing task. As the markers were handed from marine to marine, the question popped into each mind "Is this my grave marker cross?" The possibility was very real.

The days were spent checking our gear, camouflaging our gear, and receiving new equipment.

Marines needing glasses to see just did not exist during this time, except for me. Here I was, in the marine infantry — a front-line marine, successful in pulling off this hat trick. I imagined that everybody wondered how the hell I got there. A superior officer in our regiment saw me wearing glasses. Lieutenant Evans, my commanding officer, finally ordered me to the field army hospital on the island of Baneka to have my eyes examined. There were only two more weeks before we boarded ship for our next blitz.

Early the next morning, I went down to the dock and boarded a Higgins boat for my trip to Baneka. I wasn't worried. I was confident of remaining a front-line marine, and I did not dare think otherwise. Waiting for the Higgins boat, I wondered who the unknown superior officer was who had seen me with my glasses on. I had been extremely careful about wearing my glasses only when absolutely necessary. Otherwise, my glasses were only a hand grasp away, in my chest pocket, ready to provide instant 20/20 vision with a quick flick of my wrist. Grinning, I recalled the times at Parris Island, and sometimes on liberty, when, without my glasses on, I had saluted privates and sergeants. I imagined hearing them say, "What the hell is wrong with him?" The funny part was that they never failed to return my salute.

The trip to Baneka took us in and out of small island groups. It was the most beautiful voyage I had ever been on. The islands we passed were uninhabited, and each one was a picture of unspoiled, virgin paradise. The gentle waves washing the white, sandy beaches of the shoreline constantly cleansed the beauty of this tropical splendor. Slightly moving palm trees created an atmosphere of calmness and serenity. The foliage seemed to be professionally manicured, expressing nature's respect for each and every plant in this tropical paradise. The "Master Landscaper" had left out all ugliness. The demands of the human body for food, clothing, and shelter would not allow us to ever enjoy such a paradise. There was no way to enter this dimension of total human fulfillment. Only our eyes could see these beautiful islands and our minds would remember the passing of this untouched, picturesque Eden. The trips I had made through the New York State Barge Canal and the Great Lakes in my youth would never get past second place now.

Soon we arrived at Baneka, and I was transported by ambulance to the hospital area. Footsteps crunching on the beautiful coral paved walkway led me to the wooden building, and I walked confidently into the eye clinic. The army doctor who saw me must have taken instructions from all the navy doctors I knew. He was just as unfriendly and cold. The "good" doctor began his examination and became hysterical when I told him I could not see the large eye chart without my glasses. He ranted and raved in behavior unbecoming to an officer, calling me a "gold-bricker," and words of the four-letter variety. Thinking that I had been trying to pull a fast one, he threw my papers at me yelling, "Get out!" and sending me away before I could even say "Yes, Sir," "No, Sir," or anything else. The joke was on him! I was jubilant, though getting an updated eye prescription would have been great.

The trip back to Pavuvu was breathtaking. After leaving the dock area, I reported to Lieutenant Evans, who was as baffled as I was about the indifferent treatment. Taking the problem into his own hands, he asked me if I wanted to be sent back to the rear echelon (Hawaii, or the like) or if I wanted to stay with the group and make the next blitz. In other words, I had to choose between safe duty or the very real possibility of death. I instantly replied, "I want to stay with the group." However, if I decided to stay, I first had to go to every marine in the group and get their personal approval. There could be no reservations about me being a front-line marine. One by one, each marine gave me his unconditional O.K. with a strong and confident handshake. Coming from such honorable men, no compliment could ever be higher.

Cutting notches on the bows of my glasses, I tied them onto my head with two shoe strings. There was no reason to hide my glasses anymore. I was lost without my glasses, but with them I was the best shot in the company.

A Company went to Cowshit Island to fine-tune its battle skills and try new equipment. Cowshit Island received that name for obvious reasons: there was cowshit on the island. How it got there was a mystery, because I never saw any cows. This large island was part of the Russell Island group, with palm trees swaying gently, looking very much like Pavuvu. Rather than the dense jungle vegetation, though, the island had open areas with no roadways or beaten paths. There the company performed patrol-type maneuvers with live ammunition. I was a flame thrower at this time, and the rapid running movements I had to perform were difficult. The flame thrower itself was a 97-pound burden. In one practice, moving up on a makeshift pillbox, I moved in position to fire my flame thrower, imagining that some Japanese were inside the pillbox and ignited the match with my left hand and squeezed the release valve with my right hand. Pressured napalm shot through the holding metal hose hitting the ignited match and exploded, rolling on the ground toward the pillbox opening. The imaginary Japs were instantly disintegrated. Thinking that I had discharged all of my napalm, I turned 90 degrees to my left and ignited another match in the flame-thrower gun. Then I quickly squeezed the pressure valve and, to my surprise, a ball of flame shot out! The prone marine

Flamethrower and rifleman team. (United States Marine Corps photo.)

rifleman in front of me instantly dropped his weapon and shot away as if he had just been ignited himself. The one-second burst of the flame-thrower had gone directly over his head. Looking after him and gauging his speed, I do not believe he was equipped with enough braking power to decelerate. He may still be running.

Now there was time for an island jungle delicacy. Marine Bishop found some fast-running, large red ants to satisfy his appetite. He would scoop this juicy delicacy into his open mouth, taste buds jumping for joy, and red ants running up and down his hands and arms. For obvious reasons, no one joined him in this splendid repast.

Throwing grenades in practice, flame-thrower and bazooka firing, and demolition practice gave us very busy days.

Night time came and A Company set up a defensive perimeter, facing the ocean. On the command "Fire" signal, all hell broke loose. We all began firing our weapons toward the ocean at once, the tracers lighting up the sky with every fifth round, the lighted bullets giving us all the confidence that no Japs could survive our fire power.

The marines slept in hammocks strung between palm trees that night.

Like babes in cradles, they rocked, dreaming of home. Some marines, not knowing the tricks of hammock sleeping, found themselves on the ground in the middle of the night, looking up at the stars through the mosquito netting.

Morning came, and we boarded the Higgins boats for our trip back to Pavuvu. We had proven our might and flexed our muscles, and now we were ready for those Japanese.

About a week before we personally boarded the ships for our next blitz, Snyder came by to wish us all good luck. He was sorry about not going with us on the blitz, but he had lived up to his end of the bargain, living in a physical hell during the time he spent working on the docks. As fearful as he was for us, he was confident he would have life after the upcoming blitz.

Walden, with respect and admiration, approached me with his concern. Walden was always concerned about the welfare of others. Having participated in the Peleliu hell, he was a strong witness of how much death and destruction the Japs were able to cause to the first landing marines. We were scheduled to be the second wave on our next blitz. That meant the survival rate would be very low for our company. "Dude Boy," Walden said, "Why don't you turn yourself into sick bay with your bloody feet so you do not have to be in the second wave? Join us a few days later, after the Jap mortars have taken their toll."

I was silently emotional about his unselfish concern. To know that someone thought this much of me gave me a lifetime debt of gratitude, one I would never be able to repay. However, even though the tropical ulcers on my feet were very painful, I did not agree to Walden's idea. Like most teenagers, I had no fear of dying, and I just could not miss the "Big Show." Bloody feet or not, I was taking the approaching test for manhood.

One of the last responsibilities was to put all of our personal items into our seabags for storage. We were not allowed to carry any letters, and no letter writing was permitted until further notice. The last letters written would leave for the states in two days. In effect, we would disappear for a two-month period. "Killed in action" or "wounded" telegrams would be the only messages to our families. There would be no more perfumed letters to excite our motivation. The First Marine Division was ready to greet the Japs with hell, not "hello."

Summers and Tanner from B Company group were special individual marines with strong ideas of their own. Their idea of going to Australia certainly had a large degree of insanity within its framework, but with all caution ignored, off they started on their journey. Down to the docks, steal a boat, then off to Australia. It sounded simple and easy, but this was exactly how Summers and Tanner made their first step in their almost impossible journey. Soon, without a hitch, they were in the middle of the ocean.

A tramp steamer picked up Summers and Tanner in the middle of the ocean. In the insane and impossible attempt to reach Australia, they had run out of gas. Finally, the two were returned to our area and placed in the stockade. They were the lone occupants and, ever resourceful, they managed to escape. They went back down to the dock again without being noticed, stole a small boat, and headed for the open seas. Once more, the boat ran out of gas, and the two very unsuccessful and disappointed marines were returned to Pavuvu under guard. Quickly, before another attempt could be made, they had a trial for court-martial. At the proceeding, Col. Grimes asked them why they had made, not one but two, such impossible efforts to reach Australia. Summers and Tanner replied "We both believed we would be killed on the next blitz so we were trying to control our destiny." Col. Grimes, who was an exceptional veteran leader and one of the boys, fully understood their feelings. After thinking about the problem a moment, the Colonel made a deal with the two young marines. If the two marines would give their word not to escape again, he would postpone the court-martial until after the blitz. They agreed; there was no other choice.

Summers and Tanner were returned to B Company. There, they lived up to their end of the bargain, making preparations for the blitz.

And now the battle cry would echo throughout the Pacific. The time is now! Jap take notice. The impossible we will do right away. Miracles will take a little longer. The First Marine Division is on its way to hand you a terrible defeat.

8

EN ROUTE TO OKINAWA

Now we began our journey to challenge in mortal combat the cruelest and most barbaric soldier that ever devastated the islands of the Pacific. Their devastation with methods of fanatic plunder reached our very shores. It was time to take these methods to their shores.

But how could we young men, not tempered for war in any phase of our childhood or teenage life, be victorious? How could we triumph over an enemy so conditioned in mind and body? Had we reflected with any rationality on these questions, we might have abandoned this critical attempt to destroy the Japanese army. It was almost like sending a high school football team to play the best team in the National Football League, on their own home field.

However, because we young marines, sailors, and soldiers were never educated in any manner to know the "code" and the "beliefs" of the Japanese military, we had an air of superiority. Civilian movies and general conversation among the non-participating population were the greatest contributors to this air of superiority, which would be tested on the battlefield. Had we understood our enemy's dedication to war as a glorious occupation — had we known anything of their code of honor — it might have produced a fear that could have diminished the confidence we had developed in our training. Author Hatsuho Naito explains the origins of the Japanese code:

> On January 3, 1941, General Hideki Tojo, then the minister of the army, ordered that an official code of ethics be published and distributed to every member of the armed forces. This code, known as Senjin Kun or Ethics in Battle, said "A sublime sense of self-sacrifice must guide you throughout life and death. Do not think of death as you use up every ounce of your strength to fulfill your duties. Make it your joy to use every last bit of your physical and spiritual strength in what you do. Do not fear to die for the cause of everlasting justice. Do not stay alive in dishonor. Do not die in such a way as to leave a bad name behind you."
>
> Fighting to the death regardless of the odds or chances of success was a deeply embedded tradition in Japan. In fact, the greater the likelihood of defeat, the more certain it was that the Japanese would fight to the death in battle or kill themselves following defeat. To begin to understand the mentality that led Japan to make suicide attacks an official part of its war effort, one must know a great deal about her past.
>
> Until 1868, Japan was a tightly knit, tightly closed feudal kingdom ruled

by a military dictator (shogun) and an elite class of clan lords and professional, sword-carrying warriors (samurai). The shogun and the clan lords (daimyo) had absolute power over the common people, who were permitted neither family names nor the right to travel.

This system had existed since the year A.D. 1192, when Minamoto Yoritomo leader of the famous Genji clan, which had defeated the other clans in a war for military supremacy, prevailed upon the Emperor to appoint him shogun and recognize his right to administer the affairs of the country in the name of the emperor. The professional warriors maintained by each of the clans and the shogun at that time were already an elite hereditary class, and soon came to be known as samurai.

The code of the samurai was a mixture of Shintoism, Buddhism, and Confucianism. Shintoism taught the warriors that they were descendants of divine beings and that upon death they, too, would become "gods." From Buddhism they learned to accept the transitory, fragile nature of life and to view death as crossing into another plane of existence. From Confucianism came the concept of absolute loyalty to their lord.

With the fall of the last shogunate dynasty in 1868, and the restoration of imperial authority for virtually the first time in 676 years, Shinto, the native religion on which the divinity of the imperial house was based, became the state religion. The people were taught to believe that the Emperor was a living god, and to treat him accordingly.

Yasukuni Shrine on Kudan Hill in Tokyo was established in 1868 as "The Patriots' Shrine" or "The Shrine of the Religious Souls," where the souls of those killed in war were enshrined. It was considered the guardian shrine of the country, and next to the Emperor himself in importance.

Shortly after the Meiji Emperor's administration took over the country in 1868, a constitutional government was formed, with power invested in a prime minister, his cabinet, a House of Councilors, and a House of Representatives. Despite these intimations of democracy, but in keeping with deeply entrenched tradition, the military, primarily the army, began asserting itself, and by the early 1930's had total control of the government. General Hideki Tojo, who became prime minister in 1941, was a latter-day shogun. His highest henchmen were the new daimyo, and military officers were samurai — in khaki instead of kimono.

From early childhood, the Japanese were conditioned to believe that the Emperor was divine, and the spiritual head of the nation. They were also taught to accept the will of the Emperor (in reality, that of the ruling cliques) as both divine and absolute. Like the military fanatics of many countries, the ultra-nationalists among the Japanese believed they had a spiritual mandate to conquer and "Japanize" the rest of the world. Hence their wars against China, Russia, Southeast Asia, and eventually the United States were thought of as divine wars.

Very much like the Muslims of Iran in 1970's and 1980's, Japanese servicemen were taught to believe that if they died in battle, especially if they died heroically, they would instantly become "gods", and join the guardian spirits of the nation at Yasukuni Shrine on Kudan Hill.

All during Japan's long feudal age (which actually did not end until

1945), to fail in battle or to be captured was not acceptable. In clan wars it was common for the losing side to be slaughtered to the last man — and often the women and children of the losing side as well. Enemies captured alive were routinely killed in painful and gruesome ways.

Suicide became the accepted way of expiating the disgrace of failure, and death by one's own hand or the hand of a trusted friend was eminently preferable to the double disgrace of being captured and made to suffer an ignoble death at the hands of a hated enemy.

As the 1941-45 war against the United States and its allies continued, the Japanese were constantly told that their primary purpose in life and the greatest glory they could achieve was to give their lives for the Emperor. They were also harangued with the warning that they should not allow themselves to be captured — that men would be tortured and killed, and women would be raped and then dispatched.

Eventually an edict was issued actually forbidding servicemen to allow themselves to be captured, making it, ironically enough, an offense punishable by death....

As this situation worsened for Japanese troops on the various islands of the Pacific, both servicemen and civilians were ordered to fight to the death and to kill themselves if they were wounded and unable to fight. The *banzai* (literally "10,000 years" — a word expressing group resolution) charge by outnumbered and outfought Japanese troops became dreadfully commonplace. Mass suicides by civilians astounded the Americans. They did not know what to think of such an enemy. Nothing in their history, nothing in their experience, had prepared them to understand such behavior.[6]

Our company (A Company) boarded LST 71, our vehicle of transportation to our next blitz. It was one of the first LSTs built, and her seams had cracked and her engine was tired. Paint could not cover her worn appearance.

The First Marine Division boarded all the LSTs, then went to Guadalcanal to make three practice amphibious landings. The practice landings were always very confusing — landing on the wrong section of the beach and not being able to locate our assigned outfit as rapidly as possible. We had the latest in amphibious tractors that allowed us to go out the back, rather than over the side. This was great; going over the side with a 97-lb. flame thrower had been rather difficult.

Our convoy would form with three LSTs abreast and four LSTs in depth, giving a total of twelve. Usually, there was one company per LST, plus the supporting personnel. All LSTs had a LCT (Landing Craft Tank), riding piggyback on their open top deck. Ammunition and shells were stacked in every opening. We were actually a small ammunition ship, as well as a transport. An LST hit by any type of exploding weapon would be blown to dust with all its contents.

Aiming the convoy north, the determined marines were on their way to deliver a blow to the Japanese diseased empire and to make history.

In about two weeks, we rendezvoused with many other ships at Ulithi, a large group of small islands in the center of the Pacific Ocean. The area looked like a very large metropolis with all the ships' lights on at night.

My cot was on top of the deck of the LST, underneath another small boat, an LCT that was riding piggy back on the LST. I was totally exposed to the elements, so I prayed daily for good weather. Tropical rainstorms were not welcome. I put a line of grease on the bottom of the piggy-back ship to repel the constant water flow so the rain would not soak me and my cot. It was a miserable existence, and I was certainly getting in the mood to kill anybody who got in my way. I was cold, wet, hungry, and lonely.

There was no room on the ships for exercises, or even briefing meetings, and we had plenty of time on our hands. Some of this idle time was used talking about good times and good things. There was a special place near the rear of the LST on the left side, where we could sit together and converse for hours, undisturbed. Because our conversations were personal, one-on-one was the usual gathering. The calm ocean, the moonbeams reflecting off waves, created a relaxed feeling for sensitive conversations between teenage boys talking about the home life they had left behind. These conversations might prompt an eavesdropper to ask, why? Why do these young men have to be involved in this activity, one that is so opposite to their upbringing, lifestyle, and home life? An activity almost worse than slavery, with death a common occurrence.

The intimate personal conversations would not be remembered. We were like chaplains to each other. Listening was a method of embracing a buddy in need. Time would dissolve the listening memories, soon to be replaced by a silence of anxiety when time drew closer to L-Day.

With no provisions for showers, the daily exercise routine was thankfully postponed. Our body odors were strong enough to ward off any enemy that might come in range.

When we entered the China Sea, the storms made the ships roll violently. This would send geysers of water straight into the air from openings on the pontoons that were hung onto the side of the LST. This was my naturally formed shower. Even during the storms, I would stand on the deck of the ship in position for the water to fall directly over me.

I had on my nature uniform, and I noticed the sailors on the bridge, inside that nice protected area, surely thinking I was some kind of nut.

But those sailors had nice clean showers, slept between nice clean sheets, and their bellies were comfortably full 24 hours a day. My only responsibility was to survive.

I used to hang around the mess hall in the early morning hours, arriving about 2:30 A.M. That was the time when the cook made cinnamon buns. I was a beggar, looking for a handout, and sometimes he would take pity on me and give me some of the still-warm and fragrant buns. They were the most delicious buns I have ever tasted in my life.

Our LST had dropped back during one of the storms at night, leaving the convoy. Two U.S. destroyers did not know who we were and were ready to blow us out of the water. However, the radio operator came into the mess hall area and told us how he had convinced the two U.S. destroyers we were the good guys. He was still pretty nervous, sweating like a pig. We had come terribly close to being members of Davy Jones' Locker. However, the delicious cinnamon buns dominated the scene.

Two inches of water was rolling back and forth, with the LST's rough sea motion. My clothes were soaked with the cold water. My cot was totally waterlogged. I was completely exposed to the ravaging elements. A voice said, "I have a clean pair of dry socks." This was Walters' way of saying "we" had a pair of clean dry socks. With shyness and complete unselfishness, he gave the dry socks to me. I felt indebted to him for life. A spoken "thank you" would be inadequate to the emotional uplift of the moment.

As I pulled the dry socks on, I was immediately bathed in the splendid feeling of warmth returning to my body. The welcome warmth instantly energized me. Animatedly, I said to Walters, "When this is all over, you need to come visit me at home. We could explore the canals and the Great Lakes." I had been a seaman on the Great Lakes at 16.

Walters gazed at me with his slightly apologetic timidness, saying, "I'm sorry, I won't be able to go with you."

I sat stunned for a moment, wondering if he had deliberately insulted me, or if it was just a part of his shyness. "Why?" I demanded.

He dropped his head in embarrassment and said softly, "I won't be coming off this island."

Silent sadness captured my feelings and, with respect, I did not challenge his feelings. The honor code among us demanded that we never question these premonitions. These premonitions came true too often to doubt their accuracy and validity.

I spoke with what I hoped was authority, attempting to comfort him. "Wherever you are, whatever happens, I'll come to help you," I promised. Walters and I fell into silence, knowing there was nothing more to say. With a sudden rush of adrenaline, I realized my glasses were gone. Looking for them in panic, I saw my glasses half floating under my cot. I was glad they did not end up in the China Sea.

We arrived off the coast of Okinawa three days before L-Day. We could see the shelling at night, and silence seemed to be the theme of the day. I saw no fear in any other marines, nor did I personally feel any anxiety or fear. Waiting seemed to be an exercise in frustration. The night before landing, no one slept, and there was little conversation. We just kept looking toward the island in awe at the bright fireworks of the shelling. We hoped that all the Japs would be dead by the time we arrived. But we knew the chances of that were very slim; those slimy, creepy little Japs would be waiting. The greatest moment in their life was killing at least one of us; this would ensure their place in their so-called heaven. Unfortunately, this would be the worst time in our lives, whether we lived or died.

OKINAWA: THE
FIRST FOUR DAYS

The action that preceded the landing on Okinawa is well summarized by Henry I. Shaw for *Leatherneck* magazine:

> The Americans assembling from all over the Pacific to capture Okinawa were told to expect a fierce and vigorous defense by the Japanese. Intelligence agencies had a pretty good handle on the nature and strength of Ushijima's major units. They knew that the 32d Army held the southern part of the island in force and that its hills, ravines and ridges were honeycombed with defenses in depth. They expected all approaches to the Shuri hill mass would be covered by enemy fire. It was apparent that the Japanese were dug in and prepared to repel an assault anywhere along the southernmost coastline where they held the high ground overlooking any plausible landing beaches.
>
> In a spate of wishful thinking, the enemy hoped the Americans would land there, since a successful lodgment appeared to open a path into the rear of the Shuri stronghold. Even those Japanese staff officers who correctly guessed that Yontan and Kadena airfields would be the prime targets of an American assault were not ready to give up the favorable defensive positions they occupied in strength to attempt a determined defense of the western beaches. Gen Ushijima would wait for the Americans to come south where every avenue of approach into the Shuri hills would be killing ground.
>
> Ulithi Atoll in the Carolines was the assembly point for the armada of ships that began converging on Okinawa in February. The overall naval commander was Adm Raymond A. Spruance, Commander, Fifth Fleet and Central Pacific Task Forces, who had held the same position in the invasion of the Marianas and Bonins. As the atoll's extensive lagoon began to fill with ships of all types, the embarked troops were treated to a sight almost beyond belief. Everywhere one looked there was a ship of some sort — carriers, battleships, transports, landing ships, destroyers, cargo vessels — all in all 318 combat and 1,139 support vessels were involved, and they all seemed to be at Ulithi.
>
> In crew and passengers, the attack force and its follow-on echelons and the carrier covering force numbered well over a half million men. While some of the troops and crewmen got ashore on the islets of Ulithi to stretch their legs, toss a ball around and have a few beers or soft drinks, most men remained on board ship, bored from the long approach voyages

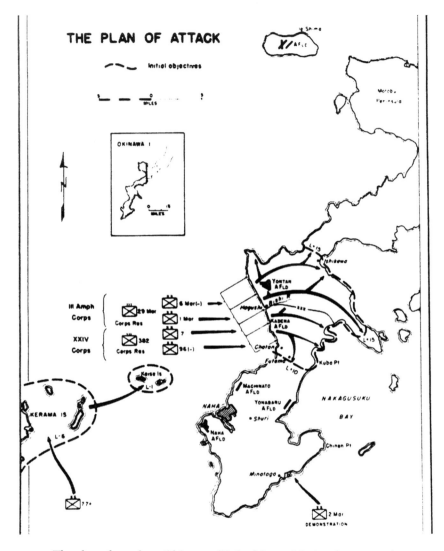

The plan of attack on Okinawa. (United States Marine Corps map.)

from the Solomons, the Philippines, the Marianas, the Marshalls and all points between and beyond. When the big carriers and their escorts disappeared and slower-moving landing ship groups loaded with assault troops, amphibian tractors and tanks got underway, everyone knew that the landings were only days away.

In their briefings on board ship, the assault troops knew what their objectives were once ashore, and if they were attentive and fortunate they had a general idea of what everyone else would be doing on L-Day. In the IIIAC zone north of the Bishi Gawa, the Sixth Marine Division would seize Yontan Airfield and drive north to close off the Ishikawa Isthmus. The 1st MarDiv [Marine Division] would drive east across the island and seize the peninsula which closed its right boundary on the east coast. South of the Bishi Gawa, the XXIV Corps would send the 7th Infantry Division across the island on the First Division's right to secure the east coast. The 96th Infantry Division would drive east and south approaching the outlying defenses of Shuri. As the demonstration landing force on L-Day, the 2nd MarDiv would fake a landing on the Minotogawa beaches on the southeastern shore in an effort to hold the Japanese in known defensive positions well away from the Americans' chosen landing area.

True to schedule, the 77th Infantry Division handily seized the islands of Kerama Retto on March 26 and 27. In places the landings were preceded by scouts of FMFPac's Amphibious Reconnaissance Battalion. The opposition to the 77th's multiple landings was scattered but intense in spots from a mixed force of about 400 suicide-boat operators and base troops and 600 Korean laborers. The veteran 77th's infantrymen made short work of the defenses and as a result destroyed 350 suicide boats which, had they been allowed to launch, might well have raised havoc with the approaching troopships.

The reconnaissance Marines scouted the island of Keise Shima on the night of March 25, and a battalion of the 77th secured it without opposition the next day. Before L-Day, the Army's 402d Field Artillery Group brought its 155-mm guns ashore on Keise in time to support the XXIV Corps' landings. The seizure of Kerama Retto, which was soon alive with antiaircraft defenses, gave the invasion fleet a relatively secure anchorage close to the objective, a virtual necessity as the Japanese were already reacting to the approach of the American ships with intensity.

Japanese suicide planes, kamikazes, crashed six ships in the naval bombardment force before L-Day, including Adm Spruance's flagship Indianapolis. Two warships were lost to mines, and mine-clearing operations delayed close-in naval gunfire while extensive sweeps were conducted. Along the proposed landing beaches, naval underwater demolition teams destroyed 2,900 wooden posts set as obstacles in the reef offshore.[7]

Now our story can be told.

Dawn came, and D-Day was upon us. But today D-Day would be called L-Day (Love Day). We all made preparations for our individual roles in making this invasion an ultimate victory. As we waited to board the amtracs (amphibious tractor that carries troops from the sea onto land) that were in the belly of the LST, Jap airplanes were trying to discourage our imminent arrival on the beach. One Jap airplane went down in flames between our LST and one next to us. That was too close!

Three Jap airplanes tried diving at a ship, or ships. They would start down, then chicken out and go up higher, then start back down. Finally, they went down low enough for the navy to blow them out of the sky and send them to their heaven. One navy gunner on our LST started shooting at a British catapult airplane. He came uncomfortably close to shooting the British aircraft down. I could very well imagine the confused look on the face of that British pilot and the verbage that was directed at our gunner. We went below deck to board the amtracs. In my quick movement, one of my grenades fell from my gear. There was an anxious moment as excited eyes looked to make sure the pin was still safely intact. As I reached over and picked up the grenade, everybody started breathing, and hearts started beating again.

The marine-filled amtracs went out of the mouth of the LST and into the water. They maneuvered around in a circle, until they were in position, and it was time to go toward the beach. We were assigned the second wave on Blue Beach 2. This is the most dangerous position to be in. Usually, the relentless pretargeted mortar fire was very intense by the time the second wave arrived. There was no way to prevent this slaughter of marines.

While maneuvering in a circle, we were underneath the guns of a battleship that was releasing broadside salvos. The concussions were frightening. The concussions felt like we had all been lifted out of the water, and a numbness overcame us. The amtrac seemed to slam back down, and it felt like we'd been hit by a mortar shell. The navy did not have time for consideration of our nerves.

Suddenly, a tremendous cover of aircraft appeared overhead. At precisely 8:00 A.M., hundreds of airplanes were criss-crossing over us, protecting our landing. It was a sight that gave us confidence that this day would be a good day and only the observing pilots or a spectator held a preferred role.

However, this was L-Day (translation: Dying Day, Easter Sunday, April Fool's Day, and thousands-of-miles-away-from-home day all rolled into one). A large aircraft flying over us created a wonder as to how this aircraft could physically be there. Maybe this large aircraft came from China or Iwo Jima. It was too large for an aircraft carrier launch. Another wonder from the American-ingenuity bag of tricks. It was a motivation force to make a marine feel proud and confident.

Now we could feel the amtrac digging into the dirt, crawling on land like a giant crab. None of us looked at each other, possibly afraid of seeing the fear on someone else's face, a reflection of one's own fear. The sergeant yelled "lock and load!" (prepare your weapons). The back of the amtrac tail gate came down and we rushed onto the beach. I yelled "Give 'em hell!" with no trembling in my voice. There was no fear, only the rush of adrenaline in our bodies to kill some Japs. The Japs had invited us on their land via the invitation that was delivered at Pearl Harbor. This was our RSVP. This was our finest hour. Maybe for some, our last hour, but that Jap would not be allowed to spread his agonies to our homes. We were marines. We had come to stay and to be victorious.

As my legs started carrying my 120-pound load, I thought someone had replaced my muscles with rubber. Thirty-plus days without exercise gave an unwelcome effect. I was carrying too much weight, with too little muscle to support it. April Fool's Day was playing a joke on me. If some Jap had come out of hiding at me, there was no way I could protect myself. I could not even see to fire my tommy gun. I was a pack mule, not a capable, defensive or offensive marine. My dumbhead Sgt. Rizzo should have realized this dangerous condition I was in.

I hit the sandy beach but decided I had to make a slight adjustment in order to survive a possible dangerous moment. My so-called teammate, rotten to the core, would not carry his share of the rockets, so I left three of the bazooka rockets on the beach. Otherwise, it would have been impossible for me to continue, much less survive the approaching conditions.

It was Easter Sunday, and the beachhead was "cold" with no Jap resistance. This day, we were given a special blessing by almighty God. No mortar shells or artillery was falling upon us. This was an unbelievable day!

Two days prior to D-Day, another group of marines made two landings on the southern tip of this island. The Japs, thinking we were going to try landing there, sent all of their troops to greet us. Surprise, surprise, surprise! Once again, we had outmaneuvered the Japs and many of us would live longer than we had planned.

The first night, we reached the south side of Yontan Airfield. The preplanned effort was to have taken the airfield in four days. I was on the extreme left flank of our outfit, along with two other marines. We dug a large foxhole and could view the air field easily. About dusk, three Jap airplanes landed on the air field. Suddenly realizing something was not right, they took off again immediately. The Jap airplanes flew directly toward our ships, and this was a grave mistake.

The navy put up the welcoming sign: antiaircraft fire that was unbelievably intense. It looked like the Fourth of July. It seemed almost possible to walk on the tracer bullets, that lit up the sky. There were so many tracer bullets; it was impossible for the Jap aircraft to survive. The Japs all found their seats in their so-called heaven. This exercise was nothing more than target practice for the navy. Later on, this exercise would not be so easy.

Then the darkness and silence fell upon us, and we were alone. Shortly after midnight, a "condition red" was given. This meant that all marines were to stay awake and alert. Not knowing the reasons for a condition red always created considerable anxiety.

Girard, one of the marines in our foxhole, chose to ignore the warning and continued sleeping. This caused me anxiety, because I personally believed in taking every precaution in order to stay alive. I did not fear death or the Japs, but I certainly did not believe in giving them an advantage. Sleeping, not staying alert, would definitely give the Japs the upper hand.

I kept on telling Girard that we were in a condition red and he needed to be awake. He said, "Go to Hell, I'll sleep if I want to." Several abortive attempts to wake him finally aroused the Lince spirit. I believed another pair of alert eyes could possibly save my life. I wanted to insure that my mother would not receive a telegram. I placed my tommy gun to Girard's temple and pulled back the bolt. This was serious business. Girard was going to be part of my safety net, willing or not. He sat up instantly and managed to stay awake and alert all night. As a result of that night, I was kicked off Girard's friendship list. It was no great loss. I probably was never really on his friendship list, and he remained the stupid jerk I first believed he was.

That night, young marines who chose to sleep, may have never woke up for the promises of the day. Infiltration at night with killing an American was a glorious delight. The Jap had invented the reason for mothers having to receive telegrams. My mother would not receive a telegram, thanks to the Lince spirit and Easter Sunday, 1945.

At daylight, we met in a group to get our rations, water, and ammunition. Then we started our scenic tour across the island.

We went up and down every foot path on the island, looking for Japs. We came upon some Japs cleaning their small arms. They were totally surprised and started returning small arms fire. As a bazooka team, we were called to fire on their position. Running low and fast to get into position we dashed down the dirt road. The marine in front of me went down, and the marine behind me went down. It was time to dive for cover, and I dove partially into the bushes. Very soon, though, I realized that both marines had been hit, one in the arm, the other in the head, peeling his helmet right down the middle. I had dove for cover just in time. I was in some Jap's gun sight. Rotolo arrived on the scene as all "goof offs" do. He could only offer the sarcastic remark "What the hell you doing, Lince?"

As I looked down the road from my cover, I saw a bulldozer heading for the cave where the Japs were. In their panic mode, the Japs fired at the bulldozer, the bullets ricocheting off the blade. *Ping-de-ping, ping, ping-ping, ping-ping* they went, sounding like an untuned percussion instrument in a weary sound of dancing death, seeking a hiding foe. The Seabee did not deviate from his path, but now had a better in-line target as he gunned his bulldozer engine to its maximum speed. In a few seconds the Seabee buried the japbastards with gleeful triumph. The japbastards' song of death to Americans would play no more *ping, ping* rings on the Seabee's bulldozer's blades.

Toward evening, during a fire fight, a very good-looking marine machine gunner took a hit through his eye; the bullet came out the back of his head. We knew he had been hit by a "dumb-dumb" bullet by the size of the exit hole in the back of his head. We all started making "dumb-dumb" bullets, so that the Japs would receive the same welcome. Dumb-dumb bullets are made by etching cross notches in the nose of the bullets.

An hour before darkness, I saw Col. Grimes coming toward our lines. This action made us confident and proud that we had a high leader who was right along with us and not way back behind our lines. That night, I would receive a welcome from a Jap that was so close I thought I was wounded.

The mental makeup of Rotolo, with my naive belief in him as a real sensible survivor, almost resulted in me becoming a numbered casualty. Goofing off, as usual, Rotolo did not express nor lead the initiative to dig in. My teenage thinking dominated my good sense, and I followed his lead, laying on top of the ground. Rotolo directed his attention toward another stupid marine, Powell, who was dug in. Exhausted, I laid on top of the ground completely exposed to any bullet traveling routes friendly or hostile. Then, after an hour of feeling naked and unsafe, my concerns became a frightening reality.

In a split second, about 8 or 10 bullets found a traveling route over my body. I yelled hysterically, "I've been hit, I've been hit!" placing my hands on every body part I could but not finding any blood. Rotolo yelled, "Where, where?" I said, "I don't know, asshole, I am trying to find out where!" My search for a blood source was in vain, placing me in an embarrassed mood.

The bullets had started their travel past my body so close that they gave me a feeling of being whipped. The bullets actually stung my face. They made a stinging path, entering between my open feet and then going the complete length of my body. A half-inch lower in trajectory would have provided a hit for a Jap. No doubt Rotolo was disappointed that I was still alive.

Rotolo again ignored my presence as a team member and did not cooperate with the needed 50 percent watch buddy system. He slept most of the night.

In the middle of the night, I kept hearing "a grass movement." Not knowing what the sound was, I said to Rotolo, "Let me have your .45, there is something moving out there." His lack of interest that accompanied his stupidity allowed him to give me his .45, and he went back to sleep.

All night long I laid prone and scared, pointing the .45, cocked and ready to fire, in the direction the sound was coming from. The night was pitch black. I could see nothing but heard every movement. Rotolo slept on.

The sound kept getting closer and closer. I was getting scared and more scared, staying motionless all night. Dawn began to break through the trees. My thoughts were many. Would this Jap jump me when he could see me? Who

Marines traverse a rocky path. (United States Marine Corps photo.)

will see the other first? Will I beat him to the punch? All of these thoughts were flashing back and forth on my mental screen. Rotolo slept on. Then, I started making out a form. I could see part of it. It was dark. It was black. It was large. It was a damned horse. I dropped the aimed .45 in exhausted relief. Rotolo slept on. I did not share this experience with Rotolo. He would have shot the horse, smiling all the while.

The following morning, when packing up to move out, I was given extra machine gun ammunition to carry. Someone thought I was a mule. A machine gun ammo box weighs 20 pounds.

However, an inconsiderate Peleliu veteran from Alabama, Cpl. Sibley, would provide me with this unbelievable task. There was so much weight to carry that I actually got stuck in the mud. There was no way I could lift my feet up enough to get out. Two big marines came along and gave me a heave-ho by the elbows, and I was on my way up another steep hill, still looking for the hiding yellow Japs.

Cpl. Sibley was a beady-eyed little weasel who used his stripes to express his absence of leadership capabilities on me. His total carrying weight was probably 50 pounds compared to my carrying weight of 120 pounds. A real asshole.

While walking through areas of possible Jap caves, we twisted and turned our eyes, focusing like searching beams of light looking for those Japs. Sgt.

Murray, an experienced combat veteran, knew the importance of keeping ten-pace intervals between marines. Any gatherings would invite without warning, a Japanese Nambu machine gun life-destroying power. Sgt. Murray kept yelling in his convincing voice, "Keep a ten-pace interval."

Sgt. Murray's marine combat dress seemed to be disguising an intelligent looking president of a bank from a large city. Maybe he did not reflect the features of a role model marine. However, he performed his duties with meticulous responsibility.

I met Nappy when I was with the rifle company. He was a busily moving Italian, full of life and spirit, a tribute to the Marine Corps and the American youth. All Italian, he was respected and loved by all marines.

The third day we were on Okinawa, we shared the "point" (the farthest from line position on the front). I was on one side of a hedgerow, dug in, and Nappy was on the other side, dug in. Nappy said, "The Japs will be coming right up here." I almost shit my pants, I was so scared! But, knowing Nappy was there gave me a sense of security. I was with the best of the Marine Corps. Nappy was like a big brother, always watching over me. He was a 20-year-old veteran teamed with an eager, scared 18 year old. Realizing who I was with gave me confidence. Digging in, we got into position, ready for any Jap attack. We had two-hour watches for survival, and Nappy was prompt and alert, carrying his end of the responsibilities without a murmur. Working as such an efficient team, we both got some shut-eye.

All through the night, we could hear the Japs moving around. They would throw stones, hoping to draw the fire that would give away our positions. Like silent veterans with nerves of steel, we did not give in to their tactics. Only the black night knew whether the tactics of the Japs would tempt the watchful young marines into gambling with their lives. There was nothing but the pitch black night and youthful courage between us and the Japs. We were marines, and we proved to the Japs that we could win without firing a shot. A boy afraid of the night had no light to turn to, nor a security blanket to hold. He could only hold on tight to his tommy gun, motionless with strict discipline. My security was in Nappy's quiet voice saying, "Hey, Lince." A voice out of the pitch black gave me all the courage I needed to survive.

It was the fourth day when we finally reached the other side of the island. The pitch-black night was falling fast, and we hurriedly started to dig in, while we could still see our silhouettes. Suddenly, a grenade exploded in the distance, and everybody stopped and looked toward the direction we thought it had come from. We could see four dark figures moving quietly down the road. We hollered "Toamati!" (Japanese for "Halt!"), and they started running even faster toward us! The four of us, highly trained, scared shitless, young marines, opened fire, and watched as they all fell in their tracks.

Then, a piercing scream broke the black silence. For a split second, we all froze. Someone was still alive! Then, driven into action by the sound, we ran to the fallen forms and found that they were all civilians. We had killed civilians! We had shot innocent people.

The continuous screaming was coming from a baby, still tied to its mother's back. A bullet had pierced the mother, killing her instantly, and severing the baby's arm on the way out. Shocked, my mind and body turned to ice. I was literally frozen with horror. I wanted to run, to disappear, to hide forever from the shame! God, please wake me up from this nightmare!

There was no choice. God forgive us, there was no choice! Against our will, we did the only thing we could. We ended the baby's life quickly, the cries stopping suddenly. In the silence that followed, we buried all of them. Sweat took the place of the tears we could not shed. I felt empty, lifeless, stripped of the ability to feel any emotions. The last shreds of our own innocence died that night; the sound of a baby's cry would awaken that horrible memory, forever.

Many of the Okinawans would move at night and nervous young marines, unable to distinguish friend from foe in the darkness, would shoot the civilians. The following morning, we came upon another casualty of just this type. We found an old man, dead, sprawled flat on his back, still clutching his carrying bar for the baskets of rice in his hand. As we stopped for breath, our Japanese interpreter suddenly appeared with two little children. They were brother and sister, no more than five or six years old. As he interpreted for us, it slowly dawned on us that this was their grandfather. What a way to start the spark of hatred in the enemy. This sight would remain forever in their minds.

That night, I had point position at a crossroads. About 2:00 A.M., during the stillest part of the night, I saw many forms down the road, moving toward me. I stood alone, the memory of the baby fresh in my mind. If I opened fire, these people would be dead in a hurry. They could be civilians, or they could be soldiers. I hollered out "Toamati!" and the civilians? Jap soldiers? started running toward me. Were they Japs or innocent people? With the greatest of efforts, I held my fire. Thank God, they were civilians! I was light-headed with relief and gave a quick, silent, thoroughly heartfelt thanks. I had avoided adding another baby's cry to my nightmare.

Not everyone would have been foolish enough to gamble his life on being that lucky, though. Most young marines, their nerves already stretched to the breaking point, already terrified half out of their mind, would have opened fire.

Our goal was to reach the other side of the island in seven days. We had accomplished our goal in four days and were now ready to swing north.

As we started north, I had to make a decision. My feet had been bleeding profusely for some time from tropical ulcers and jungle rot. At night I would try to get some relief from the pain by rubbing my feet, but this was unsuccessful. I needed medical attention.

After talking this problem over with Walden, I turned myself in to sick bay. There would not be a better time.

The main force of the Japs had swung south, and they were being pursued by four Army Divisions. Our main activity had not begun, so we were in a semi-rest mode. The corpsmen bathed my feet with some purple liquid several times a day, and this really helped. However, I still lived in a foxhole, with no special privileges.

The next morning, the corpsman brought a white-haired lady near me and attended her wounds. She was on a stretcher, and she stayed there all day and night. The following morning, she was dead. She had died during the night. I saw her picture in many magazines and books after the war. She was not our enemy, but, who was really responsible for her death? Was it the frightened young boy far from home, just trying to stay alive? Or the smiling and laughing Japs at Pearl Harbor?

After a few days, or even hours, the actions from a young marine are like a maddened animal, with no regrets or quarter given or thought of. His youth has vanished forever and is replaced by a hardened anger that will always remain part of his emotional makeup. His loved ones will never understand why he has changed. He has found an animal anger that he never wanted.

Maybe in his subconscious mind there will never be a day of true laughter again. The immediate transition from teenager to adult killer will create a mental block neither enjoyed nor welcome. Who is the victor in war? Maybe the ones who die and are relieved of the nightmare memories. Or is it the one who is destined to relive over and over again the horrors that man's folly brings? Or is another day of memory just a day of agony? God intended the years from 17 to 21 to be enjoyable — a time for maturing, a time for happiness. Extract this from a young man's life and his adulthood becomes too rapid a transition for him to achieve proper development. Like all things that temperature changes abruptly, the new formation has a rough texture, with cracks of disfiguration. A young person's brain can be scarred for life; the result of which is warped growth. Where would my dreams go after this day of dying youth who had no glory in killing in an unwanted war? How would I be able to look into the mirror of life and see my youthful smile? Only ugliness of death of mankind would reflect my being. A curtain of instant aging would hide all my feelings of despair and helplessness. Time would not erase my mental scars. Who sacrifices these once-upon-a-time teenagers? Anybody's son will do.

10

THE SWING NORTH

A Company made a swing northward to establish a line across the island just before the mountain range. The civilian farmers started coming back to the fields after a few days to tend their crops. The crops were mostly corn, sweet potatoes, and a type of scallion. All the fields were fertilized by human excrement.

Orders were given not to eat these crops because of the fertilizer used on them. Like all good teenagers, of course, we obeyed. And we paid the consequences. Our rations were horrible, with only two different kinds of slop, served with hard crackers. All came in small cans, the rejects of rations used in World War I. However, we had to improve the taste somehow, so we added the local scallion-type onions. This had an everlasting effect. The gourmet repast was warmed over a fire made of wax-like dynamite. The dynamite would burn, but one had to be careful not to cause the lightest of shocks, or you would be history.

We went on daily patrols to find the hiding Japs. One day when our patrol was returning, a young Okinawan girl jumped from the side of the road and grabbed a marine, jabbering unintelligibly. Our Jap interpreter came back and said she was saying that the marine had raped her.

That night, while verbally accepting the password and the correct reply, we were given an addition to the password. The word was, "If they shoot Smith at dawn, we kill the C.O., pass the word on." Evidently, the C.O. was going to have this young marine shot without any kind of trial, just because an Okinawan girl said she was raped by him.

The word got out to our C.O. that the troops were upset, and Smith was flown to a rear area. His disposition was not known to us. Did they carry out the battlefield's orders? Only God knows the answer.

About this same time, we learned that President Roosevelt had died. There fell an emptiness all around us, and there was no discussion about the new president. It was like losing our father, not a political figure. President Roosevelt seemed to have been a close personal friend of everyone.

Instead of depressing us, this news only strengthened our attitudes and determination. But we were all saddened and somber.

The next morning, we looked into the fields and noticed that someone out there was causing a problem. A man was swinging a type of club, hitting women and children. About six of us ran to the field and started shooting at this troublemaker. He went down, but when we arrived where he had fallen, no one could find a trace of him. So, back to our area we went to keep up the watch.

Marsh came to me and asked to borrow my tommy gun. He and my so-called teammate Rotolo went off to the field, hoping to find the fallen Jap. Their hunt was successful; they found him lying on his back, wounded, a cycle-type knife still in his hand. The Jap was dressed in civilian clothes, disguising his real identity. According to Rotolo, Marsh took my tommy gun, put it on single shot, and proceeded with his insanity. Slowly, Marsh shot off the Jap's fingers, then his toes, then his ears. Each time he used only one shot, and he seemed to enjoy the hell out of himself. Marsh finally blew the Jap's head off, sending him to his special heaven. This insanity, the insanity of war, had just been expressed by this teenage boy who was far, far from home.

There was no expression of anger; only insanity was ringing the bell in Marsh's head. The careful spacing of each shot dramatized the event. The applause of brutality and torture echoed inside Marsh's head. This was insanity in its purest form. The drums of insanity were beating louder and louder with the crescendo of blowing the Jap's head off with automatic fire as a final climax.

I angrily protested this action to Marsh himself, and we almost came to physical blows. I knew I could take him easily with one arm tied behind me, but I also knew I had to sleep sometime. He would wait for that moment of weakness to exact a horrendous revenge. To survive, I had to kill Marsh, or stay clear of him. I stayed clear, regretfully.

Another time Marsh struck again, and Rotolo, as ugly as he was, would begin the confirmation of our belief. Rotolo had just left Marsh, who was in the process of murdering an Okinawan grandfather. Marsh was plunging his K-bar (a six-inch knife) into the chest of this helpless old man. The old man tried in various ways to push the descending knife away. But each time, Marsh would just ignore the old man's attempts for mercy and shove his knife into his chest, up to the hilt. Marsh's eyes were fairly bulging with madness with every thrust. There was no reason for this brutal murder. Even Rotolo had to leave the scene. The old man had been trying to protect his granddaughter from being raped by Marsh. Marsh knocked the old man aside and proceeded with his brutality. Marsh returned to us with no expression of remorse or anxiety. He had killed a Jap, and he found insane happiness in this victory.

In days following this insanity, Marsh and I had taken a Jap prisoner. We took him back to the battalion, and the officers refused him as a prisoner. I was told if I wanted a prisoner, he was all mine. I did not have enough food or water for even myself, what was I to do with a prisoner?

So Marsh came to the rescue, making the Jap dig his own grave. The Jap knelt next to his grave, asking for no mercy; the Jap was totally silent and totally unemotional as he knelt down. Marsh "borrowed" my tommy gun and blew his head off. The sound of that burst of gunfire would ring in my head forever. There was no music of victory. There was no sound of applause. Only the thud of the fallen Jap, with the sound of bullets tearing through flesh brought an end to this horror with absolute silence; the silence of despair. This was not war; this was murder. This was madness. This was insanity. There was no hero; there was no cheering of crowds.

Marsh would die, in a few weeks. His death would bring a collective sigh of relief from the marines who knew of his insanity, as well as the rest of civilization. It removed the burden from our shoulders, because we would have been responsible for making sure he would never be returned to civilized society. Was he ever a civilized person? Only God knew.

The next day we walked about a mile to pick up our rations, water, and ammunition. I remember using my physical strength. I carried two five-gallon cans of water back to our machine gun emplacement, one on each shoulder. Five gallons of water in these heavy metal cans weighed about 50 pounds each. I won no cigars with my personal pride.

My teammate Rotolo and I, per his invitation, decided to go into a small Okinawan village. He was always looking for trouble. I always tagged along but somehow never paid the penalty for his irresponsibility. In one house we visited regularly lived a pretty young woman in her 20s. She would unashamedly breastfeed her baby, while we watched with young teenage eyes. Her breasts sure were pretty. However, all romantic intentions diminished to minus zero when she started picking fleas and bugs off her other children's heads. She was very friendly in our efforts to communicate, but we did not need the company of her bugs.

On this particular night, after returning from a patrol, Rotolo had to release some nervous energy that seemed to be always present. So off we went to our favorite off-limits village to visit the pretty Jap mother and her bug-carrying children.

On our patrol, we had some skirmishes, killing Japs who seemed to be second-class soldiers. Souvenirs were available, and I was able to get pictures from their pockets. My innocent teenage mind saw no harm in showing this picture to our newly acquainted Jap friends that lived in the village. What a foolish mistake. Showing the pictures, then physically demonstrating what we had done to the victims brought no applause, only stares of hatred.

Suddenly, around the side of the house a tom-boyish type Okinawan woman came charging at me with a knife. Rotolo was facing me and saw the Jap woman, knife in hand, coming rapidly toward my back.

Rotolo knocked me to the ground, pulling his .45 from his holster. The Jap woman stopped in her tracks, then retreated into a shed-type part of the house. I was forced to be thankful to Rotolo, but this would not improve our personal relationship.

We looked down to the road and saw an army jeep coming with two army MPs in it. Rotolo and I, using our professional marine training, vanished from the area faster than vapor dissipating in the air.

Being close to a village — and its livestock — had one notable benefit, thanks to a marine named Lareau, known as the "company butcher." Lareau was the typical young American boy far from home. His curly blonde hair dominated his youthful features. He was a very pleasant person who never engaged in arguments, yet his attitude of rolling with the punches did not diminish his capacity as a strong and brave marine.

The nickname of "company butcher" was synonymous with his extracurricular activity, which was butchering goats and pigs that strayed around the deserted Okinawan villages. It was a type of artistry witnessed by few. Lareau was cunning and slick. Before the goat or pig could squeal, it was butchered into small portions of high protein for hungry marines.

We needed and craved that meat. The "C" rations from World War I provided no energy source outside of their vintage cans. That food had more life in the can than on its journey to empty Marine stomachs. God bless Lareau, who gave us all our shares of butchered homeless animals. We carried this treasured meat in our unrefrigerated sacks. After a few days, despite the darkened color, the meat rivaled the most delicious cuts offered by the finest New York restaurants. Our C3 (dynamite) provided a fire that destroyed any bacterial poisoning. Charcoal was the flavor on the menu, and we enjoyed every morsel with no checks to pay and no waiters to tip. At such times life seemed almost livable.

Returning from a patrol one day, we came under an air attack. Moving across an open field, I somehow was the only marine who had not taken cover. I was moving rapidly but not taking advantage of the surrounding trees and bushes. Hearing the searching aircraft approaching, I ran faster, my heavy gear bouncing like a loose pack on a scared jackass.

Then from an area 100 yards away I heard a very convincing and commanding voice yelling, "Hit the deck! Hit the deck!" Within seconds I was hitting the dirt. The Jap plane went zooming over my head, looking for the target that had been bouncing in his sights. Sorry, you Jap, I could not oblige you with your ticket to heaven.

I lay there on the ground in momentary exhaustion. Raising my head to see if the anxious moment had passed, I suddenly realized who had been yelling at me, possibly saving my life. There he stood with his hand on his chin, staring at me, while my mind kept whispering, "Wow, that was close." I looked at him and our eyes locked momentarily. I was saying "thank you" without a word spoken.

I was filled with pride and grateful humility. My rescuer was my C.O., Lt. Blinco. To realize how concerned my C.O. was for me made me more confident of my future survival and left me with an everlasting feeling of honor to have been a marine in his command.

The air bursts of the 90-mm antiaircraft rent the skies around our heads, searching for the Jap intruder. Then silence fell. I had been given another lease on life and was deeply grateful that someone cared about my survival.

One bright sunny day airplanes were flying high in the sky. The distance gave no advantage for recognition. The sound of machine guns firing told us we were watching a live dogfight. There were about 20 airplanes zig-zagging across the sky. We saw two Jap airplanes crash into the ground about two miles from us. The next day our teenage curiosity got the best of us. Armed to the teeth, we started on our stupid and dangerous journey. I had one clip of 20 rounds in my tommy gun, and Rotolo was armed only with his brazen stupidity. We came to a farmhouse and asked the Okinawan civilians if they had heard the crash. We communicated by gesturing and drawing pictures in the loose dirt. They were very helpful, pointing in the direction from which they had heard the sound. So down the dirt road we went, and within a half-hour we had located the crash site. However, the excitement of our discovery suddenly turned to disappointment. The Jap plane had crashed nose first, creating a hole into which the rear of the airplane and the pilot had been pulled. There was no way to locate the dead Jap pilot and his souvenirs — a prize pistol, a personal flag and a Samurai sword. They were all there, under about six feet of dirt. But all was not lost. We cut aluminum strips from the wings to give to our favorite craftsman to make watch bands.

We left rather quickly, afraid that a Jap patrol might find us. After all, we were about two miles into the Jap lines.

About a half-mile down the dirt road, we passed Okinawan farmers in the field to our left and saw an Okinawan man stop in the field and stare directly at us. He was frozen in place, apparently trying to make our journey unpleasant just by the way he stared. He was successful. We moved on quickly, watching for any movement he might make. There were definitely no welcoming gestures visible, so it was time to move out.

Moving down the road rapidly, we saw an older, small, thin Okinawan lady trying to put a basket on her head. Of course, here were two big hairy marines that could help out this lady in distress. So to her rescue we went. Each of us grabbed one side of the basket. With a good strain on our muscles and a heave-ho, we placed it on her head. She gave a little grunt and down the road she went. We stood there in total amazement. The basket was heavy, heavy! How did she do it? We stood there, looked at each other and said, "I don't believe it."

Down the road we went with all caution to the wind. Looking behind we saw two older Okinawan men approaching us. My idiot so-called marine buddy, Rotolo, forced the old men to give up their money. He grabbed their money belts from their bodies. He pulled out their money and threw the money belts back at them. I rushed over and yelled, "What the hell you doing?"

"Getting souvenirs, stupid," he answered.

"You're robbing them, you thief," I said. I saw the money, some falling on the ground. Suddenly it flashed through my mind that maybe the money was only good for souvenirs. I reached in my pocket and took out my occupation money. It looked like their money, but had a guarantee that it could be used like good old United States currency. I had bought this occupation money before we left Pavuvu. Now I had it to give to the bewildered Okinawans. Understanding my hand gestures, they handed me their money for mine. I gave them more value than what their money was. They put on their money belts, gave me a thank-you gesture and continued down the road. Asshole Rotolo stood in the background watching with his silly sickening grin, probably mumbling. "Chicken marine." I said under my breath, "Your day is going to come."

Soon we were at our area, two teenagers who would live another day.

Even the circumstances could not change the fact that we were still teenagers. Our immediate responsibilities, which consisted mainly of driving the Japs off the face of the earth, did not change this fact. And what would a well-trained young marine do to express his dedication to duty? Go into Jap lines about three miles, maybe, to go swimming? Prove that you had no fear by not even carrying a weapon? Absolutely! This was true teenage behavior, especially for a young marine named Rotolo. He was my idol, my teammate, the experienced veteran marine who was to teach me how to survive and kill. *Wrong!*

I followed him the three miles into Jap lines. Rotolo badgered me unmercifully: "Why are you carrying that tommy gun, huh? Are you chicken?" I did concede to his insanity by having only one clip (20 rounds) in my tommy gun, and this did seem to express some sort of bravery to him. At 18 years of age, I did not realize the difference between a brave marine and a stupid marine. So off we went, no thought given to the Jap patrols that were out there.

Our several successful trips convinced other young, innocent marines to join us. Soon, there were six of us regularly visiting the swimming hole. I was the only "chicken," carrying my tommy gun, loaded with one 20-round clip. Maybe we all thought that this was John Wayne's war and we had nothing to worry about. It's a good thing our mothers didn't know what we were doing.

My grandfather would have said we were "climbing up fool's hill." What a place to climb fool's hill, in the middle of a war!

Fortunately, Sgt. Rizzo got word of our insanity and put a stop to it. It was time we were serious and acted like adults, even if it meant being killers. Taking our situation seriously was our only path to survival. My idealistic belief in Rotolo began its diminishing journey.

One time, while swimming, we heard someone approaching. We thought our insanity would be the end of us then and there. However, we lucked out. It was only an old Okinawan, one that could speak a little English. We talked with him for quite some time. He said he had worked in California and Hawaii. He liked California better, because he could make $1.25 a day there. In Hawaii, apparently, he would get only $1.00 a day.

He was a handsome elderly man with gray hair and a pointed white beard. Certainly not a "Jap." We left the area, never to return again.

Time and distance would become a vacuum in the relationship between Speedy Dorn and myself. Then I would be in a firefight where a lieutenant would leave his manhood by receiving one of the most horrible wounds. He was a married man of 21; if he lived, this would give his wife a test of loyalty and understanding. How cruel can war be?

My group had followed Dorn's into battle. We had moved into position, expecting more enemy fire. I looked to my left and saw Dorn on a stretcher, lying on his stomach. He had been wounded during the previous firefight. Dorn had been hit in a tender spot, the buttocks, and the bullet had lodged in his stomach. I knelt down, seeing the wound and realizing the consequences. Giving him my most precious commodity, water, I didn't even consider that there would not be enough for me that day. He was also aware of the consequences; his eyes said it was time for the unspoken goodbye. No more Coke and beer to barter. Here was one bullet, one boy, one life, one war, one marine, one friend, one telegram, one goodbye, and one memory.

Dorn died, leaving a memory in my heart for a lifetime. There was no time to grieve. Only time to move fast and forward to find and wipe out the disease that kills young heroes.

Now I was "Asiatic" and understood what Speedy had been telling me. I was an "Asiatic" adult Jap killer.

Oh, you defenders of democracy and freedom! Why do you not write home before you say goodbye?

Now was time for action. We went on patrol and soon found ourselves in trouble. We had been pinned down by machine gun fire from a Japanese pill box. The rifle platoon called back for help. We were two bazooka teams, Lamotta the head of one team and I the other.

When the word came back, Lamotta looked at me. I looked at him. His look was saying, "Send me, I am ready." I said, "Go ahead, it's your turn." I watched Lamotta and Marsh get into position to blast the Japs to their heaven. Lamotta put the bazooka on his shoulder and aimed it at the pill box. Marsh placed a rocket in the tube, wrapped the wire around the igniter, tapped Lamotta on the shoulder, then crouched over to avoid the blast.

The bazooka fired. Lamotta hunched forward, but I saw no rocket leave the bazooka tube. This was common; usually, only 4 out of 6 would explode on target (if we were really lucky). So we often ignored any non-report of an explosion at the target. Marsh quickly inserted another rocket, tied the wire on the igniter, tapped Lamotta on the shoulder, and crouched to avoid the next rocket blast. There was a split second of the sight of the rocket blast, then a tremendous explosion. Marsh's body shot straight up into the air and came straight back down. We rushed to his position and could not find Lamotta. He had disintegrated into dust particles. All we saw was a puff of smoke. There was not one splinter of his helmet, one splinter of his bazooka.

Everything had vanished, like it had never existed. We found only Lamotta's ring finger, with the ring still on it. That was all that was left of Lamotta, physically. Marsh was sitting there, temporarily blinded by the blood coming out of his eyes, caused by the concussion.

I went to help the nearby marines who were wounded by the shrapnel from the exploding bazooka tube, the bazooka rockets, and Lamotta's helmet. One marine had a large piece of shrapnel in his neck, and he was gasping for air and life. We quickly carried him out. He did survive.

Even in our mass confusion, we were able to annihilate the Japs. Meanwhile, after almost three years in the Pacific, death had reached Lamotta. His mask of abandoned dreams had now become an invisible mask of death. It happened so quickly, there was no time to say goodbye.

The cause of this tragedy was that the first rocket was still lodged in the center of the bazooka tube. Marsh, ever irresponsible, never cleared the breach. A look-see through the bazooka tube must be done before inserting another rocket. Marsh never looked through the bazooka tube. Had he completed his responsibility, he would have seen the lodged rocket in the bazooka tube. Instead, the second rocket collided with the first rocket and caused the tremendous devastating explosion, killing Lamotta instantly.

Now Marsh was killing his own buddies. Not one tear or ounce of remorse did he express.

Thus another marine hero passed into oblivion, while no flags waved or bands played to announce his departure. Only memories and prayers from his witnesses would remain with the survivors. Only death would bring silence to this horror.

There were 10,000 Japs in the hills dedicating themselves to making sure young marines did not reach their twenty-first birthday. To fight them, we had set up a perimeter with two machine guns in cross-fire and another machine gun pointing toward our flank. Barbed wire, grenade booby traps, and Bangalor torpedoes were in front of our position. A telephone tied in with our mortar support gave us fire power and light when needed at night. All the luxuries of home, but killing and hate dominated the scene. I was with my so-called buddy Marsh, whom I hated in every respect. Marsh did not inspire confidence in his abilities as a good partner. The cold, cold rain settled in, and there was no way to think about being warm again.

My hated buddy and I went to a deserted Okinawan village and found some straw. We put the straw in between two ponchos, snapping them together, and hoped this would help keep some heat in our shivering bodies. How wrong we were! We could do nothing all night long but just shake with the cold. To top it off, we had a Jap trying to find us to put us out of our misery. I could smell him and hear him breathe, but the night was pitch black and we could not see him. Apparently, he couldn't see us either, and after several hours, he gave up and suddenly stood up and ran like hell. His feet could be heard pounding in the mud as he ran away. I had no fear or anxiety during those hours; most probably I would have welcomed death as a way out of this living hell. My priority at that time was to try and stay warm, not to kill Japs. I had never been so cold in all my life. My hated Marine buddy was an unbelievable animal, and he didn't seem affected by either the hunting Jap or the bitter weather. I comforted myself with the thought that the war had made him such a monster, and that possibly in real, civilized life he had been at least marginally human.

Marsh, more than anybody, probably contributed most to my intense dislike of smoking. Each night while doing our watch on the machine guns, he would smoke. He would cup his hands around the cigarette, assuring me that no one could see the glow from the lit end. Somehow, I didn't believe him. I knew that the Japs spent all their time and talents trying to hunt down marines. I knew that even the tiny glow and smell of that cigarette would catch their attention.

While on watch one night, my fears were justified. About 30 Japs converged on us. A trip-wired grenade went off, and we quickly called for a flare to light up the area. The flare light was not very effective, and the Japs stayed hidden and quiet. We, in turn, did not open fire, because that would give away our position. Marsh, an absolute jackass, kept on smoking!

Our patience provided a stand-off until daybreak. At daylight our group went into the small ravine looking for the Japs. The Japs had dragged off their dead, and there were many bandages lying on the ground. We followed their trail, and found three dead Japs and a dead Doberman pinscher. The dog had killed the three Japs, losing his life in the process. Another unsung hero whose name and heroics will never be known.

A day or two later, we were standing as part of a road block when we saw some civilians slowly walking down the road toward us. Among the civilians, we noticed a couple of men dressed as women, young and healthy-looking, good enough to be in the Jap army. We stopped the group, took the men aside and roughly stripped the clothes off them, noticing rough army bandages on their wounds. There was a brief and furious argument about their future among us, which turned out to be a very short trip to a nearby tree. One Jap woman had argued with us, saying that one of the two Japs was her son. Regardless, they were no doubt part of the Japanese that had sneaked up on us a few nights ago. A short machine-gun burst eliminated these men from any future sneak attacks. There was no time for a trial.

We saddled up and moved out early in the morning, walking half the day to an Okinawan village. We checked the area for Japs and saw no evidence that they had been there.

Our numbnuts of a sergeant saw no reason for us to enjoy this safe and relaxed time, so—can you believe this?—We had to pick up trash in and out of these Jap houses. I started beating my gums in irritation. I was angry. Probably part of the plan. I was saying, "What the hell is this? Whose bright idea was this? I came here to kill, not clean their houses!"

Walking through their doorless and windowless, dirt-floored houses, I continued my barrage of discontent, our numbnuts sergeant hearing every word. Finally he had had enough, and he said with an irritated and trembling voice, "Lince, if you don't like this, then report to Patterson. He has a hole he wants dug."

I moved out angrily without a word in search of my awaiting penance assignment. Patterson wanted a hole four feet deep, four feet wide and six feet long. Maybe I was digging my own grave. My blood was still boiling with anger.

I grabbed a large shovel and proceeded to the desired location. I dug and dug, more rapidly than a backhoe, looking like a mole in heat trying to find its mate. I finished in record time with no stop watches to time me for the entry into the Guinness Book of World Records. Walters came by and saw how much I had dug in such a short time. He said, "Lince, you must have been pissed!"

The hole was dug, the Jap houses "policed." Sgt. Numbnuts had a piece of my ass. I reached a peak in my anger. Lucky for the Japs they were not there.

I turned in the large shovel and joined my group, the sergeant ignoring my presence. We saddled up, then moved out and back to our established perimeter positions.

The sergeant this day gave support to the reason he never ventured to the front lines very often. He could be mistaken for a Jap by his created enemies.

As a machine gunner on the last watch, I saw a show that seemed to be staged expressly for my personal enjoyment. The island was secured by P-61 Black Widow aircraft at night, forming a perimeter of protection. However, some Jap planes would occasionally get through this shield and fly directly over the island, looking for targets to destroy. At night, this effort by the Japs was usually ignored by the American aircraft. But when daylight came, any Jap planes foolish enough to be around became easy targets.

Suddenly, daylight was showing through the trees and I stood from my uncomfortable position to stretch my weary muscles. There it was! A "Black Jack" type airplane, flying at treetop level, its motor sounding like a washing machine, right in front of me! The red meatball insignia was so close, I could almost have hit it with a baseball. The Jap pilot may have seen me; however, he flew by so fast, I couldn't get a glimpse of him in his jet-black aircraft. Then, all of a sudden, there was a highly tuned roar of an engine, like the full-throated rumble of a great cat ready to pounce. The powerful sound came from a marine Corsair, flying just above the treetops, pouncing on a motor-stuttering aircraft. We used to say they had washing machine motors.

"Here comes washing-machine Charlie!" was the cry that came simultaneously with their appearance. The washing-machine Charlie, now in sight, had only a few seconds. Without warning, the pouncing Corsair aircraft aimed its machine guns and squeezed the trigger. The unsuspecting Jap aircraft burst into a fireball. The Corsair whizzed past the disintegrating aircraft and pilot, not dipping his wings in a honorary salute. Another cruel and vicious Jap had lost his life, with no respect earned in his departure.

This was like being on the 50-yard line at a football game, with someone just making a touchdown. I was there, and saw it all happen — the ultimate victory exercise that was used over and over again. I was there, and I cheered with the other beleaguered young marines. Wouldn't it be nice now if we could pick up our marbles and all go home? But our job was only partially completed. We still had to dig these diseased killers out of their holes.

It was on Okinawa, while setting out some booby traps and mine fields, that Corporal Powell demonstrated what appeared to be a miraculous ability to survive. Powell placed a grenade, with a trip wire, on the side of a hole in the middle of a field. This would be the logical place for anyone to take cover if they were under fire. I saw Powell walk in one side of the hole and out the other, tripping the wire, the grenade exploding while he was still in the hole.

This explosion should have blown him to pieces, but, unbelievably, he received only a slight leg wound.

Did he do this stunt on purpose? Did he attempt suicide or just forget what he had done? Considering his pretzel mind, it was surely the latter.

Powell was completely numb as to why he was in the Pacific, or to any event that might be happening, for that matter. The only thing Powell was concerned with was expressing his meanness in all directions, to everybody. Powell was unbearable most of the time, if not all the time.

All of his "virtues," which included only meanness, would provide a "missing at roll call" while on a ship in the China Seas. There was a collective sigh of relief at the completion of a job the Japanese had failed to perform. The effort was necessary, humane, and appreciated by many. His watery grave forever silenced his rotten mouth.

Powell was never missed. There were no salutes of goodbye, only a mumble of "man overboard." The ship sailed into the night. A telegram would be received, with no explanation. An unexplained casualty of war. Still, it would have been nice to have known Powell before the Japs killed his youth. He may have been a smiling youth like most of us, but now he was a casualty of an unwanted war.

As for Powell's rotten buddy, Rotolo, the last association I had with him was when he and Powell were going to duel with me with their knives. I knew I could take them both at once, but Sergeant Rizzo broke up the duel. The duel had been instigated by me because I had finally had it with Rotolo. We were supposed to be a team and share our responsibilities in trying to stay alive. Being patient and mild-mannered in nature, I can take a lot of bullshit before I have had enough, but then there is no return. Then the volcano erupts.

The night before, Rotolo had refused to act as a buddy team, so I was left alone to survive the night. We were in a Okinawan village. When I realized he was not going to team up with me once again, it was too late to dig a foxhole. This was an absolute necessity if we were to survive the night. The foxhole was the only protection from ground fire. Thirteen inches of dirt would absorb a bullet's velocity.

I left Rotolo, cursing him, looking for an alternative to a foxhole. There was a Jap house nearby, and some marines were inside. I was not too friendly with them because I was so frustrated and ashamed of my predicament. I did not coordinate a plan with them as to who would watch and when.

There was an open porch on the side of the house, and in my anger and pride, I decided to try and survive the night alone. This meant staying awake all night long. With a buddy, I could have gotten at least half a night's sleep.

I laid my back against the wall. I stuck my knife and Jap bayonet into the wall, where I could get at them quickly if necessary. Gripping my tommy gun,

I cradled it along my arm, ready to use. There was a full moon that night, and I stayed in the shadows of the porch. I stayed awake as long as I could, but eventually I dozed off. A sixth sense woke me suddenly. I had company.

How long had I been dozing? There on the side of the so-called open way, a new tree had grown in hours. I froze and tried to control my breathing. It was a Jap. Did he see me? Could he see the whites of my eyes? Could he smell me?

I stared out at the camouflaged Jap for what seemed like an eternity, not even daring to blink my eyes or breathe. I could have taken him out very easily with one burst, but he could have buddies on the adjoining hill who would then be able to mark my position. Staying awake would be no problem, ... *wrong!*

I woke all of a sudden to bright daylight. I had actually dozed off again. Fortunately, the Jap "tree" had disappeared, and I had survived the night. But now the anger began to grow. Now I was ready to annihilate a marine named Rotolo!

All that day I was yelling at him, until the knife duel started. There was nothing that was going to stop me from removing Rotolo from the face of the earth, once and for all! Ole Walden knew of my ability and told me to go for it. Even Rotolo and his crazy buddy Powell did not know of my plan. However, when we had our knives drawn and were maneuvering toward each other, the sergeant interceded and sent Rotolo back to the rear area. I was given another team member. He was another boy from New York City. How lucky could I get?

Many events had contributed to my hatred of Rotolo. While on Guadalcanal, he would steal from fellow marines. He would go into their tents while they were on patrol and help himself to anything he wanted. I used to tag along with him, not realizing what the hell he was doing. I was 17 years old, blind and naive, and he was my hero. Digging all the foxholes while he watched. Carrying more than my share of ammunition.

But he was so rotten. One of his favorite games was a particularly macabre form of Russian roulette. Rotolo would step suddenly in front of a marine, staring at him, deliberately placing a .45 between the two faces. In a split second, he would insert the obviously loaded clip into his pistol, skin it back and cock the pistol for firing, put the pistol against his own temple, then pull the trigger. *Click!* Rotolo could plainly see the effect on the face of the other person, who would be standing frozen, his heart not even beating, as he waited for the horrible result. Rotolo would laugh gleefully, or stare at the other with a scornful expression that said all too plainly, "Don't you have the guts to see someone blow his head off? What kind of chicken-shit marine are you?" If a marine turned his head at this disgusting display, Rotolo would openly ridicule him with, "Hey, you chicken marine," and other degrading remarks. No one particularly wanted to see him blow his brains out, although his constant irritation did make it an entertaining thought. Rotolo wore a marine uniform, but he was a poor example of a marine, and an even poorer example of a young boy. Rotolo did not contribute anything to the war effort, but he was a dangerous distraction to the young brave boys who did.

The last I saw of Rotolo, he was wandering around Okinawa, avoiding combat whenever possible. Maybe even stealing from the dead and injured marines.

Now was the time to erase the court-martial that originated for Summers and Tanner at Pavuvu. Now was the time to realize premonitions were real and too often proving time. Summers had carried out his agreement with Col. Grimes to make the blitz then have the court-martial continued after Okinawa. However, this was not necessary because Summers stepped on a land mine, making his premonition a reality. Tanner followed this path of predetermined doom by tripping a leaping lena flare that put a 3,000° F flame in his head. Thus Summers and Tanner met two horrible deaths that laid their fears and daily anxieties to rest. These two young men, not 20 years old, had known and believed an executioner was in their daily shadow. Their escape from death would only have been possible if their attempted ocean escapes had been successful.

A sadness engulfed our group when we were told Summers' and Tanner's premonitions had come true. Col. Grimes, I am sure, wished it had been in his power to create an ending that would have made a mockery of premonition. But death was too frequent and too real. Today was a day for killing, dying, and maybe weeping. All our destinies were really in the hands of an unwanted foe. To the Japanese empire and its inhumane soldiers, I gave a cry of, "You rotten Japs!" We were too young to die. Too many songs would never be sung.

All these events gave indications that our job was done on Okinawa. The four army divisions were pushing the Japs southward and appeared to be in control. We were told by our elite sergeant that we would soon prepare to invade Formosa.

Two days later, we were told the Formosa invasion was the farthest thing from the truth.

Admiral Nimitz was totally dissatisfied with the army's progress and their extremely high casualties. Nimitz said, "If the army does not move forward in three days, I will send in the marines." In three days we were on trucks moving south to do a job the 27th Army Division was not doing; annihilating Japanese. As war correspondent Ernie Pyle had said, if the war could be accelerated to its victorious end by cocky and swearing military soldiers, the marines were the ones to do it. Marines were the most swearing and cockiest soldiers he had been with.

Ernie Pyle would die with our marine group on Ie Shima. A Japanese machine gunner found this unarmed target leaving the remainder of his stories told.

Oh death, you rescuer from unbearable pain, why do you avoid me? How can I find death so that my suffering will end? My eyes refuse sight of the pain that takes these friends from me. Why should there be in God's eternal plan such agony of ending youth? How will I be able to seek pleasure in memories of the past when my past will hold such terror? My life without these heroic youthful marines will wander, searching for the pleasures we could have had.

But now, the marines are coming, you Japs; prepare yourself to fight to die. We will fight to live.

11

SOUTHERN BATTLES

At the southern tip of the island, the Japanese soldiers waited for their tickets to heaven. The 27th Army division, from New York State, was stalled in its futile attempt to grant the Japs their wish. Heavy American casualties in the 27th were the result of total absence of discipline caused by poor leadership and lack of motivation. Casualties were extremely high, overflowing the 31st Field Army Hospital with so many wounded, that many formalities were ignored in order to save lives. Even the recording of names was abandoned, allowing an extra few precious seconds so that a life might be saved. The unbearable strain was obvious. The 1st Marine Division arrived to relieve the 27th.

As we moved up through the 27th Army Division, Dumley started with his mouth. "I thought marines were all heroes running up hills and charging the enemy. They are no different than anybody else. They are scared. They are cautious. They even pull back when they have to." On and on he went with his verbal nervous digestion of fear. He said, "Where are the big fearless marines that the movies portray?" I said, "Back at the movies where they belong with the rest of the non-participants."

I noticed the soldiers looking at us with curiosity and amazement. They had never heard such a swearing bunch of teenagers before. They just stood there looking at us in motionless stupor. They knew we were winners by the nature of our verbiage that characterized courage, confidence, cockiness, and a determination of victory that would not be denied. Dumley's mouth represented his true character, and he later demonstrated with the absence of the daily heroics that real marines perform. Yes, he was looking for the marines from the movies, and he found one in himself. He may have never seen a real marine, because he had a fear of being where they were and of becoming a real marine.

We left the soldiers with their puzzling glances and moved forward to fill the void of the disorganized and demoralized soldiers. The Japs were waiting to greet us with their uncivilized methods of death and destruction. They were not aware that this day not only would be their glory to heaven, but also, their retreat into an unglorified hell. Marines had landed, and now they would face the real marine, never portrayed in any movie.

Then, in a panic mode, the soldiers abandoned their positions, running to our trucks, while the Japs ran to the abandoned positions. At an unbelievably and totally unnecessarily high cost of life, the marines were finally able to turn back the Japs. The Japs now faced a group of young marines whose minds had been instantly tempered by the virtual baptism of fire. Those young marines, who were not already adult killers, became instant killing machines. The Japs faced a determination they had never seen before, as the veteran marines expertly guided the inexperienced young marines to ultimate victory. The 27th Army Division left in humiliation and defeat. It gained the reputation that day of being one of the poorest examples of a fighting force. That night we dug in, in a rough semi-circle with no particular direction for defense. During the night, we moved up from the beach area, under a red alert condition. About 2:00 in the morning, I started trying to call to other positions for assurance, hoping that we were not alone. There was no response. The young marines were either sleeping or too frightened to reply. There was highly intensive fire by the navy at the seawall area. When morning finally came, some of us were ordered to the seawall area. As I approached, I saw other marines leaving the area with blank expressions. Too soon, I saw what had brought this look to their eyes; about 300 Jap corpses were strewn all over the seawall area. Pieces of torsos, arms, legs, hands, and feet were all lying haphazardly around, everything so grotesque as to be unrecognizable. I saw a tall Jap marine lying dead on his back, with no visible wounds besides having a hand blown off. Sickened, I looked up from the carnage and saw a Jap running in the shallow water, an amtrac closing in on him. It didn't last long; they soon overtook him and brutally ran him down. The intent of the Japanese had been to get to our airfield and destroy it and all the airplanes. The Japs had no small arms or knives of any sort but were carrying demolition only. They never even got close, all at an unbelievable cost of human life.

A Company was in reserve, with B and C Companies on the front lines. Sgt. Rizzo told our group, "Dig in on top of that ridge," pointing in a southerly direction. About ten of us started to climb the coral rock ridge. It was a gentle grade with good footing. There were a few short pine trees with two-foot high bushes scattered about pleasant surroundings that appeared good enough for a peaceful camping area.

We peeled off our gear in a relaxed manner. However, in a few short minutes we were welcomed by Jap artillery. *Boom!* The first shell exploded. Then a second shell, then a third, then bingo they hit us. I was knocked down the steep side of the ridge, and I saw several others on the ground. I picked up my body completely intact and ran with lightning speed to more protective cover. I was not alone.

Other marines saw my intended vantage point. Looking like football players streaking to the goal, we all dove for this remote natural protection from these Japs. The shelling increased its intensity, but somehow we were now not in the target area. As quickly as the shelling started, it stopped.

Six teenagers, looking at each other with a scared-shitless expressions, burst out laughing bordering on tears of thankfulness. We had survived our baptism of fire. Miraculously no one had been hit.

Going back up the ridge, we saw the casualties, one flame thrower and one bazooka blasted out of usefulness. Shrapnel had torn large ripped holes in the coral rock that I had been standing near. Reaching down to pick up my helmet had saved my life. When I had my helmet on during a crisis, my mental feeling was that nothing could harm me. Without my helmet during a crisis, I felt as though I were naked in Times Square. My helmet was my security blanket. This time was the only time laughter was heard while shells were bursting. This game being played by young boys found no more time for laughter.

When we were at Pavuvu, we had been shown a very unbelievable secret weapon. A black light was developed that was unseen when shown in the dark. However, looking through a special scope mounted on a carbine rifle, it was possible to see a lighted outline of a figure. Looking through the scope, a Jap outline could be seen in total darkness. Even though only the outline of a Jap was visible with bright green light around him, it was possible to put a bullet into his useless head. A yell of, "Surprise, you Jap!" would be appropriate and satisfying.

Dumley, the goof off, and myself were privileged to use this weapon on Okinawa. Ignoring the previous Jap artillery welcome, we dug in on Sgt. Rizzo's selected ridge. We came there to stay.

As usual, Dumley expressed no energetic reason to try this weapon. During the night, I tried looking through the scope for Japs crawling to find us. There was difficulty in seeing below the two-foot high bushes. That area did not disclose any silhouettes, just a black area. The light provided by burning phosphorus parachuting from the sky gave a brighter affect with less shadows for Japs to hide in.

So off and on that night, I used the scope, not having full confidence in its intended capability. No Jap crawled near us that night, so maybe we had no chance to prove its full potential.

The next morning, we saddled up and began to move toward the center of Okinawa. The 6th Marine Division would now be on our right flank. Their time in hell would begin.

After about ten minutes of column-moving, I asked Dumley, "Where the hell is the nightscope?" Because I was carrying the heavier load, Dumley was to carry the nightscope. He looked at me with a blank stare. I said, "Get your ass back there and get the scope!" He ran back, picked up the scope, and joined us without being noticed. Another teenager showing teenage-type responsibility.

As we left the view of the China Seas side of the island, an artillery duel and small arms fire greeted our approaches to Dakeshi. Laying on the ground for temporary cover, I could see the broadside salvo of a battleship. Then, low overhead would go one red tracer. As the red tracer went directly overhead, the sound could be heard from the battleship salvo. The sound was earth-shaking and dramatized the enormous power of the destructive shells traveling overhead. Then, without warning, a five-inch shell landed short among the marines, causing no casualties.

This must have ignited the energy fuse in Walden's and Dutt's shovels. They had dug the largest foxhole I had ever seen. More like a bomb shelter. We all started digging in, not knowing we were preparing for our biggest and deadliest battle of Okinawa. Just a few yards away, the valley, as beautiful as it was, would earn, even with its own innocence, the name that tells of tragedy, Death Valley. Too many marines would die here with acts of heroics that would diminish the witnessed acts of the much publicized all-time hero Audie Murphy. Only God and a few survivors would see these unmedaled heroes in their finest hour. Even the final victory would not express the real valor given to the heroic deeds by young men in the next few days. History would only record the event and the numbers with the coldness of a non-participant. Some historians would even distort the facts to please themselves and their readers.

"A" Company and "C" company were already in position with intensive fire fights with the Japs. Our group moved up to the edge of a large valley and waited for word. There were many sounds of fire fights, but we were not under fire.

In almost a panic cry, Sgt. Rizzo yelled out, "We need stretcher bearers." Not having to point or select any particular person or persons, marines just automatically responded with instant movement. All we needed to know was where and when. We dropped any packs and gear that we did not need so that we could move low and fast.

Waiting at the edge of the immense valley, possibly 200 feet deep, and 1200 to 1500 yards, from ridge to ridge we could see the advantage the Japs had from the commanding ridge. Marines lay wounded in the valley below, needing medical aid. We had to get them out soon, before they bled to death.

As I moved toward the edge of the ridge, a marine came toward me with streams of blood covering parts of his face and arms. I went to assist him, but he waved me off and kept moving toward the aid station. What a display of determination and courage.

We started down the gradual slope. Small arms fire was bouncing around our feet. In teams of four, we started running low and zig-zagging toward the wounded marines.

The area looked like some rural areas in New York State. Some marines said it looked like Ohio. Whatever it was, it was a type of hell, later called "Death Valley." Running through a dry creek bed and taking cover at isolated hedgerows, we were able to reach the wounded marines. Placing them on a stretcher, four of us would use one hand to support the stretcher. Then, we would start running like hell. Sometimes we would be running only a few feet, then down would go one of our stretcher bearers. Of the four marines on a stretcher team, usually at least one marine would be wounded or killed. So we would pick up one marine and lose another in the process.

It was a vicious game of death and dying. Up the slope we went, not stopping on the way. Each trip took about 20 to 30 minutes up the slope and to the top. Then, as quickly as we could turn around, we went down the slope for more wounded marines. Each time down, I saw this familiar face. It was a cook I knew from the mess hall on Pavuvu. Seeing him every day, I somehow could not forget his friendly, pleasant face. There seemed to be not one ounce of dislike or hate in his expression. He seemed to enjoy helping people. Serving and preparing food, and carrying out wounded marines. He and I made approximately eight trips together bringing out wounded marines. I believed he deserved a medal of some kind.

However, the responsibility of a cook in combat is to be a stretcher bearer, so his actions were not considered "above and beyond the call of duty." If I had been politically acceptable to my NCO, Sgt. Rizzo and Lt. Evans, I certainly could have been considered for a medal, however, I was not a "brown nose" so no thoughts of an award would be entertained even though my actions were above and beyond the call of duty. Basically, I was a demolition specialist, and my responsibility was not as a stretcher bearer. After all, who could embrace a four-eyed marine with the Navy Cross? In the movies the bespectacled ones are the weak ones. No hero actions intended. The movies do portray the truth and reality.

The cook, anonymous to me, remains the hero of the day. With no handshakes or pats on his back saying, "Well done," he would slip into oblivion with God as his only satisfying witness. I cherish the time I spent with him, in his finest hour.

About a hundred yards down the decline, we came under fire. Some Jap tried hitting me, but his automatic fire was just below my feet. I pulled up my feet, and the bastard tried again. I moved away, and he gave up.

I had a wound on my foot, and a corpsman named Ski bandaged it for me. He was later denied the Congressional Medal of Honor, or any medal, for his dedication to his duty and his buddies.

TOO YOUNG THE HEROES

A medical aid person, called "Corpsman," was a super-hero, unknown to the world. Corpsmen were assigned to the marines by the navy. They were respected by the marines as angels of mercy, the cry of "Corpsman!" echoing day or night meant a marine was down. The Japs, with their unmerciful ways of fighting a war, often hit a marine in the legs, knowing a corpsman plus four marine stretcher bearers would come to the fallen marine's aid. These fanatic schemes now produced five more targets, rather than just one. Heroes were born suddenly, with only a basic principle of helping a wounded marine. In many theaters of war, this humane treatment was respected by gentlemen and soldiers with integrity. A red cross signified medical aid people and not weapon carrying soldiers. However, the Japs had no humane feeling about anybody, so disregarded giving neutrality to the corpsman, killing or wounding the unarmed corpsman at every opportunity. All of our corpsmen were wounded or killed on Okinawa. Marines were given a crash course about medical aid for the wounded to provide for our medical needs during the ongoing blitz. There were no navy replacements to fill the void. One of the super-heroes, "Ski," a corpsman, performed above and beyond the call of duty. The real crime of not awarding any kind of medal to this super-hero should be entered in the unwritten book of shame. Those witnesses who could have enacted this honor posthumously should weep with shame every time they look in a mirror.

Ski and a group of marines were caught in the middle of extremely intense Jap firefight. Every marine in the immediate area was down and wounded. Ski was able to find cover in a large, empty shell hole. He was safe and sound where he was.

Then he saw wounded marines needing medical attention. Crawling out of the shell hole, exposing himself to enemy fire, he began dragging one marine after another into the shell hole, bandaging each one and providing the cover they needed to survive the relentless enemy fire. Soon he placed so many marines out of harm's way, bandaging each one, that he now had no place to take cover. The Japs, taking advantage of the situation, targeted a hail of bullets into this unarmed youthful body. Ski was dead in a split second, while the bandaged marines watched in awe, his lifeless body falling on the living bodies that he had saved. Maybe there was no medal high enough to honor Ski. Could this medal of honor only come from God? We all held our heads in dismay when we were told Ski would not be receiving a medal.

I was privileged to have Ski bandage the wound on my foot. Yes, we were under enemy fire too. Bullets were dancing at our feet. He never sought cover. His concentration was only in bandaging my foot. Where do these heroes come from?

The second time I came down to pick up a wounded marine, I went

Marine Corps artist's rendition of corpsmen aiding wounded marines in the battlefield. (Painting by Tom Lea.)

almost the same route. One path I had been on now had a small mortar hole, with blood in it exactly where I had been. The Jap missed me again. One stretcher team I was with went through a dry creek bed, and then we crawled on our bellies through some high grass.

As I was crawling through the grass, I heard a shot in the dry creek bed. I yelled, "Hinton, Hinton are you hit?" There was no response. I repeated my concerned yell, still no answer. I thought he had met a Jap. But what really happened was Hinton had shot himself in the leg on purpose so that he could go back to the hospital ship. We knew he had shot himself because of the powder stains on his dungarees.

I continued crawling through the grass until we found cover behind bushes on a hedgerow. One Jap shot at us, hitting the marine next to me in the wrist. The bullet glanced off his wrist past me into the heart of the marine next to me. The young marine fell to the ground. He kept moving spasmodically, and we saw no blood. We felt useless and helpless to try and save him. He kept moving. Then he was still.

The letters from home that he treated like gold were still in his pocket.

Every chance he had he could be seen reading those letters over and over again. Now there would be only one letter: a KIA telegram to his mother. He died the loneliest boy in the world. They would shove one dog tag in his mouth and keep the other one for the records. Some Jap had just insured his place in glory. How horrible life could be.

The corpsman tried to revive the dying marine, but the marine's last nervous movements of life only frustrated the corpsman in his desperation. Then, suddenly, I looked up and saw Napirino with no shirt on, with no weapon running toward us. He bounded with panic, yelling, "The Japs have broken out." "Get the wounded out of here!" Without hesitation, I grabbed a stretcher with three other marines and started running like hell across the bottom of Death Valley. Across the dry creek bed we ran and started up the slope. The Japs were firing at us all the way. Then, without warning, we came upon an obstacle. A very narrow one-person walkway was across the gully. The Jap fire was increasing in intensity. I grabbed both handles of the stretcher and another marine grabbed the other handles. I gave my tommy gun to a standing marine and said, "Hold it, I'll be back." Then we dashed across the wobbly walkway, not stopping to access any danger or sanity. We were going to save a buddy marine and maybe our own asses at the same time. Everybody else had taken cover and later comments were, "How did you ever make it with so many bullets hitting all around you?" We were going so fast, the bullets just couldn't catch us. In my concentration, trying to get across that stupid walkway, I did not realize some jackass was trying to kill us.

While we were running for a life and evacuating the wounded, Walters, Walden, and James were carrying wounded under intense heavy fire from Jap machine guns. Walters, while on a stretcher team, was less fortunate than I. His youthful body caught the full destructive power of a Jap machine gun. Now, he was on a stretcher fighting for his life. Although he was extremely strong and youthful, he was dying.

Walters was so strong; he even raised up on his stretcher and waved good-bye. Walters died in less than five minutes. I had made a promise I would come to him if he was hurt, wherever he was. Unfortunately, due to circumstances, I was not near him when he was hit.

Walters may never have seen a live Jap. They were all underground with a network of caves and firing positions that were engineered for the ultimate in defense. Many marines who died or were wounded never even saw a live Jap.

After carrying a wounded marine from "Death Valley," I arrived on the top of the secured approaching ridge to Dakeshi. I looked to my left and saw a tank with a large 105-mm Howitzer firing on the Jap positions. This was a most deadly piece of machinery. Nothing but a direct hit in the right place could stop this tank.

The Japs were feeling the tank's destructive force and began trying to destroy the tank by sending artillery round after artillery round, just hoping for a direct hit.

Now was the time to dive for cover! My choice was a shell hole nearby. The odds were very low that a Jap shell would not hit the same place twice. Using my helmet as a sort of security blanket, I placed both hands on top of it to hold it in position. The Jap barrage was tremendous, and I bounced around like a ping-pong ball against the sides of my protective hole. Luckily, the Jap barrage ended as quickly as it had started. Hopefully, this meant we had been able to zero in on their position, and they were too busy protecting themselves to respond.

Silence fell, and I began to hear voices. They sounded very near. I looked around and saw a telephone, wires still attached, lying on the floor of the shell-hole. I picked up the phone, and listened. "We must have reinforcements or pull back! I have 36 dead already and if we don't pull back, we'll all be dead in the morning!" This was the voice of my Company C.O. Lt. Blinco. "I'll call the Regimental Headquarters right away to get their permission," said Col. Grimes. "I'll call you right back!" said the voice of my battalion C.O. Keeping silent, scarcely breathing, I heard the regiment C.O., Maj. Snodgrass, relaying our perilous situation. The Regimental C.O., from a very remote location and not anywhere near the front lines, replied, "We must hold the high ground, regardless of the situation!" Considering the distance from the front lines, it was easy for him to say "we." The phone went dead. At that moment, young boys were dying and some were as dead as that phone line. The regimental C.O., the one that so casually used the word "we," lived on to receive his medals for the type of "heroism" he displayed that day. It must have been a tremendous strain, not to mention dangerous, for him to say "we" from his position so far removed from the fighting.

I dropped the receiver and lay there totally spent. Then I saw someone looking down at me. It was my special weapons lieutenant. "Where is your weapon?" he asked. I explained that I had handed my tommy gun to a nearby marine, in order to free up my hands to carry a wounded marine across a small bridge. During the intense activity, I never saw the marine or my tommy gun again. Lieutenant Evans left then, returned with a M1 rifle, and quickly walked back to his foxhole. He would never venture to the front lines, for fear he might mistakenly get into the line of fire of his many enlisted marine enemies.

There was an airdrop of ammunition, and I went to help distribute this most precious commodity. As I approached the parachuted ammunition, I saw Lt. Blinco leading our men to a rest area. They had been relieved, either by their own initiative or by the battalion C.O. The "we" commander was not close enough to accurately assess the situation to reach a proper decision. Thank God our immediately involved commanders had the guts and brains to ignore that "we" decision.

As the rifle company secured the high ridge at Dakeshi, our group moved into position for immediate support when needed. Intense fire fights were only 100 feet away. Suddenly from their cave of hiding, about a hundred Japs came at us in a miniature Banzai. This unorganized mob was running like mad dogs in July, only lacking foam gushing from their mouths. Their voracity was as intense as a raging bull. Unknown to these short-lived warriors, they would be on their way to their heaven with rapid ascension. Sgt. Owens and I had our sights aimed with a deadly resolve. *Pa Pa Pa rat-a-tat!* went the machine guns, like pins in a bowling alley down they went on top of one another. They were firing madly and shouting "Banzai Banzai," meaning hope you live for ten thousand years. But their cries were in vain. And even the battle itself was total insanity; their blind tempers driven by blind beliefs. Barnes fell over with blood gushing from his neck. Sgt. Owens grabbed the machine gun, keeping deadly rhythm, not missing a beat. We dragged off Barnes and called "Corpsman!" The Corpsman would only temporarily deter the reward of death. The remaining Japs abandoned their idiotic battle and literally dove back into their hole. Fifty Japs lay dead, piled like football players who did not make a touchdown. These players had played their last game.

Barnes would die at the aid station, but Sgt. Owens, who was a buddy of Barnes for a lifetime, would have memories he would never forget. No medals were given or thought of. It was a job well done with the loss of another young boy.

Dumley and I checked a slope to the ridge for Japs hiding in spider traps. We found no Japs, but they found us. Unseen and impossible to locate their hidden locations, a Jap opened up on us with his Nambu. Not obliging this honorable Japanese with his glory, we zig-zagged to cover, imagining the bastard cursing us for not staying in his futile gun sight aim. Dumley was quiet as a mouse, and I yelled out in panicked anxiety, "You rotten bastard." Scared shitless, we regained our composure, staying in our selected shellhole for several hours, knowing we were literally pinned down.

Ammunition, food, and water were dropped by aircraft. The aircraft came so low we could see the pilot. The slowly falling parachutes made an easy target area for the anxiously waiting Jap artillery.

With all caution and abandon, I ran zig-zagging all the way to retrieve the needed commodities. As I reached the area, the Japs greeted us with intense artillery and motor fire, right on target. While the intense shelling was raking the area with no indications of letting up, I heard someone crying. About ten minutes later, the shelling stopped. I began to raise my prone, limp body and saw a young marine near by. Embarrassed by his actions and now knowing I was within hearing range, he tried to hide his shame from me. I pretended not to see him, and I began picking up ammo to carry to the ridge. Marsh joined me, and we made several trips to the rifle company positions. Later on, I was joined by Big Archie, and we made several trips together. On our last trip, darkness began to fall. As Big Archie and I approached the ridge, some Jap aligned us in his machine gun sight. Bullets bursting away at us, we were like cats on a hot tin roof. Those bursts were too damn close. My irritation reached its peak, so I started cursing at that Jap, "You bastard, what are you trying to do, kill us, you son of a bitch!" Then I heard Sgt. Rizzo say, "Hey, Lince, knock it off!" I saw him moving toward us waving his arm in the direction we should move to get out of the line of fire. This was a most welcome unusual gesture by Sgt. Rizzo, "Numbnuts" for short. Big Archie and I found a ditch that had protection on all sides like a foxhole. Too exhausted to think about a 50 percent buddy watch, we collapsed into the natural foxhole. There was no energy even to hold our weighted eyelids up. God would have to stand our watch tonight. Daylight seemed to break even before our exhausted eyelids reached the bottom of our eyes. Big Archie bounced up and joined his rifle squad. I would not see Big Archie alive again. Yes, Big Archie was big in many ways, 6 feet 5 inches tall, nineteen years old, big in heart, big in stature, big to the Marine Corps and his buddies. Too big to die so young.

The rifleman from A Company reached the top of Dakeshi Ridge, laying down an intensity of machine gun fire, BAR fire, and rifle fire that had the Japs running in a panic escaping mode. I could see groups of fifty Japs running with no evidence of organized resistance, some falling down as the bullets found their targets. As I returned to find cover, there seemed to be a break in the action. Then, suddenly, all hell broke loose. Artillery was landing on our marines, but this was not Jap artillery, this was our own artillery. The army division on the left of us, not believing we were marines on that ridge because we had done an almost impossible task in a very short time, zeroed in our own artillery on us. We had taken Dakeshi Ridge in three days and, being cut off from our rear communication, we were alone. We were victorious, but we were dying by our own artillery.

The Japs zeroed in on our own artillery bursts. Burst after burst, with all of us wondering who the hell were our friends at this moment. The shelling ceased and panic cries for stretcher teams echoed through the devastation. Not many were wounded, but many were dead.

As I rushed around an embankment, I stopped in my tracks. Dutt was in a shellhole moving Sgt. White off a blood soaked stretcher. Sgt. White, an old marine 23 years of age, his body a mass of blood, had died. There was nothing more we could do. His children and wife from Tennessee would mourn him the rest of their lives. He was a veteran with almost three years in the Pacific. Dutt and I grabbed the blood-soaked stretcher, then ran to pick up more wounded.

Coming back to my foxhole, I looked up and saw a parade of heroic marines pass by. They were not marching in dignified marine form, but lying prone on stretchers with covered heads, arms swinging lifeless in a grotesque way of maybe waving goodbye. Eight veteran marines, all having almost three years in the Pacific, paid a very high price for our freedom that day. Possibly, all had been killed by our own artillery. Marine Cpl. Bailey followed the parade, hunched over and looking like a man 80 years old. While waiting alongside the rows of his dead, close buddies, a corpsman gave him a shot of morphine to help him survive this horrible tragedy.

As I looked down the slope toward Bailey, I felt helpless and despondent. Bailey had his shot of morphine, and now he was alone, walking around his dead buddies. They had all been together in the hell of the Pacific for over two years, and now he was a survivor, with memories of hell for a lifetime. I dared not look under the ponchos to see their faces, but I knew who they were. They were my buddies also. Some I knew by their faces only. Some I knew only by nicknames. One thing for certain, they were lifeless. They were still. They were at peace. But why should they die so young to become a casualty of an unwanted war? A number in a history book and not even mentioned by a non-participating historian. But the truth was before us: In order to stop the killing, we had to kill. We had a job to do whether we were 17 years old, 18, 19, or 20. On our watch, we had to stop the killing. So I turned my head away from the sadness, put on my pack, grabbed my tommy gun, and started up the slope to the top of Dakeshi.

Mentally, although the smoke had cleared and the dead and dying had been removed, we as marines were there to stay, and our angry determination overshadowed our sadness while we increased our intensity of killing those Japs.

As C Company, 1st Battalion 7th Marines came down into the valley, there was no resistance or any kind or any welcome by the patient waiting Japanese. Positions were taken on both sides of the road that led to a gradual incline. The valley was an ideal trap for any opposing force. Numerous caves faced the valley for an ideal defensive position. After all of C Company was in the valley, all hell broke loose. Machine guns, rifles, mortars, and grenades all came at once at the unsuspecting marines. The cave positions were well camouflaged by the natural terrain, so easy detection was not apparent. Only flashes from gun bursts made the cave openings visible. The marines opened fire with everything they had, but the Japs had the advantage. Red-blooded marines had to find these caves and destroy them before every marine was dead. One by one, the caves were blown into submission. Uncommon valor was a common virtue. This was where men and boys became marines. This was where marines died and marines were wounded, but up the gradual slope they went, sometimes having to move back and regroup to go at it again. The marines were relentless in their determination to kill the Japs that were killing their buddies.

G.G. Olson was there with his water-cooled machine gun, picking targets in an attempt to turn the tide of battle. Intense would be a mild word to describe the action. Our own artillery fell short, killing some marines going up the incline. Japs were running out of caves, two or three at a time, throwing grenade after grenade. Jap mortars were hitting their intended marine targets.

Tanks were brought in with flame throwers finding their Jap targets. A tank commander yelled down at G.G. "Can you drive a tank?" G.G. said, "No, but I can learn." The tank commander said to G.G., climbing into the tank, "Just push your feet left and right." G.G. said, "O.K.," putting a new wad of tobacco in his cheek. Up and down the road they went, pulling wounded in through the bottom hatch. They would take the wounded back to the aid station, then up after more wounded marines. Soon, G.G. was an expert tank driver. G.G. was wounded himself, but nothing like the marines he was helping.

After getting the wounded and dead marines out, G.G. went back to his machine gun position as night was beginning to fall. Marines needed to be ready for the infiltrating Jap tactics.

About midnight, four or five Japs came down the road right past G.G. G.G., not giving away his position, let them pass by. Then, at the end of the road, the Japs found the end of their glorious military journey. Marines cut them down with automatic fire, bringing silence to the deadly fight. Later, Japs could be heard jibber-jabbering all through the night, but no significant fire fights occurred. Then daylight came, and the goal for the day was in front of the marines. Take the ridge was the silent battle cry.

As G.G. and his group started up the gradual slope, three young girls came out of a cave, yelling at them in Japanese. What a surprise! One of the marines understood some Japanese and believed they were yelling "Go around, go around." The Japs had a trap waiting for the marines. The young girls were evidently angry at the Jap soldiers, so they gave away the Japs' secret of the waiting ambush. The marines accepted the warning of hidden danger and went to the right of the waiting honorable Japanese.

The civilian girls went back into the cave and innocently avoided the

A marine mourns a buddy killed in action. (United States Marine Corps photo.)

unsuspecting Japanese. Unfortunately, the young girls no doubt died a horrible death alongside their undeserving companions.

But G.G.'s toothache was better now. While he was driving the tank, he traded a Jap flag for a pair of pliers. What do you do with a pair of pliers in the middle of battle? Pull a tooth! What else? After all, G.G. is where no dentist dares to tread. So take the pliers and pull the aching tooth. Then stuff it with a chew of tobacco. G.G. says, "I am from Virginia, and that's how we do it there."

Now, it is up the slope we go. Firing on our way. Tanks and artillery fire was closing up the caves, with the Japs still in them. G.G. and 46 other marines reach the top of the ridge. Their Captain makes it also, even though his leg is broken. Only one BAR man makes it to the top of the ridge. Now the valley is known as Death Valley and C Company is now about platoon strength. This was a day and half of pure hell. The impossible was done right away. Future miracles will take a little longer. G.G. is one big reason why the 7th Marines was awarded the Presidential Unit citation for those days of uncommon valor. Billy Siegfried from Rome, New York, was there also. He was a veteran of Peleliu.

After securing Dakeshi Ridge and the Shuri Castle area, which took our 1st Battalion ten days, the remaining marines were formed into a company. From about 900 combat marines, our total battalion strength was reduced to about 350. The regiment had lost over a thousand marines in ten days.

SOUTHERN BATTLES

Seventh Marines,
First Marine Division, Fleet Marine Force,
C/o Fleet Post Office, San Francisco, Calif.

20 May, 1945.

MEMORANDUM TO: Seventh Marines and Attached Units.

1. It is with great pride that the regimental commander publishes the following dispatch from the Commanding General of the First Marine Division:

    THE 7TH MARINES HAVE EVERY REASON TO FEEL PROUD OF THEIR GALLANT CONDUCT WHILE IN THE LINE & CAPTURE OF THE WELL ORGANIZED AND DESPERATELY DEFENDED DAKESHI RIDGE AND HIGH GROUND TO ITS FRONT WAS A FEAT OF ARMS IN KEEPING WITH THE BEST TRADITIONS OF THE MARINE CORPS AND OF THE NAVAL SERVICE X
    WELL DONE X

    CG 1ST MARDIV

2. Each individual of the Seventh Marines and attached and supporting units share equally in this commendation. The personnel of the Seventh Marines are deeply appreciative of the untiring and unexcelled support given by supporting tanks, artillery, 4.2 chemical mortars, rocket platoon, motor transport, artillery, naval gunfire and air liaison and observer personnel, C Engineer Company, and C Medical Company. The determined efforts of all concerned and the fine spirit of cooperation existing at all times is a source of great gratification to the regimental commander and a source of great discomfort and destruction to the enemy.

    E.W. SNEDEKER
    Colonel, U.S. Marine Crops.

For the first time in the Pacific, the replacements waiting on the ships were used. Over 4,000 marines and 180 officers attempted to fill empty ranks by numbers. The tragedy was filling the ranks by numbers and not by experienced combat trained marines. The effect of the poorly trained and inexperienced marines was apparent. The casualty rate among these marines was extremely high, with death the higher percentage; it was like sending teenagers to the slaughterhouse. A typical example was an inexperienced marine who threw a case of grenades all night long. However, he never pulled the safety pin that allowed the grenades to explode. How could we place medals on generals and admirals who, through poor logistics and planning, allowed this to happen to our young men?

The newspapers and movies would not publicize these horrible personal tragedies. They were hidden in unpopular books, the only recognition that they did exist. Only God would embrace and honor these young men to the high degree that they deserved. The ignorant populace would still go to the movies and see how war "really" was.

Looking to the sky each day, we could see the close support of our own aircraft, a confidence factor that was necessary for survival. The TBF aircraft would fly so low we could see the pilot. They flew in and out of the valleys looking for places to drop our supplies of food, ammunition, and water. Usually they made one dry run, then came in the second time to drop the parachuted supplies. Unfortunately, one day one of the aircraft was hit. Both pilots bailed out about two miles inside the Jap lines. It looked like they landed safely. However, after moving forward through that area, the pilots' remains were found. The Japs had actually eaten the pilots. This was another reason never to surrender to these honorable Japanese.

Spotter planes were overhead during most of the daylight hours spotting targets for artillery and naval gunfire. They were a small, very light-weight civilian looking aircraft. Usually with one or two spotters aboard, they flew over enemy territory, an easy slow target for any Jap gun sight. While I was watching a spotter aircraft one afternoon, it suddenly burst into flames evidently hit by Jap gunfire. There were no survivors.

Like a shot from an enormous aircraft cannon, a P-38 Lightning zoomed over our head at tree-top level. The exceptional fine-tuned engine sent chills of enthusiasm and courage up and down my spine. With such a display of American engineering, I felt I was on the winning side. I knew my days of being a ragman would eventually turn into a satisfactory reward of victory.

The center pod of the P-38 aircraft enclosed the smallest cameraman in the world. "Pretzel-bones" would be a good description of his body posture. However, its swift appearance over the Jap lines had to astonish those fearless Jap warriors. The close accurate photos of Jap positions would help accelerate our quest for peace.

We moved off the ridge, going to our right, through the second battalion area. This would be a nightmare in itself. The second battalion never removed their dead. We walked through an area of dead marines in their last grotesque positions. One dead blond boy, with long hair, was arched backward. That I will never forget. Other dead marines were scattered all over. My buddy, Dumley, from New York City, and I dug in for the night. The shelling was quite intense. We were low enough that the dirt and mud from exploding shells kept falling on our Jap blanket that we had captured. There was a big bloodstain on it from a Jap who had come for an unwelcome visit to us one night.

We shook the dirt off and prepared to move out. There was a fire fight with a couple of explosions nearby. Suddenly a marine came running toward us yelling, "Pop is dead. He was decapitated by the last artillery shell." Pop was a 29-year-old man in our company. He was much loved and respected. Now he was dead, an old man of 29.

Then we heard the terrifying cry, "Blinco is dead." Our veteran leader, C.O., 24 years old, was also dead. A Jap cave, believed to be harmless, suddenly opened fire with automatic weapons, killing Blinco and eight other marines instantly. The Japs had waited patiently for this prize moment, hitting the leaders first, thus demoralizing the rest of the fighting marines. Officers and non-commissioned officers wore no rank insignia of any kind. We never saluted or referred to their rank in any manner. We used last names only. But, apparently the Japs had seen Blinco's leadership stature and possibly his visible commands of other marines. This prize would be the Japs' ticket to an honored place in their heaven.

We regrouped, and Dutt ignited a satchel charge, grabbed it, and ran for the cave opening. We all dove for cover and waited, and waited, and waited. There was no explosion. Dutt grabbed and ignited another one, and ran for the hole again. With deadly accuracy, he threw the charge into the hole, and we all dove for cover again. And we waited and waited. Again nothing happened. After a few minutes, the riflemen and BAR men started cautiously toward the opening. They were halfway there when a gigantic explosion ripped the hillside apart, spraying the approaching marines with coral rock and shrapnel. Cave, earth, Japs, and all disintegrated. The marines received only minor wounds, not enough for hospital care.

Dutt received the Bronze Star for his action that day. I asked him, "How did you do it? Why were you so brave that day?"

"I just found out that my sweetheart married my 'best' friend. I just didn't care about living that day," said Dutt. His bravery had really been anger and grief.

Blinco was dead, with no one in sight to fill his shoes. We moved on, leaving his body and the other bodies exposed to the elements. The intensity of the ensuing fire fights made it impossible to return to the area for ten days. Blinco would certainly have reprimanded us for not carrying out his orders regarding respect for the dead. Our hearts were heavy with this unfulfilled duty.

How Arthur and I ever got together, under extremely heavy artillery shelling, escapes my memory. But there we were, like two peas in a pod, and just as green in fright. Those Japs were serious about trying to blow us to pieces. I, a strict nonsmoker, smoked almost all of Arthur's cigarettes, trying to calm my nerves. He would hand me one, hands shaking like leaves in a high wind, while I puffed away like a locomotive, concentrating on not inhaling. The shells were dropping very close, scattering dirt over us, with shrapnel whistling over our heads. I had developed a kind of sixth sense of how the Japs would walk their target through a pattern of destruction. They usually fired two shells at a time, with pin-point accuracy. Arthur and I jumped from shell hole to shell hole, trying like hell to avoid the fire. Suddenly, I got that strange feeling that we were targeted and the next shell would be for us. I looked at Arthur, and he looked at me in complete understanding. In perfect unison, we dove for the next shell hole and felt a shell explode where we had been a split second before. That was enough! We started running across the shell torn field, toward a nearby marine tank, which was the reason for the Japs' continuous efforts. We made it, and I was relieved to find myself alive, to say the least. I also found that I had not developed an incurable nicotine habit, and that I had not soiled my pants. We finally joined our group, and everybody had a good laugh at my expression. My eyes were still as big as saucers, and it was obvious that I had had the stuffing scared out of me.

Artillery shells were exploding with piercing sounds of searching shrapnel tearing at the fabric of frightened young souls, tormenting minds knowing there was no defense. An unseen monster with claws was tearing flesh to instant pain or disintegration. Out of the mother's womb and the arms of love, young boys experienced a hell known only to the victims and the surviving witnesses. The inventors of war should touch and feel these moments of hell to purify their minds for avenues of thought that allow a solution not limited to war.

There was continued periodic shelling, and I shared cover with a marine I didn't know. He tried to relieve a little of his anxiety by telling me a short story. He was a veteran, maybe 23 years old. He told me about how proud he had been that morning to have helped a very young marine kill his first Jap, just to be saddened that very same afternoon by that young hero's death. He seemed to think that he lost out on that trade, that in fact we all had.

I never did have to pay Arthur back for all the cigarettes he gave me. He was under the impression that he owed me a debt for the "sixth" sense that had surely saved both our lives. I have always wondered at the circumstances that throw people together. As frightening a day as this had been, it was nothing compared to the hell that awaited us that night. Even Dumley would find out how marines die.

There were two D.C. Jacksons in A Company. The tall, curly-headed young boy was the one I became friends with. He was a tall, lanky boy from Texas who would be welcome in any American home. He brought cheer with

Marines faced challenging terrain on Okinawa. (United States Marine Corps photo.)

his smiles and was always interested in you and your welfare; just a pleasure to be around. Put a marine uniform on a boy, give him months of training, and he is still the boy from the corner drugstore.

The other D.C. Jackson was from Utah, a devote Mormon, and a strong and dedicated marine with expressions of seriousness with little room for laughter and jokes. But, do not put on the boxing gloves with him. He would knock your head clean off. It was rumored that they wanted me to have a boxing match with him. I ignored all comments so that my head would still be intact. The idea was forgotten so I lived another day. Oh, he was a good boxer and an excellent marine. A Jap mortar found him as its target. His wounds were on almost every part of his body.

During the last moments of his life he kept saying, "Daddy it's ok. It's ok, I've come home, I am coming home." Then he was silent and motionless.

We had been on Okinawa for about two months, when we were told some very bad and demoralizing news. Snyder was dead. His mother, father, and loved ones would not see his handsome face in South Carolina again. Snyder had died alone, unnoticed by any friendly person. His body was found by our "graves recorder" after we had advanced onto Jap territory. Snyder had become a sniper and had gone behind Jap lines about three miles, to kill Japs. Whether he was successful or not, or whether he volunteered, we did not know. Only God knows. We know for sure he died alone, he died young, he died hungry, he died dirty, and he died thousands of miles from home. He died with the mind of an adult killer. His young mind of love had become an adult mind of hatred with only thoughts of killing. Where do these young boys come from? They come from the bosoms of mothers' love, and now the mothers of love will be mothers of sadness and despair. If Snyder was the victim, then his mother, father, and loved ones were also victims.

Snyder's silence in death is all that remains. The world would never know or realize his quest for freedom and a life of happiness for his land. Snyder's echoing cries of despair dissipated into a pyramid of wealth rising high above the fields of terror caused by the Japs. Very often, a soldier's death meant leaving next of kin to live in a sea of poverty, while the next of kin of Japs lived in a level of economic growth unknown to mankind before the war. Would Snyder's teenage death, like all the others, be in vain? The silent yes, would register at the bank of the Jap's empire in years to come. Monuments to commemorate these loving teenagers would be torn down by Jap demolition crews. The memories of these teens would only be left with those who received the telegrams.

One of the most dangerous duties in the marines was that of being a sniper. Camouflage clothing, an .03 rifle with scope and guts of steel, were the ingredients to fulfill this above-and-beyond-the-call-of-duty mission. On Okinawa, the deadly accurate Jap artillery man was a prime target for a sniper. Now, at darkness, it was time for a sniper to make his move. The yell would go up and down the lines "Marine moving out, hold your fire." Then, quietly, like a fast moving cat, another brave marine would speed into the darkness. This young American boy was alone, scared, and brave all rolled into one. The sniper would go three miles into the Jap lines, find the Jap artillery, secure an advantage point with proper cover, then wait for daylight to see his intended targets. The cold of the night gave the excuse for shaking like a leaf. No moments could be spared to think of home and loved ones. A thought of, "What the hell am I doing here?" could ignite fast-moving legs to safe and sane surroundings.

However, marines, not known for abandoning their duties, demonstrated their courage time and time again in the unheralded and unwitnessed mission.

Darkness would hide this super-warrior, with dreams of home pulling at his very soul. The night would be long to some marines, whereas other marines would feel the dawn came too soon.

The first rays of sunlight came over the hills and through the shell-torn trees. The sound of jabbering Japs gave a signal that the intended targets would soon be in view.

Full daylight soon exposed those slimy Japs, and prime targets were picked to send a piercing bullet through their distorted brain.

As a marine sniper, you would put your rifle to your shoulder, place a Jap head in the cross hairs, hold your breath, squeeze the trigger, and suddenly one Jap has quickly gone to his heaven. Cock the bolt up and back, then forward and down, hold your breath, and squeeze the trigger, and another Jap who dared to be in your scope's cross hairs has also gone to his heaven. Repeat the above for enjoyment, sending a sound around the world that freedom is alive and well. After many shots, you notice that the Japs that are alive are looking directly toward you. Do they see you? Have you not hidden yourself well enough?

The sad part of this true happening is that the marine sniper has done his duty above and beyond the call, but the United States of America, in its vast arsenal of brains, has provided this super hero with smoking powder. Each time he shoots, smoke goes into the air, giving away his position of hiding. The more shots, the more smoke. The Jap snipers had smokeless powder, and their hiding place was impossible to find.

Seeing how easy it was to spot smoke from the brave marine sniper firing on them, the Japs directed automatic fire at his position, and he had no place to hide. Yes, the Jap artillery men were dead, but no marine sniper would live to tell this tale. We would only find their bodies in positions where no imagination was needed to tell of their heroic deed.

Snyder was one of these boys. No medal has been forged that could honor their heroism. If we forget these boys, may we be damned for an eternity.

There was no time for promotions. Only time for dying, killing, and being wounded and some time for surviving the unwanted hell. Privates dying doing a sergeant's job. Sergeants dying doing a lieutenant's job without even fair compensation for a day's work. I was a private for 2½ years. In the army, the same responsibility I had carried sergeant stripes.

Stedwick, the short, muscular, fast-moving marine, was energetic and moving about helping other marines. In combat, finding Jap targets was his specialty, and he used every available weapon to satisfy his thirst for killing Japs. On one very dangerous, daily mission, he paid a high price for satisfying his thirst. His unheralded heroics should be mentioned in the Marine Corps archives. Unfortunately, for the benefactors, all of his heroics disappeared with his life.

Moving over to the right from Dakeshi Ridge, A Company came under some heavy Jap resistance. Our rifle company had been pinned down and had many casualties. We were activated to try to pull out some of the wounded marines. It was almost impossible to advance. Darkness was fast approaching, so we quickly carried one wounded marine back to the rear. We could not reach the others. One particular marine had broken legs. While going back to the rear, I noticed a nice souvenir in front of a cave. A trap a Jap had set. I knew if I went to retrieve the souvenir, the Jap would open fire and I would be dead. To hell with you, you Jap.

Gorham, a fatherly type marine, at the age of 20, was always yelling out greetings whenever I passed his tent at Pavuvu. A veteran of the Peleliu blitz, he seemed to try to cushion the shock we would receive when we would be in combat. To be friendly seemed to be his daily chore, and he would remain a good thought in the minds of the survivors. Like all premature deaths, his passing created a void in the happiness of the world.

Walden came to me and said "Gorham is dead." Walden knew of my comradeship with him. In fact, he was one of Walden's closest buddies.

We had moved into an area where many dead Jap bodies were lying in their rotting condition. The air was filled with the smell of death. Death was an odor so distinct and repressing, that it gave the nervous system a command to the brain to "do something!" The only way to "do something" was to bury the dead. The odor was a command, from God that something horrible had happened, and if you did not destroy the odor, the smell would attack your nervous system like a virus. The area was exposed to this condition at almost every hour of the day, and our "Asiatic" attitude provided us with a sort of immunity. We completely ignored the situation and moved about in a numbed state. There was no way to control or to correct the situation.

With no immediate war activity, it was time for lunch. The Japs were getting blind drunk, making preparation for the Banzai that night. Time for lunch, with the formal setting of death and rotting bodies. There were four of us, old before our time, numbed to the surroundings, and too "Asiatic" to complain. Our wordless conversation at lunch would echo through the universe, asking why?

A rat would run in and out of one of the dead Jap's mouth, enjoying his own lunch maybe in the same degree as we were. These adult killers were now reaching down into their animal instincts to survive. This horrible effort for survival might linger as a habit for the remainder of their lives. Maybe only the silence of death could suppress these visible activities, and no peacetime experience would make citizens understand. Maybe they would believe we had gone to Boy Scout camp, where we got all muddy and where there was no cookie jar. Oh, God, please forgive ... the ungrateful living.

Sgt. Rizzo came to us and said to expect a banzai attack because the rifle company was pinned down, and there was a big hole in our lines. There were only 14 of us, and we had to get to the top of this ridge before darkness fell. We hurried to the ridge and dug in. Someone brought me a shotgun from headquarters, and we began preparing for the worst. We knew we would not survive a banzai attack, but we had to do what we had to do.

There were many dead Japs in the area, especially in front of us, only 6 feet away. We had to take inventory before it became too dark, knowing they would sneak among their dead and wait for the right moment.

The other two marines took the first watch, and I tried to sleep. About 2:00 A.M., I was suddenly awakened by Dumley asking me if I knew where the dead Japs were, saying he believed there was a new body out there. I looked in front of us when the lighted flare exploded and sure enough we had company. I could see a shiny part of his belt, or something that brightened up with the flare. Shells were landing near us, but not exploding. We could hear them come in, going "plop" in the heavy mud, sending up dirty geysers of the stuff. We could hear the Japs at the bottom of the hill, just jibber-jabbering away. Evidently, they were drunk and probably did not know we were there in the darkness. This was why the new "company" was among the dead. This Jap was the jabbering Jap's scout.

My foxhole buddy marines, especially the gutless mouth from Alabama, stayed in the foxhole, with no intention of coming out and exposing themselves. By default, I had been elected to be a hero.

During the daytime, before getting pinned down, we saw a group of Japs getting drunk on an opposite ridge. This was their preparation for a banzai attack. There they were jabbering in their drunken stupor, waiting for the word from their scout. At noon, a 37 mm cannon was put in position next to me. The marines aimed at the drunken Japs and started blazing away. The shells contained shotgun-like pellets. Of course, this is against the Geneva Treaty and the Decency of War Rules. Now we were really poking holes in them; their knives and bayonets went flying into the air from the explosions. However, this effort did not lessen their madness.

But now, flares charged the darkness with some visible light. It seemed like an eternity, watching that Jap to see when he would make his move. There was always a long period of pitch-black darkness before the next flare would begin its parachute descent to earth. The Jap would stay motionless for hours. Then suddenly, probably a half hour before dawn, the Jap was gone. Where the hell was he? Then night became pitch-black again, and I didn't know where he was. There was only one place he could be and that was behind a large coral formation to my left.

I stayed motionless, then, from the Jap's hiding place I heard a clunk. That bastard ignited a grenade. Suddenly, something flew past my head, and then there was silence. He had vanished again. The gutless wonder marine had a good night's sleep at my expense, and I hope he had good dreams of home. Dawn was beginning to break. I could see silhouettes of marines at the dawn's first light, and I began to believe I had survived another night. There were no more sounds of jabbering Japs, and the dud shells had stopped falling. Evidently, the Jap among the dead had been a scout and the jabbering bastards below the hill were waiting for him to give them word to start the banzai attack. He evidently found us ready, and he did not have the guts to go back and give them the starting signal. Our preparation had saved us for another day.

I was exhausted and drained when full daylight came. A few feet from me, I saw what had gone past my head. There lay an unexploded grenade. If it had exploded, the grenade would have blown my back off. The Jap was probably wondering what had happened.

I just wanted to go to sleep. I remembered a cave just a few feet away and went there to get some shut-eye. Unfortunately, that thought was short-lived. The Sergeant came after me and said, "What the hell are you doing here?" Little did he know I may have saved his ass and his brown-nosed buddy that night. There would be no time or need for an explanation: the sleeping hero from Alabama would probably tell all of his girlfriends about how he was such a hero that night. I never had the opportunity to beat his ass. I would have welcomed the opportunity.

As our group of 14 marines moved off the ridge where we may have prevented a banzai, I saw a life-lasting sight of the ultimate hero. The sight of Sgt. Jeffers going over a very small ridge, his silhouette against the orange blazing sunrise, burned in my mind. A picture expressing the dauntless determination of the American youth. The strapped Samurai sword to his pack told me that Sgt. Jeffers was relentlessly pursuing the Japs with his buddy marines, the best the Marine Corps and America had. His expert deployment of fire teams that consisted of four marines in each fire team was the ultimate exercise professional Jap killing. Sgt. Jeffers' expertise could destroy any and all opposing Japs. Only once that I knew, did he and his squad have to withdraw and regroup. There must have been an overwhelming Jap force to cause this unheard of action. The daily reports via scuttlebutt were always victory after victory. These victories were never photographed or published in any newspaper. The Japs knew when Sgt. Jeffers and his squad were in pursuit of their extinction. None of the Japs would survive to tell of the hell-type experience. An old man at 20 years, Sgt. Jeffers would not see his twenty-first birthday. The very day I saw his silhouette against the rising sun would be his last day. Unfortunately, some Jap had him in his gun sight and decided to kill another American as the "code" demanded. Sgt. Jeffers' heroic deeds would not be recorded in books and only in a few minds. I feel honored that I was present in his finest hour. The price he paid for the freedom of millions of people would be enjoyed 24 hours a day, for many, many years to come. Yes, anybody's son will do.

12

AWAY FROM THE FRONT LINES, AND BACK AGAIN

Now it was time to leave the front lines. Sixteen days of continued, intense combat demanded that these young teenage boys be given a rest from a time in hell.

Our departure seemed to be a blur of exhausted excitement. The 2nd Battalion had already moved into protective positions to allow us to move out with no casualties.

I, having more gear to organize than most marines, found myself the last one in our column. It had to be somebody, but why the hell did it have to be me? All I could think of was the Sgt. York story where Sgt. York shot the last German soldier, and the other German soldiers never looked around to notice that their buddies had been shot. Dumley was ahead of me, and he never looked back to see if I was coming. That movie reminded me that my marine buddy was a hell of a teammate. On each side of the dirt road, there was evidence of total war. The trees were all leveled, with blackened and smoking areas. The smell of death, from visible rotting bodies and burned powder, supported the facts that there had been a hell created for mankind by men. Regardless of my minimal abilities, there was little acceleration in my dragging feet, going to the rear of the rest area.

A Company went back to the rest area after many days at the front lines, relieved by the Second Battalion. Our withdrawal was orderly and welcome. We had no energy for, or interest in, looking back to see where we had been. All of us were filthy dirty, drained of the ability for all facial expressions and youthful smiles. Even hungry beyond the thought of food and almost at the point of believing that food didn't even exist, our energy had been drained away with the inches of our bodies. My own 30-inch waist line had been whittled to a scrawny 27 inches, the belt hanging on the bones of my hips. Youthful, unshaven faces looked like homeless hobos wandering aimlessly to who-knows-where. Those who could still muster up the energy to talk said to me, "If your girlfriends could see you now!" I had no energy for girlfriends, and I did not want to be seen by anybody. The sight of us could make our mothers cry for the rest of their lives.

Sixteen days of hell, with no feelings of victory. Our youth had gone to hide in shame, and we knew it. Light conversations included, "It was worse than I ever imagined or feared!" The previous battles welded our young minds shut, forging the new adult killer.

Rest area? This can't be real! Our rest area was under the muzzles of two batteries of 105-mm howitzers. The howitzers went Boom! Boom! Boom! Then reloaded and boom! boom! again. How could we get rest, or even sleep? It was quieter on the front lines. But here, it was safer ... wasn't it?

Our company received bed rolls and clean clothes, so we stripped naked and everybody "showered." We filled our helmets with water from a bucket, raised it over-head, and released it. Oh, that felt great! We soaped up from head to toe, rinsed, and repeated until clean. A final rinsing seemed to give a sense of being human again. Even at 50 degrees or so, and no sunshine in sight, it was great! Or maybe the cold was a sign of God's disapproval of man's folly. Once we put on clean clothes, and added a scalping from the resident barber, the world seemed livable again. After the cosmetic corrections, I was standing next to James in silent conversation. Suddenly, out of the low clouds, three aircraft appeared, coming directly toward us. We had no cause for concern; the aircraft was our own. Wrong! Wrong! It was time to be concerned. The aircraft on the left sent its rockets over our heads and into a group of resting marines. The aircraft on the right followed with its own self-propelled rockets, sending them into another group of resting marines. There was no time to think. "Shit," said James, looking up for a split second, then we both dove for cover. This was the only time I had ever heard James, a strict practicing Mormon, swear. His verbal control around the continual bombardment of marine language was unprecedented and unmatched. However, seeing the center plane's sights directly on us, there was no thought or time for control. God must have heard James and decided to give him time to repent. Luckily I was with him. The center aircraft never released its rockets. Only God knew why.

James had better cover than I did; this was his area. Not being as familiar with the human activity in the area as he was, I dove for a hole that was used as a urinal.

My brief moment of cleanliness was now history. "B.O." would not even begin to describe my condition "Young marine skunk" came closer.

However, I was alive. Ten marines were not so lucky, and the ugly process began. K.I.A., what a horrible way to surrender youth and life.

Now it was time for food. The marines, as part of the 10th Army, were beginning to benefit from how the army soldiers lived. The rations were excellent meatballs, ham and beans, even dessert! It was almost a gourmet's delight. Marines usually had only two choices of garbage, with hard crackers to go with the garbage. The army had boots while we had the leggings handed down from World War I and before. Whenever we saw a dead marine with boots on, we knew that he had been wounded before. A wounded marine would be treated at an army hospital, patched up, given new boots, and sent back to the front lines to die.

Army bazooka rockets had a 180-degree point of detonation. The rockets previously used by us had a 67 percent success rate, only about four out of six exploding on impact. The army gave us a variety of new grenades, some we had never seen before. However, the questions were unavoidable: Why did the army have such good food, better clothing, and better weapons? We were part of the same military machine, were we not? I often imagined a big, fat marine officer at the Aberdeen Proving Grounds, standing up and saying, "We have some marines who would use that" after the equipment, food, or clothing had been rejected by the army, navy, and the coast guard. Then again, maybe the marines were just too busy fighting for freedom to be present to claim those state-of-the-art materials.

That night, an orphaned marine came to me for refuge. There were rumors that Anderson had a foot odor above and beyond the call of "body odor." My kind refuge would prove the rumor a "smelly" reality.

Anderson, from Minneapolis, Minnesota, was the typical American boy so out of place as a marine. He was soft spoken, not argumentative, with a pleasing personality. He was mentally able to adjust to any sociable situation. His dark curly hair and sleepy eyes were usually accompanied by a little smile when conversing face to face with him.

Anderson and I brought front-line jazz music to our group. With helmets as musical instruments and our un-tuned sounds of "do-da, do-da, do-da," we provided the "One O'clock Jump" with an original rendition heard only where it could be enjoyed. No recordings would be made for posterity. As we would get our rhythm going, Walden would yell out, go, go, go! He seemed to be the most appreciative and polite, maybe even almost recognizing the tune that our efforts disguised. Anderson and I really had a ball doing our "thing." The joy that Anderson gave was clouded by his almost unbearable smelly feet. The absence of daily bathing made him almost unapproachable. No Jap ever got close to Anderson. His smelly feet would keep them at bay for at least 30 feet. They were our secret weapon, unknown to the civilized world.

As Dutt's flame-thrower teammate Anderson was booted out of their foxhole one night, so Anderson came to me to share his perfumed nights of bliss. I suffered through this agony for at least three nights, because Anderson was such a nice guy. How could I refuse? A memorable conversation with him was when he said, "The blitz is worse than I ever imagined and almost too horrible for thoughts." Another young boy who gave up his teenage life never to know what a real joy it could have been.

TOO YOUNG THE HEROES

A letter home:

Pvt. G.R. Lince
Hdq. Co. 1st Bn
7th Marines
c/o F.P.O.
San Francisco, CA

My Dear Mom & Dad:

I have finally found time and paper to write and let you know I am well. I am on the island of Okinawa. No doubt you have read about it in the papers. I could tell you a few personal experiences, but I think I'll wait till we get settled again. I must tell you one though.

A buddy of mine was in a sugar cane field doing his daily duty. A Jap got a bead on him and the cane began cracking around him. He made for cover in nothing flat. Boy he certainly looked funny out there though and we razz him all the time about it.

The land here reminds me a little of home. I mean the pine trees and hills around. The people are very backward. They wear no shoes and little clothing. The women do all the work here. If some of these American girls could see how they would work if they were here, they would certainly be thankful for many things. The men lay around and have a life of ease. I wish you could see the old fashion methods they use. All the land is culti-vated. It is really a beautiful island. It is very cold at night and warm in the day times.

I received your letters. The picture and newspaper clippings of Bob were swell. The picture got ruined though. I carried them with me and they got all wet.

Bill Siegfried is in my battalion in a different company. I did see him quite a bit. The last time I saw him he was alright. That was O.K. what was in the paper. It's a little fouled up though as we see each other quite often.

Jim Snyder sent me a clipping saying Art Petinelli was killed. It made me feel kind of bad. Art was a swell fellow.

A buddy and I were just discussing the good food we used to have at home. What I wouldn't give for some spaghetti or soup now.

We really have some design on our foxhole digging. If anybody hands me a shovel or pick home I'll hit them over the head with it. I have some souvenirs I'll send home later. Ray is really lucky going back to school. I wouldn't mind myself, but there is other things to do first.

It must be swell up on the lake now. I have seen enough of this salt water. You will have to send me some pictures of the boat and things you do this summer at the lake and etc. I like to receive them.

If anybody asks about me tell them I am fine and will write when I get time. I am really lucky that I am alright and thank God he brought me through this.

Your loving son,

George

P.S. *I am sorry this is such a sloppy letter but it is the best I could do considering the conditions.*

Pvt. G.R. Lince 873441

While I was at the rest area, I wanted to see if I could find out what happened to a friend I knew from Rome, New York, and G.G. Olson. I was hoping they would still be alive. I went searching for C Company, and came upon two marines pounding a stake in the ground. I told them I was looking for C Company, and they said "This is it." Out of more than 350 men, only two still walked. I never asked about my friends. I was afraid of the answer. Forty-three years later, I heard from my friend from C Company. He was living in Danville, VA. He had been badly wounded a couple of times, but he was still alive. My friend from Rome, N.Y. had also been wounded, but he too was still alive. The Japs had caught them in Death Valley and mauled them to pieces. They had been on our right flank.

We were given the alert to pack up and move out, because some marines were in trouble and needed help. They were out of ammunition and were fighting hand-to-hand to survive. Every precious moment could mean saving a young boy's life.

We moved swiftly toward the area of conflict. There were no words, only a fast moving machine of destruction. We were there in moments. We could hear the screams of butchered marines. We opened fire with deadly accuracy, killing the animal Japs who seemed to be in a sort of glorious ecstasy. They were butchering marines, who did not want to die, with clubs, stones, knives, bayonets, swords, and anything else not related to human warfare, if there is such a thing.

As we leveled this worst kind of Jap animal, we rushed to embrace the spent and dazed survivors. Their eyes held no welcome, just vacant stares. They seemed not to know who we were or who they were. For a time, they had become animals themselves in order to survive. They were proving Darwin's theory of survival of the fittest. Darwin's theory, though, never took into account the question, "Does the human civilized mind always survive?" The young silent boys seemed to be crying for a chance to go back into their mother's womb, so that this time could be erased.

We moved toward them. Their arms were outstretched; their knees were bent; and they moved with the dazed walk of an 80-year-old that told us the war was over for them. They were all given a shot of morphine, and this could be the beginning of their long trip to a padded cell in a hospital in California. This could be their home for the remainder of their lives. Mental life had ended for these 18 year olds. There were no body bags, only body tags. There were no starched-shirt generals or admirals who would absorb the blood, sweat, and tears on their bosoms. There were only some young boys who would have memories for a lifetime. There were no photographers that day, either. Tickets to this kind of movie, this kind of story, do not sell. After all, what role would John Wayne play?

A 1949 work by Marine George C. McMillian describes some of these little-known victims of the war, and the doctors who cared for them:

> The toll for what the Division's Presidential Unit Citation for Okinawa called "the bitter siege" around Shuri was not all in killed and maimed. Near Chatan there was a hospital for those whose minds had been scarred and bruised in southern Okinawa.
>
> "The doctor in charge offered to demonstrate his methods for us," writes an officer of his visit to Chatan. "He first brought in a Marine who had cracked up when a Japanese mortar shell landed in his foxhole.
>
> "The case history of this man was simple. He had been engaged in the bitter fighting on the southern front. Probably he had lost a lot of sleep and had not gotten much to eat. One night he and his buddy were in a foxhole when a Japanese mortar shell burst on the edge of the foxhole.
>
> "The man passed out and was out for some time. His buddy was uninjured. According to the doctors, the man had suffered no concussion but was so keyed up emotionally that he lost consciousness when the mortar shell exploded. When he came to, he was completely out of his head and had to be taken to the rear.
>
> "Several days afterward he was still shaking. In their treatment of the case, the doctors felt that the essential thing was to find out what was weighing on the man's mind, whether fear, shame, or whatever it might be, and then to attempt, over a period of days, by talking to him, to restore his confidence in himself.
>
> "In such cases, however, a man could not usually be induced readily to come out with what he was thinking or feeling. To produce this result, the doctors injected into the arm of the patient a solution which left him conscious but freed him of his inhibitions about talking. Also he was not aware of what he was saying. The man whom we were observing was given this injection and the doctor began questioning him.
>
> "He was asked many questions regarding what had happened prior to the time the mortar shell exploded. The doctor the whole time was very gentle in his questioning. When the man had been finally brought to the point where he and his buddy were in the shell hole together, the doctor suddenly stamped on the deck, hit the wall with his fist, and shouted, 'Mortar!'
>
> "No actor could have portrayed fear like this man did. He kept gurgling, 'Mortar... mortar... mortar...'

"The doctor asked him what he was going to do now. The man replied, 'Dig deeper! Dig deeper!'

"The doctor told him to go ahead and dig.

"The man got down on his knees and went through frantic motions of digging in the corner of the room.

"The doctor then put the man on his bunk and quieted him. Then the doctor took a new tactic. He asked the man if he read the Bible. The answer was affirmative. Then the man was asked what the Bible said about killing. The reply was that killing was forbidden by the Bible.

"The doctor asked, 'What about Japs?'

"At this, the man ground his teeth and muttered, 'Kill 'em all.'

"The doctor then asked, 'How about Jap women?'

"The answer was, 'Kill 'em too.'

"'Why?'

"The patient said the Japanese killed his buddies and his buddies were good men.

"The doctor then accused the man of being yellow. He was quite indignant and shouted, 'I'm not yellow. I want to go back.' He repeated this several times.

"The patient was then quieted and allowed to leave. The doctor explained that, of course, what we had seen had nothing to do with effecting a cure. It would give the doctors some leads on the basis of which they could continue talking to the man without the benefit of drugs and probably bring him back to normal."

Some of the physically wounded were in functional as well as organic shock when they came into the battalion aid stations. A visitor to one of the forward stations pointed to a surprisingly spry wounded man and asked his condition.

"He's dead," said the doctor with utter sadness, "but he doesn't know it. I'm doing what I can for him, everything, but he'll be dead in two hours. Yet ten minutes ago he came in here on his own two feet. And look at him laugh and talk. A lot of them are just like him. It's as if they've so steeled themselves, so keyed themselves up, that they can't stop. The books would call it 'disassociation,' meaning that they've had to separate their minds and their bodies for so long that they can't quickly put them into their normal relationships."

Against the tide of recessive losses, a system of battlefield replacements had been worked out in the planning stage, and at Okinawa for the first time in the First Division's history, fresh men were sent into the lines while the battle was being fought. By the end of May, 180 officers and 4,065 enlisted Marines from replacement battalions were received and "absorbed" during the conduct of the operation. And more were to come.[8]

The youth of America was not conditioned by the military or their civilian way of life to participate and survive mentally in a war of such a vicious nature. This was the Japs' ultimate way of living and dying all rolled into one. From April 1, 1945 to May 30, 1945, 6,315 marines became neuro-psychiatric casualties. The intensity of the battle was a destructive force on the minds of these teenagers. San Leandro Naval Hospital in California was the permanent home in padded cells for countless numbers of 18 year olds. No Purple Hearts were given for this sacrifice of the most important part of their bodies. There was no blood, and no one could see the everlasting pain. Yes, anybody's son will do.

* * *

As we left the body-tagged marines to go south on Okinawa in pursuit of the animal Japs, the fact that the Japs were fighting to die while we were fighting to live was in our confused thoughts. How the Jap minds had gotten into such an incompatible state for a peaceful existence with other human beings on this earth was extremely puzzling. Although their actions were apparent, we did have empathy that was rarely expressed to the Jap soldiers, our resolve became more determined, and our pursuit became more intense.

The Japs were on a running retreat so we had to keep moving, with no breaks, to close the gap. The Japs' most frightening weapon was being used more often to try to deter our advance. This weapon was called by many names such as "Screaming Willies," "Flying Seabag," and "Flying Boxcar." The reason these nicknames were given was because these weapons were visible high in the sky, and they appeared to be very large. The missile type mortars weighed about 600 pounds and were launched by a large tube or a railroad track launching platform. They moved high and slowly through the air, and then suddenly, after losing their velocity, came to the ground, exploding on impact. On their way down, a screeching sound destroyed even the strongest nervous system. Upon impact, the immense heat with flames caused devastation in a large area with a crater 60 feet across and 20 feet deep. It was almost like a miniature atom bomb. Our eyes were constantly searching the skies for these flying seabags. Their intensity was increasing as we gave relentless pursuit of the Japs. The countryside was covered with Jap bodies. Many thousands of Japs had come out of their cave networks and were caught in the open by our many battalions of artillery. There was so much artillery whistling overhead, that the short rounds created a very tense feeling. Short rounds are exactly what they are named. The short rounds fell and exploded on our own marines. The thought of being killed or wounded by your own artillery was extremely demoralizing.

As we moved rapidly toward the southern end of the island, our environment became more difficult. Flies and mosquitoes, acting like kamikaze insects, began to make life miserable. Swarms of flies would hover about three feet from our heads, attacking us in an unmerciful, continual attempt to aggravate the hell out of us. Eating our semi-garbage food became not only unpleasant, but the persistent flies made eating almost impossible. The flies wanted our food more than we did. Holding a small can in one hand, eating utensil in the other hand, and swatting and swinging with both hands, still did not discourage the kamikaze flies. If I left my mouth open too long, they would follow the food into my mouth. There had to be a better way. Marine ingenuity developed a plan whereby one marine ate while another marine discouraged the flies from attacking by swinging arms and hands continually over the hungry marine. These swarms of flies were on the attack all day, then, just before dark, the mosquitoes changed shifts with the flies, and it could almost be heard from the retiring flies the order of the day. Attack! Attack! Attack! While the Japs were retreating, these airborne insects had somehow read "The Code" and were attempting to kill as many Americans as possible. The war was known by the Japanese to have been lost, but now even the insects were enjoying an attempt to destroy us.

Add to this almost intolerable situation, our daily and sometimes hourly job of "digging in" was done with great difficulty. The soil was a clay type soil and digging a foxhole became very, very difficult. Being a fox hole excavator, however, was necessary in order to be a next day survivor. Thirteen inches of dirt was all that was necessary to keep the bullets from hitting our bodies. Like moles hiding from the impending darkness, with a small shovel, youth, and a strong body, in minutes a marine would prepare to survive another night.

Days of doom seemed to accompany our spirit. Each day youth seemed to escape our insane desperation.

Then, without warning, I heard that someone was leaving our time of suffering to go directly to civilization. He did not have to be torn apart by a bullet or a shell, or bandaged by a corpsman, or go via an aid station or hospital. This selected political hero was going on a "bond tour." He would go directly to a world of love. He would not have to pass "Go" or collect $200. Just "Go" home.

I could not accept this unfair act of rescue. Who the hell did "he" know? I almost went into a rage. I knew this glamour boy and mostly all of his heroics. In a class rating of marine heroics, he would be at the bottom. However, he would be called "marine." He would surely make a handsome marine poster. He still had his smiling youth, that he had never exposed for destruction by man's foolish folly. I can still see his wavy black hair and olive skin, a smile that glistened with teeth and a body well fed. I still feel my envy of his unearned ticket home. I realized the unfairness of life at its peak that day. There was a hatred in my body that I felt toward a fellow marine, and there were thoughts of killing him to remove the possibility of the situation so it would not be real. I turned my head, hoping this moment would disappear as quickly as it had appeared. Going back to the flies, mosquitoes, garbage food, fox holes, dead Japs, and dead marines, I became the ragman of the day. The clouds of war were overhead, and the clouds of despair were drifting away my youth that contained love and hope. Full of hatred and energies of despair, I picked up my tommy gun, the bazooka rounds, checked my grenades, and started putting one bloody foot ahead of the other. Maybe this was the day I became a real marine, a killing marine. Maybe this is how a real marine is made. All I could say was damn it, damn it, damn it, and cry without tears in a frightening rage.

Rain was coming down in cold proportions. Our pursuit brought us to an abandoned Jap quartermaster compound. We found hundreds of Jap hooded raincoats. All of us grabbed one and put it on. As we continued our fast pursuit, I had thoughts of a possible disaster. If our own aircraft came upon us and saw all these Jap raincoats moving rapidly down the road, we could have problems. However, we were lucky our innocent wearing of Jap clothing gave us no unwelcome consequences.

After two or three days of pursuit, we established a temporary position next to a stream. There was time and it was safe enough to take a bath. Stripping off our clothes, we braved the cold water. The cold water was so refreshing. We drank the water and filled our canteens. I was in the middle of the stream that was two to three feet deep and eight feet from bank to bank. A marine walked by and said "I would not swim in that water. There are three dead Japs in the stream just around the bend!" I was out of the water before he finished his sentence. Our Jap contaminated bath, however, refreshed our spirits as well as our body, regardless of this news.

A discussion of, "How did we beat these Japs?" was ignited. The Japs had many advantages. Because they were smaller in size, they required less food and water than we did. Smaller in size also made them smaller targets. The Japs faith that gave them a fight-to-die attitude was a distinct advantage. The Japs were professional soldiers, and we were just teenagers from the corner drug store, far from home and loved ones.

So what was the determining factor? All our conclusions were the same. Our love for our home life and our families gave us a strength unmatched by any military training or military experience. This strength gave us enough courage and determination to be victorious over these Japs. And now we moved out again, in our relentless pursuit, leaving our needed support far behind.

Because it was still raining and no Japs were in sight, A Company decided to set up a perimeter and dig in.

As we approached our assigned area, a short round exploded 30 feet from me. My nervous reply was, "You bastard," and I walked on with annoying contempt for the possibility of what could have happened.

The genius of the Japanese Empire calculated and summarized that to create a soldier who would be victorious in every battle, he must become cruel to its extremity, obedient with blindness, dedicated to suicide missions, and have a false faith that gave rewards for killing. Enjoyment in killing and raping women and children would be part of the macho soldier's make-up. Torture was an added feature of the soldier's development. The rape of Asia and the Pacific would be the proving grounds for this genius of military prowess. Years of conquest proved this theory to be valid for the Japanese Empire's quest for world domination.

Then, without warning or suspicion of presence, an opposite unplanned military deterrent evolved. The spirit of youth, love, dedication to principles, a true faith where rewards are based on love, not hate, was awakened to prove that the simplistic "right over might" was alive and well. The unpreparedness for war was not a dominant factor. The sacrifices necessary to protect love, a good life, home and family became the victorious factor.

Personal initiatives resulting from these virtues created a soldier unmatched in world history. This human development factor created a uniformed soldier that could defeat any military force.

Why did I see so many dead marines? Scattered like toys of death on carpeted remains of unwelcome soil. How will I be able to embrace my mother, who knows nothing of this game of horror I have played. Now I have been part of a real war, and I hang my head in shame for my ignorance of its aftermath. Where can I go to cleanse my memories of an ugliness that destroyed the very fabric of the soul?

The mind and all of its power could overcome evil when love remained the controlling feature.

The Japs had made a great military blunder. American youth had proven the Jap "codes" and "beliefs" were a self-destructing theory.

13

OKINAWA: THE LAST DAYS

The rain kept falling, with brief periods of letup. Cold, damp, wet, sloshy, exhausted, tired, no energy, no hope, no dreams, no smiles seemed to be the drumbeat of the day. Standing alone with no conversations, no one seemed to even want to look at each other.

The Japs were running. The artillery kept swishing over our heads like bowling balls in a massive bowling alley. With so many short rounds now, a numbness to their horrible effect became the only thought we had. Out of 450 of us, plus about 100 replacements, there were less than 70 able to be combatants.

Seeking cover from the rain in our pup tents was our only partial escape from this dismal hell. In a sense we were hiding temporarily, hoping to find some energy to make the final push. Maybe we would soon be going over the last ridge.

Night had fallen, and we tried to get some sleep in our soaked-to-the-bone condition. We still had to keep a watchful eye for any energized Jap. And here he came, running through the slushy mud trying to find that ticket, down the embankment toward us, small arms fire dancing at his feet. He kept coming. We could hear him, but we could not see him. The mud was slopping from his feet along with the searching bullets. Now he was right in front of the Greek. Sure-shot Greek will put him down. The Greek does not fire! What happened? Is he sleeping? But now that Jap is in front of me. I can't see him! He is ten feet away. Slosh, slop, slosh, slop. He is going to run into me! Does he have a grenade? A knife? or what? Then three feet away he slopped right past me, slopping off into the night.

If I could have wiped my brow of perspiration I would have. That Jap must have had night vision radar. He saw me, but I could not see him.

But what happened to the Greek? A most dependable marine with a chance to annihilate a Jap, and he failed.

The dawning daylight hours came, and Greek's tale would remove the mystery.

The rifle company was on the other side of the ridge, and there was no further small arms activity. So now maybe it was time to get some 50 percent shuteye. The wet hard ground, however, gave no feeling of a Serta Perfect Sleeper, and there were no thoughts of sweet dreams.

Marines march past a fallen soldier. (United States Marine Corps photo.)

Somehow, during the night I lost my glasses. In the morning, they were nowhere to be found. During the Korean conflict I would meet my buddy Dutt and he would tell me how Walden had stolen my glasses. Walden had finally succeeded in saving my life.

Of course, I did not know that this morning. But I did know things could not get much worse for me. Only death could be my real rescuer.

[143]

Then, here comes Greek! Smiling and almost laughing, he was a shining gem in the darkest of darks. He started out with a little laughter and a smile showing his beautiful white teeth. "Hey Lince, you know what happened?" he said apologetically without waiting for my reply. "I was pulling on the trigger guard and not the trigger." We all had a good laugh, feeling sorry for the Jap, who did not find his place for honored glory in battle. Greek, a silent hero, was wounded on the last ridge.

Even with the temporary laughter, the importance of having good eyesight without glasses was staring me in the face.

I said to Walden, "What to hell do I do now?" Walden, not discussing his life-saving secret, said, "You better go to sickbay."

Sickbay was right behind us on a little knoll.

The rain had let up, although the day was dark and dingy. My mood was very Asiatic, so I began to walk toward the knoll with a heavy heart. My long range dream was coming to an end.

I was sitting on a stool, appearing not too energetic, when the doctor approached me asking me what my problem was. I told him, "I lost my glasses." The doctor looked at me and casually said, "So what?

I sat there in temporary silence, then I said, "Well, I carry a tommy gun, and without my glasses I cannot tell if you are a Jap or my doctor!" The doctor said, "Wow! We do have a problem!" He looked at me with a smirk and said, "You will have to go off the lines."

In the meantime, Walden came in with Dutt. Dutt was wounded and also had an extreme case of diarrhea. He was beginning to dehydrate. Going back to the battalion aid by myself could be very dangerous. Walden thought it would be a good idea if the sick and wounded Dutt went back with the blind and wounded Lince. Like a remote camera from above, I saw Dutt and myself leaving, and Walden walking away very slowly. There were no handshakes or hugs and no waving or saying goodbye, just moving on regretfully and sadly. There was no joy in this moment. We dared not look back for fear we would lose all desire to do what we had to do. We were leaving our buddies, some for the last time. This was a hell in itself.

Dutt and I had quite a trip to make. We went through a desolate area where war had ravaged every foot of earth. A river separated us from our past hell and the possibility of hope. We wanted to survive, so we swam the river. Vehicles were not reaching our wounded because of the river, and at least four of our buddies would bleed to death because they could not be transported to the aid station or hospital. Japs were shooting at us all the way. We could see the dirt and mud being kicked up by bullets all around us. With our Asiatic attitude that expresses no real interest in life or living, we did not seek cover. The fear of death or wounds was not present in our minds.

Dutt and I walked doggedly down muddy roads lined with trucks and marines trying to get to the front lines.

I saw Rotolo briefly, wandering away from the front lines so as to insure his survival. This effort expressed his true character, as he was a lousy marine and a lousy human being. After receiving directions from advancing marines, we arrived at the Battalion Aid Station. I was directed to a tent for shelter. My companions in the tent were two dead marines, their bodies bloating out of their uniforms. The smell was nauseating. I spent the day and night there in unbelievable despair. A chaplain came to me and invited me to his area close by. Probing me with many questions, he tried to get me to talk. His nonsense only deepened my feelings in despair. The chaplain offered no comfort, no food, or refreshment, but seemed to be appalled at my looks and my unexpressed feelings. After his futile attempt to get me to smile and laugh or possibly even to talk, I returned to be with my dead marines.

Their clothes were bursting at the seams from their body decay. I dared not to look at their faces because I feared that they could be someone I knew or could recognize.

That night we boarded a truck and went over some rough terrain. We were told that the area was still being fired upon by Japs, but we had to give it a try. The truck bounded over the road with night lights dimly lighting the way. We eluded the Japs and, after an hour, we arrived at the 31st Army Field Hospital. The nurses and doctors went to work on us right away. Bandaging my foot, removing the dirt and grime from the wound. There was a feeling resurging through my body that someone cared that I was alive.

Then I had the most delicious cup of coffee I have ever had in my life. The coffee was warm and so refreshing. Maybe I would feel like talking again. Maybe there was reason to be alive.

In a couple of days, we were able to attend the hospital movie. Dutt and I hobbled over to the movie with blankets around us to keep warm. At the movie, I met a friend Stuart Rounds from Rome, New York, who was a jeep/ambulance driver for the hospital. After the war, he would tell me how skinny I looked.

Each night, when I came back to my cot after the movies, I was approached by a medic who insisted that I take pain medicine. The pain was not that bad, but I went to sleep like a rock.

Why was this medic doing extra duty? He had already been there all day.

Sometimes a certain pretty nurse, the pain pill, and the empty sack next to me were combined ingredients for romance. How naive I was. She was just too pretty to be a whore, but I guess she was there to make people happy, especially her friends. Not having any enemies, she was quite busy. At $50 a throw, many nurses would live in luxury for the rest of their lives. The Post

Office had to limit their money orders that they sent back home to $500 amounts. They seemed to never run out of customers nor pay any income tax.

As I flew away from Okinawa, on a C-54 hospital transport aircraft, I could still see the Corsairs flying the short bomb run, killing Japs. I had left the place where many heroes had died so lonely, so tired, so dirty, so hungry, so scared, so thirsty, so far away from home, and so very young, where love had left the scene, to be replaced by hatred and killing. Death gave the only relief to pain and suffering. Courage and bravery gave way to the silence of death as the marines tried to put out the flame of a disease named Jap.

As I looked out the airplane's window, I was engulfed in pride knowing I had been with many great heroes during their finest hour. I had thoughts of happiness and joy, not because I had survived this victory, but rather because I had known these young heroes. I had known them only briefly, but I had memories for a lifetime. There was a loneliness for those who had died. There was even a feeling that maybe being a member of the elite (those who died) could not be such a horrible consequence. After all, what more could a young boy do for God and his country? We would cry because of their passing but not of their accomplishments. Their names would echo in triumph in the heavens forever. As we flew away, the island became smaller as my pride became larger and larger with knowledge the job was "well done." The last battle of World War II had come to an end.

There was no time to say goodbye.

However, the last ridge remained to be taken even while I was flying to a hospital on Guam.

Thanks be to God that there is a God to reward these unheralded heroes in their everlasting silence. Thanks be to God that I am a survivor and a witness to these real heroes so I can tell the world about the overwhelming courage of the American youth.

In the publication *Marine Corps Gazette*, Joe Douglas Dodd wrote:

> During the first few weeks of what would be the final campaign of World War II, the supreme effort of the soldiers, sailors, and Marines involved in the ground action on Okinawa for the most part went unheralded in the world's press. President Franklin D. Roosevelt's death, took most of the front page headlines in the beginning. Hitler's death, and the collapse of the Third Reich three weeks later, also relegated the fighting on Okinawa to page two. Probably the biggest news concerning the Okinawa fighting was the kamikaze attacks against Adm Raymond A Spruance's 5th Fleet.
>
> Another reason for a less than fervid interest in "The Last Battle" was Okinawa's benign beginning, which literally became a gigantic April Fool perpetrated by desperate, fanatical enemies determined to protect their homeland at any cost.

OKINAWA: THE LAST DAYS

The Marines who went ashore on 1 April 1945 (Easter Sunday) 50 years ago were mostly unopposed except for sporadic mortar and artillery fire. The ease of the landing came as a pleasant surprise to veterans of earlier campaigns, and was considered "a piece of cake" for those expecting a type of hell on D-day. It was only much later that the expected resistance materialized, turning Okinawa into a bitterly contested, bloody battle.

Most of the hard fighting developed after the Japanese high commander, Lt. Gen Mitsuru Ushijima, withdrew the bulk of his army to positions south of Shuri. Here his soldiers would make a last ditch stand in the coral ridges of southern Okinawa.

One of these ridges near the town of Kunishi has been described as "the scene of the most frantic, bewildering, and costly close-in battle on the southern tip of Okinawa." It was also the scene of one of the few night sorties by Marines in World War II, as well as a most successful, improvised armor operations by Lt Col Arthur J. Stuart's 1st Tank Battalion. Both events helped to accelerate the end of the war.[9]

A confirming letter from Walden while I was in a Naval hospital told me how tragic this necessary effort was. Our personal loss of buddies, the unmentioned heroes, would give us sadness for the rest of our lives.

> *Cpl W. Walden*
> *"Assault Plt"*
> *August 22, 1945*

Dear Lince,

Well, I received your letter yesterday and I was glad to hear from you. I knew you would write "Dude Boy."

I let several of the guys read it, say when you write Jensen (name change?) his initials are R.R. and not D.C. Remember D.C. was killed and in able Co.

Yeah, Dutt said you had gone home and I figured on a discharge for you. I see no reason why they should keep you now — since our fighting days should be over — it has really come as a surprise to me!!

I am glad you ran into Hinton — Yeah, Greek caught one through the fleshy part of his shoulder — A clean wound and not serious at all.

Well, I am proud you got out when you did, because the shit really began to hit the well known fan.

We lost good ole James and Lodge on the last ridge a day before we were relieved (June 22) by the 8th Marines. The island was secured two days later. The first BN. Then was formed into a company and we along with a recon outfit hit a small island about 40 mi. from here named "Ie-Shima" — not much of anything was there — "Thank goodness." We stayed there a mo. We really have a nice area and good tents here now.

Dude Boy I would sure love to make a liberty there with you — Sure you done any good with the women. Ha! I imagine there are plenty of cuties there — But getting it is a different story — eh what? Are you still hearing from the cute chick that wrote a corker of a letter?

I think your sea bag was over to Hdg. property but has been opened and turned in.

You can write Dot at Box 925, Alney, Texas and maybe she has another one of those pictures of me and she will send it to you. Well I will close for now — keep me posted on how things are going with you and ("the records"). I see you have made PFC (ear banger).

Write again when you can. Take care of yourself and so long for now.

Your Cobbler,

CPL W. Walden

What makes one division of fighting men fight better than another? A post-war correspondent found some answers:

Few of the 1st Marines were surprised when it happened. In the three-year trail westward from North Carolina, [the 1st Marine Division] had been so often on the small end of the horn that their position seemed normal. A camp in some miserable field, no tents, no drinkable water, supplies irrevocably lost in a rear echelon, sunk in a typhoon or vanished into an impenetrable mist, a movie machine that won't work — those are the things the 1st Marines are made of.

Pedro A. Del Valle, a Puerto Rican graduate of the United States Naval Academy, had been commanding a Marine Artillery Regiment on maneuvers in the Caribbean Islands in the winter of 1941–42. The returning unit was unloaded at a southern American port. Although they were even more short of transport than Marines have been since, the battalions were sent on a two-hundred-mile overland march to New River, North Carolina. Dirty, tired, eager to see their families, they were directed over a dim trail to a selected spot in the middle of a swamp, far from the rest of the mushrooming military camp. They looked at trees, at soggy ground underfoot, and at nothing else. No tents, no lumber, no buildings. "This, " said their guide, "is where you live."

Del Valle, now a Major General, says, "Most men would have felt abused about it. I did. But those boys, instead of turning sullen about being miles from anywhere — we had to pile all the cooks into a truck for a nightly ten-mile ride, so that they could get baths and we could be sure our food was clean — buckled right down to make something out of the place. I don't know that anyone actually said it, but their attitude was, 'Well, we're the toughest outfit here. We can take things that would drive other guys nuts. Let's show them how it's done.'

"They were tired and they had almost nothing to work with. But you should have seen that place change. The only way a man could get a pole for his tent was to go out into the woods and cut one, but they built a camp. A few mornings later, I heard a horrible racket outside my tent.

You know what I found outside? A house. A whole house loaded on a truck. Some boys had got it for me. I never asked them where, but I used to wonder a bit about how the owner felt when he came home to find his house gone."

That artillery regiment, then the 10th, eventually became the 11th regiment and a charter unit in the 1st Division, along with the 5th Infantry, one of two Marine infantry units of great World War I fame. With cadres from the 5th, the dormant 1st and 7th Regiments were added to make up the division.

The 1st Marine Division did not win the war in the Pacific, no matter what its veterans may say in bars. People will be arguing for generations about whether ships or armies, planes, submarines or atomic bombs actually won that war. But the most rabid disparager of Marines would hesitate to name a single fighting organization that did more than the 1st Marine Division toward winning it or to deny that the division took both the first and the last combat steps toward Tokyo....

The echoes from the cries of the Japanese in 1924, "We must fight you someday" were now buried in the very soil that staged this horrible unwanted war.

The young boys and men of the First Marine Division had played their part in making this cry of 1924 a reality.

Were the Japanese satisfied with the outcome or was this part of their culture to fight, to die, and to devastate the land of the human race? The curtain had fallen for many Americans, thinking this was the last act of a horrible reality play, but maybe this was not the last act, for this real-life Jap play would have acts and scenes already written for the next 200 years.

Let us not forget those young boys and men in the 1st Marine Division who kept this Jap real-life play from our homes and loved ones in the 20th Century.[10]

14

HOSPITAL TIME, AND
THE END OF THE WAR

Our hospital aircraft landed on Guam, and the wounded were ambu-lanced to Naval Hospital III. The hospital was overflowing with wounded. Many bandages had been on too long, and the stench signaled the need for immediate relief. Naval personnel came to our sacks to get our names and to award the Purple Heart to everyone who had been wounded. I refused the Purple Heart because I could not find it in my conscience to receive the same medal that had been awarded to the dead marines. There was no comparison. I could understand a Silver or Gold Heart for the dead and the Purple Heart for the wounded.

> *Pvt. G.R. Lince 873441*
> *June 20, 1945 Fleet Hospital 111 TC*
> *c/o % F.P.O.*
> *San Francisco, CA*

My Dear Mother & Father:

I wasn't going to write for a while, but I thought I had better. I haven't glasses now and I am having a little trouble with my eyes. I got cut on my heel by shrapnel. It's alright now. You may get a telegram saying I was wounded in action, but don't worry. It's nothing.

I saw Stewey Rounds. I was sure glad to see him. He certainly has an easy and good life.

The doctors said I should be home soon. I know I must get some good care for my eyes or it may be a matter of time before I lose my complete sight. I know I shouldn't be telling this to you. It will make you worry all the more. Try not to because there is no sense in all of us worrying. I'll be alright as long as I get home.

On the lines I heard I made P.F.C., but I'll remain a Pvt. until I get official word.

I am in the Marianas now and away from that "hell hole." Thank God.

I don't know what is going to happen or when, but I know what I need.

Don't worry about anything.

> *Your loving son,*
> *George*

HOSPITAL TIME, AND THE END OF THE WAR

While hobbling on crutches outside the hospital tent, I noticed a great number of marines, sailors, and soldiers waiting in line for a nice cold Coke. The Red Cross was selling Cokes for 5 cents, and I did not have a nickel. I felt sure that the pretty Red Cross lady would let me borrow a nickel. After all, I was a handsome, young, wounded marine, far away from home, and besides, I looked real thirsty under that hot sun. Oh, how a cold Coke at that moment would change my view of this horrible world!

I went to her with a great, big smile and felt confident of total success. Then, suddenly, without even a return of my smile, she coldly, flat out refused me with an incredulous and resounding, "No! "Wait till payday!" With a look of frigidness, she was colder than the Coke. Payday was an eternity away. I developed a strong aversion to pretty Red Cross women, the Red Cross organization itself, and to cold Coke.

All of the military services were represented in the hospital tents. I met Curtis from Ohio whom I had buddied with on the ship going overseas to Pavuvu to join the First Marine Division. Curtis was assigned to the 5th Marine Regiment. He had been hit in the shoulder receiving a wound that did only flesh damage. We played games to try and satisfy our boredom.

I became friends with an army soldier from Minnesota. His ethnic background was Finnish. He taught me some Finnish language, and he conversed in Finnish, talking about the pretty nurses. Glancing and glaring eyes gave us a clue they knew we were talking about them. Curious and squinty smiles satisfied our youthful pleasures.

Our little group of walking wounded had a very special buddy. He was a very young army soldier shot through the mouth. The bullet's entry and exit could actually be seen. It had destroyed his inner mouth, and his jaws had to be wired shut. Our conversations, therefore, were in sign language and head nods. He told us he would be on liquids for two years. That created a challenge he had in his future. I was transferred from the tent area to a permanent-type building hospital ward. The doctors were very concerned about my diminishing eyesight.

After many days of boredom, a new patient was placed in the bed next to me, a 20-year veteran marine who had been mangled by a Japanese mortar. This marine hero was blind, his mouth was wired shut, one of his arms was gone, one of his legs was missing, and excruciating pain dominated his very breath for life. Moaning and intelligible mumbling was his only communication. A nurse from Ithaca, New York, kept giving him an extremely hard time. She harassed him, complaining about how much of a pain in the ass he was, and just generally treated him like shit. The nurse was an ugly person with black hair that partially covered her ugly head. Before make-up, she would probably frighten the most poisonous, vicious reptile. Her meanness was in every wrinkle of her face. Her eyes were flashing thoughts of plans for mental torture, and her mouth could only extrude sounds of a mentally deranged scumbag. A nurse she was not. A complete asshole she was.

After several days of listening to this abuse, I finally snapped. I jumped up, grabbed her, and roughly shoved her across the hospital room. The officer of the day came in to see what the commotion was all about, and within a few hours I found myself in the air, on a hospital aircraft to Hawaii.

While on Guam, a team of movie actors and actresses came to entertain us. Who the hell needed entertaining? We needed medical attention, daily refreshments, and an appreciative, humane, sensitive nurse to tend our wounds. We did not need to see some half-dressed girl wiggle her ass (which we could not touch) in front of us. They teased the troops and pounded the officers all night long. Is there any worse mental torture?

While walking between hospital wards, I almost ran head-on into one of the frillies. She jumped aside as if she had seen a snake. She knew I was off limits and exercised the maneuver to express her knowledge. I could die and be wounded for her, but don't touch or say Hello.

I did not attend the shows. I had already received the message loud and clear. To add to this frustrating and irritating phony effort, Eddie Bracken, the movie star, seemed to think his presence and blessings would provide everlasting happiness. A group of us walking wounded were on an ambulance going to the airport to be flown to Hawaii and the naval hospitals there.

Suddenly, the ambulance rear door opened, and there was Eddie Bracken, movie actor, or maybe movie asshole. "Have a nice trip, fellas," he said. He closed the door quickly, avoiding pukey stares. And a possible reply should be, "You too, fella."

The aircraft landed at Johnson Island and later Kwajalien Island, in the middle of the night. Our landing pattern appeared as though we were landing on the ocean. When we landed at Henderson Field in Pearl Harbor, I could still see the bullet holes in the pillars at the entrance.

The ambulance transported us to AIEA Heights Naval Hospital. This hospital overlooked Pearl Harbor, and the view was spectacular. I could imagine what the Japs must have thought as they spread their disease of destruction.

There were eight young marines in my ward, the eye ward, that had no eyes at all. Their eyeballs had been removed because of injuries, but I saw no scars around their eyes. I often wondered how their injuries happened, but I never voiced the question because I was afraid of the answer I may have received. At the 31st Field Army Hospital on Okinawa, the doctors said I would be blind in six months. The navy doctors, indifferent about marines, wanted me to go to Honolulu and buy my own glasses. I told them to stick it — full Commander and all. The commander became rather irritated, but I didn't give a damn. Rank didn't mean anything to me anymore. I practiced a little reverse psychology; "If the marines cannot afford glasses for me," I said, "Send me home!"

Not pleasing the doctors and their ungrateful demand to buy my own glasses, I soon would feel their dissatisfaction with me. At $50 a month for total income, the navy or marines could at least buy me a pair of eyeglasses. I was insulted and mentally depressed to think my importance to anyone was so trivial. But the navy doctors said, "To hell with you, teenage marine" and sent me back to duty. Unbelievable! My first assigned duty was guard duty. Can you believe that? Good thing I was not in a combat area. But the inconsiderate navy doctor would have put me on the front lines if he could. What a terrible situation. As my mother would say, "Blind in one eye and can't see out of the other." Guard duty was nerve-racking. I could not tell a private from a general. It was a good thing I had no loaded weapon. However, with no consideration of my eye problem, I was assigned to the Officers Club at Camp Catlin, a marine base between Pearl Harbor and Honolulu, set among the hills that gave a picturesque splendor for an enjoyable duty post. Washing dishes, waiting on tables, and preparing the snack bar provided semi-entertainment and extra income. There appeared to be some interesting times ahead. Famous people visited the club. One special time was when Admiral Nimitz and the Secretary of the Navy attended a night of festivities. We went to the abandoned, artillery shell, bomb-proof storage. These bunkers were located in the hills. Instead of storage for artillery shells, these bunkers were storage for New York champagne and all sorts of booze. We loaded the truck with the precious cargo and off to the club we went to prepare for the special evening. At 10¢ for a glass of champagne, the dignitaries exhausted our abundant supply. Ladies, and their escorts of high level brass, were bubbling all over the club. Bob Crosby, Bing Crosby's brother, added music for the dancing celebrants. As a waiter, I found the tips very generous, and everybody was champagne friendly. Before the festivities began, Admiral Nimitz reviewed our platoon of Officer Club Marines. Although I preferred being reviewed by Admiral Nimitz under more honorable circumstances, I welcomed the opportunity to be eyeball to eyeball with the admiral. When he stood in front of me and looked directly at me, I felt a rare moment in my life was happening. I saw a kind, loving face that welcomed admiration, respect, and love. Only the face of God could diminish this feeling. It was difficult to believe that this beautiful, kind face could muster so much courage, with intelligence to command loving, young men in the destruction of one of the most cruel civilizations that was ever on planet earth. I have been honored and blessed to be part of Admiral Nimitz's Command. This was a time to be proud and thankful.

Two marine buddies at Waikiki Beach: John (left), wounded in Iwo Jima, and the author, recovering from the Battle of Okinawa.

HOSPITAL TIME, AND THE END OF THE WAR

While at Camp Catlin, I became good buddies with young wounded marine from the 5th Marine Division who had been on Iwo Jima during the blitz. All of my new buddies had been wounded at Iwo. One particular buddy I went on liberty with had a steel plate in his head. This was very sad because his short-term memory was affected. One day he would know me, then the next day he would not. This did not affect our friendship. We still maintained a good relationship.

Liberty one day in seven still gave us opportunities. I chased (mentally) a Japanese American lady until she caught me. We had no intimate relationship, and it was interesting to note, at 19, I had no hatred for the Japanese in my heart. My mind would not accept any memories of the immediate past. My Iwo Jima buddies and I never discussed the battles that we were in. Maybe we believed at 19 all these horrors would be erased someday forever. At the best steak house in Waikiki, I met Jean, a Japanese girl. Her beauty supported the fact that war was man's folly. A young American man attracted to a Japanese girl. Why should life be any different? Time would evaporate our relationship, but those days may register on the conversation of the world as a time well spent in love and respect between a Japanese lady and an American young man. They both lived happily after.

* * *

While we were loading ships for the invasion of Japan, with many nights of cooley-type labor ending in the early morning hours, news came from Japan. Their preparation signaled an immediate need to end this horrible senseless continuation of the unwanted war. Did we have the means to promote our quest for peace, or should the slaughter continue to the conclusion that was known both in Japan and the United States?

Japan was defeated. Why continue such a slaughter when the only immediate goal by the Japanese was to kill as many Americans as possible?

In *Japan's War*, author Edwin P. Hoyt describes the Japanese mood:

> Taking note of the invasion of Okinawa, so close to the home islands of Japan, on April 3 the government announced the establishment of the "National Volunteer Force," which would be headed by the prime minister of Japan. It was to be a People's Army, or organizing every citizen for the defense of the realm. The old, very young, and women began learning to drill and use such primitive weapons as the pike and such complicated ones as explosives.
>
> This mobilization was assisted by news from Okinawa, picked up from the reports of American journalists via Lisbon and other neutral centers. One United Press Association report told of eleven women charging an American position with rifles and machine guns. Another report told of

American tanks running over civilians and crushing them. "They would never surrender anyhow," was the justification of one tanker. There were virtually no medical facilities for civilians or soldiers. The instructions went out from General Kurabayashi's defense headquarters: those wounded too badly to fight will kill themselves. Articles in the press and tales on the radio of the no-quarter battle raging on Okinawa strengthened the determination of the civilian population. The Americans had shown themselves to be barbarians in Japanese eyes. The barbarians must not triumph over the Japanese people. Americans, who continued to marvel at the deadly fear in which enemy civilians held them, simply did not understand what had happened elsewhere and how effective the Japanese use of the facts had been. Particularly telling were the unthinking dispatch of Japanese bones back to the United States, as souvenirs, and the wholesale bombing of civilian populations. One was repulsive in spirit; the bloody, mangling results of the other were apparent every day. Americans were monsters and death was far preferable to falling into the hands of the monsters....

[By the spring of 1945 the Allies] had Okinawa. They were poised on the front doorstep of Japan. The Japanese had been primed over the past six months to believe that if the Americans conquered Japan the men would be reduced to slavery, the women would suffer unspeakable tortures, and the children would be brought up in foreign ways. The Japanese were not willing to accept that. More and more of them were willing to die instead. Their wish, encouraged by the government with all its might, was that they might die so valiantly and hurt the enemy so much, that he would stop his efforts to kill off the whole population and would give Japan a peace with honor.[11]

On two separate nights I was awakened by moving marines, going to the next barracks, where there was a large radio. We heard news about the dropping of the atom bombs. There were no comments from anyone; there was absolute silence. These were the young marines from Okinawa and Iwo Jima who had seen life and death in its worst dimension. We all felt that this would not erase the memories that would be with us for a lifetime.

Now that the Japs had been brought to their knees, and with the possibility of the war coming to an end, these very teenagers listening to this gratifying and horrible news had a chance to be fathers and grandfathers in their lifetime. We would not become one of the projected million American casualties that would be a blood bath in destroying the Jap disease on their own soil. The *Enola Gay*, a B-29, dropped atom bombs on Hiroshima and Nagasaki in the attempt to end the war. Did this act really kill innocent men, women and children?

Two million Japanese people had lined the streets in Japan paying their respect to the designer of the attack on Pearl Harbor. Maybe some of these same people were from Nagasaki or Hiroshima. Maybe even relatives of the residents of Nagasaki or Hiroshima. Could these supporters of the actions at Pearl Harbor and the bloodshed in the Pacific be considered as innocent people? Were they enemies or just bystanders giving cheers and support for vengeance of Admiral Yamamotos' death? Ask the boys who lost their minds or their bodies on Okinawa and any other Pacific island. Was there a reason to show mercy and stall the end of the war? Was there a reason to give more chances for the Japs to fight to die and to kill innocent young boys in the process?

Innocence was not exclusive to the civilians of Hiroshima and Nagasaki. Young men and boys uniformed their bodies to express the strong beliefs in our peaceful lifestyle. War was not part of our upbringing or nurtured in our culture. As innocent as apple pie, we went to war only because our homes and lifestyle were threatened by a ruthless enemy. Our beliefs were never vacated or abandoned to afford an enemy a foe that glorified a willingness to fight to die.

Our innocence remained with us as part of our soul. Pearl Harbor and all the battles in the Pacific, did not remove this inherent quality of American boys. Brutal American military tactics did not drop the atom bombs. The invitation was given to us on December 7, 1941. There was no dancing and victory yells in our quiet surroundings as the Japs did on their carriers after returning from Pearl Harbor. Who are the innocent? The frantically yelling Jap craze of death and destruction or the young boys from the corner drugstore who put an end to this madness of intended premeditated murder? We did not want to be marines to kill Japs. Our main purpose was to preserve our own freedom. Killing Japs was the means and not the end.

After several days, on August 14, 1945, the unconditional surrender treaty was signed by the Japs on the USS *Missouri*. Then came the cheering, the parades, and the bands. Alone, I sat on the roof of the barracks and saw a fantastic air show celebrating V-J-Day, flying past Diamond Head, Waikiki Beach, Honolulu, and over Pearl Harbor. I was alone and did no cheering. How could I cheer for the friends I lost, the memories in my mind, and the teenage life that would never be? We had been working for more than a month until the early hours of morning, loading ships for invasion of mainland Japan. Now there would be no invasion, and only the thoughts of home were on our minds.

The duty at night at the Officer's Club without glasses started taking its toll. Headaches were with me 24 hours a day. I had to see an eye doctor. The base doctor sent me to the Naval Hospital at AIEA Heights again.

While at AIEA Heights Naval Hospital, overlooking Pearl Harbor, my thoughts began to drift toward home again. The doubts about never seeing home again began to slowly leave my mind. The war was over and so were my combat days. The first attempt to turn back the clock to embrace youth, love, girls, and home life was beginning to appear on the horizon of my thoughts. I began the exciting campaign of making my future full of happiness and joy. My combat experiences and the tragic loss of friends was pushed to second place. Death and destruction were behind me and the future, filled with love, was in front of me.

I spent hours just thinking about, and remembering, the young life I had before the marines. My thoughts began again to embrace my childhood sweetheart, Mary. I began to write her almost daily, pouring out the love and devotion I felt for her. She responded instantly and passionately, expressing mutual feelings. Our bond of innocent youthful love had been rekindled into roaring flames. Our physical reunion was all that remained to bond us to each other forever. I started counting the days and hours until we would finally be together again.

The navy doctors, once again not sympathetic to a young marine, did not really attempt to find the true problem. They washed their inconsiderate hands of me and gave me a ticket to the USA on the USS *Saratoga*. Strong mixed feelings went through my mind because I had been fairly happy at the Officers Club.

So now I begin my journey "back home" to the USA. The aircraft carrier *Saratoga* was known as the "Flying Carpet" because 72 hours was all it needed to go from Pearl Harbor to San Francisco, making many trips back and forth with the wooden decks filled with homeward-bound, happy servicemen.

Excitement left us all sleepless, and any time of the night or day servicemen would be walking back and forth almost in a silent prayer of thankfulness to God for having escaped the jaws of destruction of the diseased Japanese Empire.

Many servicemen would stop and look with awe at the record of victories displayed on the conning tower. This steel lady was busting with pride of her unbelievable feats of victory. But the unappreciative bean counters, who had no feeling for living and breathing, still would express their absence of compassion for the survivors and all the heroes who made the supreme sacrifice by sending her to the bottom of the sea at the Bikini atom bomb test area. All of us who had shared in her glorious moments in life had part of our souls buried with her. What a glorious monument she could have been to remind us all of the gallant victories and to the men who served with her.

The ship heaved to and fro in its 72-hour race to San Francisco. At night, it was possible to imagine the sounds of the aircraft, the firing of her guns, and to hear the men running on the wooden deck. Now only the echoes of these sounds could be heard in a time warp out in the heavens, where the sounds of victory would be embraced forever. Only the beast of mankind would forget that these days, this ship, and these men ever existed.

HOSPITAL TIME, AND THE END OF THE WAR

Time suddenly engulfed our imaginations and San Francisco could be seen on the horizon. The Golden Gate Bridge stretched out like welcoming arms, and the tears of joy would silently say, "We are going home." The Golden Gate Bridge was getting bigger, bigger, and bigger on the horizon. The fog was rising like a curtain on a stage to the Greatest Show on Earth: The USA. Then we were under the Golden Gate Bridge and all eyes were on the antenna on the conning tower. Would it clear the bridge structure? All breathing stopped as the antenna and the bridge structure appeared to be on a collision course. Then, the two metal opponents passed within a few feet of each other. The ship was always confident, never slowing down for any possible misjudgment factor. Everybody started breathing again and all eyes were now looking toward the bay.

Like guests at a surprise party, the docked ships and moving boats of all kinds blew their whistles and horns, welcoming our arrival. Water spraying in the air, boats going by us blowing their horns, gave us all shivers of delights. Goose bumps were a welcome experience. Our long-awaited sounds of appreciation had arrived. Our shouts of happiness we hoped for, could be heard above the sounds of "Thanks."

15

GOING HOME

With "thanks" still sounding in the Bay, we rode a bus to the San Leandro Naval Hospital on the other side of Oakland. The one-story wood-framed hospital was on the crest of picturesque rolling hills. Wards and rooms were joined by long empty hallways that echoed rapidly moving feet in every direction.

There were no pills to take, no X-rays or tests for bodily functions were needed, only interviews by psychologists to find out "why" we were there. My only reason was because I had rejected the insults of a commander back at the Naval Hospital in Hawaii. In my almost three years in the marines, I had developed a resistance to taking shit from anybody. So now I was to be psychoanalyzed and have further studies made of my eye problem. The diagnosis had been made by a naval commander who did not know anything about marines reacting to degrading personal insults. He put this marine in the corner, and I was ready to tear the commander's head off. Evidently he did not know "Fight" was our middle name. His intelligence did not allow him to realize what marines did for a living.

So here I was in beautiful California. Christmas was a few days away, and I was 3,000 miles away from home. No Christmas presents from home this year either.

However, a beautiful family invited me, through the hospital, to their home. This was American hospitality in its finest hour. The day was spent in perfect satisfaction of appetite and a homey atmosphere.

New Year's came and off to Oakland for Sweets' Ballroom for dancing with a new pretty girlfriend, for companionship only. My heart still pounded for my childhood sweetheart at home.

Idle time at the hospital was spent learning to type. The doctor saw no reason to waste time waiting for my discharge, so he granted me with a precious gift: a 30-day furlough at home.

The 30-day furlough did not bring happy hysteria to my mind. Fear, of acceptance, rejection, whatever, overshadowed my enthusiasm. Two years, two Christmases, from home had created a large void in my life, one that would never be filled.

Special fares were given to servicemen, so it was very reasonable to travel by train. The Red Cross loaned me $75 to go home. I expected a gift, but I was lucky to get the loan. I did not make a phone call home, because a $5 phone call was beyond any rational reasoning.

The train was a modern-looking streamliner with comfortable seats to stretch out on. It was 72 hours to Chicago, then a transfer to the New York Central, and sixteen fast hours and I would be home in Rome, NY.

The food on the train, in the dining car was excellent. It was reasonably priced with courteous service. I tried bringing on a bottle of whiskey, for party time aboard, when we stopped in Arizona. The MPs made me smash it on the concrete. Five dollars of precious fun-filled whiskey flowed under the train. I said some mumbled words to the MPs that I hoped they did hear. The train conductor called "All Aboard" and I approached my anticipated pretty partymate with the discouraging news. Our friendship dissipated faster than the whiskey seeped into the ground. I saw in her eyes, "No free booze." A thankless thought from a "cheap date." Dreams of home were more appropriate anyway.

Standing between the cars, hearing the clang of the tracks, gave a feeling of serenity. Who am I? Where am I going? Where have I been? echoed with the rhythm of the guiding railroad tracks. The moon was bright while my mind was dull with loneliness.

I had been part of the biggest show on earth, and no spotlights were ever on me. No applause deafened my cries of why!

The dry desert air rushing past like a vanishing buffalo stampede, I looked and looked for a smiling face. There was none. Maybe I saw the reflection of a broken smile that was mine and only mine. I looked for my future and maybe my dream, but there was none. There was only a train racing in the night while the world could now sleep in peace.

Apprehension was my close companion on the five-day train ride. The only way to sleep was sitting up. Pretty women, attracted to my uniform, afforded me some attention on that boring trip. I felt there would be no one waiting for me at the train station at the end of the trip. No bands, no flags, no cheering crowds. Not even a dog to give a howling welcome. Life seemed as empty as that train station would be. Now I knew I had gone to the wrong war.

The train stopped at the small station, and I stepped onto the empty platform. No goodbyes ... no hellos. No "welcome home" signs. No one there to hand me a refreshing drink, shaking my hand with a heartfelt, "Thanks!" and "Well Done!" The war had been over for five months and had been quickly forgotten. I gave my teenage life for this. Did I get off at the wrong stop? The wrong country? The day I had dreamed of was disappearing with the train, moving fast down the track, blowing its whistle of haunting regrets. I turned and saw the smoke billowing out the factory smokestacks. I saw no war-torn streets, no demolished buildings, and no war-weary people. There were only young, broken hearts returning to an empty station.

A taxi gave me a ride to the corner of my street. I told the taxi cab to stop at the corner so I could walk home. The only thank you I got was for the money I handed him. No free rides for the victims of circumstance!

The street was almost deserted. No kids were playing. No cars were moving. No flags were flying. No bands were playing. Peace and calmness surrounded the streets and houses. No Japs were knocking down our doors and raping our women. Within me I felt proud of "a job well done."

Our home was a real home, with grandfather from my father's side and grandmother from my mother's side living with us. My mother was the best cook in the world, and my grandmother was the most nervous dishwasher that ever lived. Your dish would be extracted for washing as your last morsel was enroute to your mouth. A cousin would find an empty bedroom with a reason to freeload as long as she could.

We had seven bedrooms with 1½ baths, and room for impatient waiting lines for the bathroom in the hallway. Waiting lines at the bathroom doors were part of daily activity. Sometimes, anxious knocks and words of "Hurry up I can't wait" were common.

One telephone was in the front hallway where listening ears were in every adjacent room and an impatient operator always waited for our call. Three neighbors shared our telephone line, so gossip was better than any TV show ever dreamed of being.

The mailman came to our door by foot twice a day and provided newsworthy gossip with every delivery. Life was friendly and homogenized with all of the neighbors.

My father was ambitious and worked seven days a week in his service station. He would have never forgiven me if I had been killed in the marines. He disliked war and the military, especially me in the marines. He wrote me probably three times in three years.

I bounded up the side steps and stood at attention yelling "I am home." My grandfather jumped to his feet with joy, making sounds of utter happiness. My mother, surprised by this reaction, walked into the room, her face lit up like the sunrise when she saw me. Beaming, crying with delight and relief, she held me; her teenage son was home. Goal accomplished; I had brought home a mother's son, alive and well.

My 17-year-old dog, Queenie, had waited for me to come home. My 10-year-old brother, Jerry, was running around with a marine sweatshirt on next to my room where my drums and music were still in place.

Then, upstairs for a bath in the old bathtub. Showers were not in homes during this time period. The Saturday night bath was still the ruling habit.

GOING HOME

The return of 13 million servicemen and women who showered every day would change the Saturday night bath ritual forever.

My mother's special dishes were spaghetti and hot sausage. Next was vegetable soup. With no recipe to follow, each time it seemed to get better and each time I ate too much, making my stomach ache. The pain was ignored by my dancing taste buds. The ultimate in American dishes was apple pie, cheese and milk. Wow! How could I have given that up for over two years? These daily pleasures were worth fighting for. The Japs did not know of this secret weapon. There was a desire to live and love. If the Japs had known, they surely would not have attacked Pearl Harbor. This was their great military blunder.

I stuffed myself with my mother's delightful cooking until my stomach ached and groaned. Now, I was ready for my ultimate dream, a night with my childhood sweetheart.

I bounded to the telephone and called my girlfriend. She would be jubilant to see me. The clock was ticking. My heart was pounding with happiness and joy. I shined my shoes, put on my pleated, starched shirt, and pulled in my waistline and tightened my belt. I was trim and I was sharp. I then put on my ribboned jacket, buckling my large belt. Then I put on my hat at an angle and looked in the full-length mirror. I saw a marine. A proud marine. A survived marine. I was ready for my ultimate in blitzes. I was going to land on my childhood sweetheart's doorstep. Oh you dreamer, you. All my blitzes may not be in victories, but now is the time to go across the street, up the steps, and knock on the door. As she said in her letters, she would be waiting.

Out the front door I went and across the street, making the shortest invasion route in history. The giant white house with its large bay window, where she had watched me in my every boyhood movement, looked like a giant welcome home sign flashing thoughts to me of how good life and God had been to me. I knocked on her door, and her large collie started barking. I knew I was home. The door opened, and there she was, prettier than a picture. I thought of her as an angel on earth, our time had come, we were together again. The door opens and a new life begins.

The moment had arrived. A beautiful smile, just for me, a hug, a kiss, and a pretty little hand fingering my hero ribbons. It was worth all the sacrifices I had made. There would be no more lonely days and nights. My dream would be with me forever now, the nightmares would be in the past. I could go on with life again.

But suddenly, a friendly and verbal mortar fell on me, wounding me forever. My love, my childhood sweetheart, could not see me tonight. "So very sorry, you see, but I already had a date for tonight that I cannot break," she said calmly. The words were like screaming mortars flying at me from all directions. I had come home just to receive the longest lasting and most cruel wound of all. Death at the hands of the enemy would have been better by far than the death dealt by this unbelievably pretty girl. That night destroyed any remaining fiber of confidence I still had. The endless days and nights of feeling ugly began. I felt as though I had committed a horrible crime and hoped that no one would find out. The guilt of being part of a war that had no rewards dominated any feelings that might have been left in my mind. Did my sweetheart know what we really did in the Pacific? Did she believe that we were criminals and disregard the real conditions that we lived with? Did ugly rumors invade her innocent lifestyle, and make her feel that our youth had passed unnoticed, untouched, or even unknown? Did she see what I saw when I looked into the mirror, an old ugly head? There was no reason to smile anymore. There was only a tired old man trapped in the body of a teenager.

The casualties of war were not confined to the battlefield. The fearful society, in disbelief of the reality of war, and the devastation caused by war, rejected the participants and their return to society. Their love for the smiling teenage boys diminished when they never came home. These young minds lay among the dead, but with no body to bury, or mourn over. There was no evidence of the thief that had stolen their young smiles — no witness to bring the criminal to justice. The crime was not even identified or recognized. Like blind knights, these young heroes came marching back home, arms extended for the love that was only for the dead. These casualties would never be counted; no generals, no admirals, would know. Only the physically dead and bleeding counted after all. No one wants to hear how heroes die. It was just another day.

It was time to return to the hospital in San Leandro, California. Ten days of traveling gave less than three weeks at home.

I left home disappointed and rejected by a love I believed existed.

Walking up the long wooden corridors that led to my ward, the pain of loneliness had overtaken my being. As a teenager, I was unable to understand the aftermath, and it began to be more frightening than combat.

The doctor, not experienced in real war, found difficulty in understanding why I was in his hospital.

With a compassion of imagined understanding of war and its effect on teenagers, he wrote a letter of heroic content that could diminish any dialogue or content in the Medal of Honor Award. I was embarrassed and honored. This letter was noted and accompanied my honorable discharge. Now was a time to celebrate! San Francisco, here I come.

I was transferred to marine barracks, Vallejo, California. The duty was great. Marine living at its best. The base, all fired up for reenlistment prospects, gave us special picnics. We picked the spot in the hills and rode horseback out there. A cook with a truck brought us beer, hamburgers, hot dogs, and all the goodies. We had to get the girls. That was no problem. Oh, this marine life was so good.

We had a dining-room where we ate on real china plates with portions of good food on the table just like home.

My duty was escorting dishonored sailors and marines in civilian clothes to the front gate, coaxing them with a loaded shotgun. If any escaped from me, I would have to serve time in the brig until he was caught. No one escaped for the apparent reasons.

We had free bus tickets to San Francisco, and all the pretty young ladies were waiting for young marines on Nob Hill. Cozy little lounges provided an atmosphere of celebration and welcome home. No one insulted our dedication to our country's freedom. They only embraced us and told us how great we were. Maybe they never went to the movies or had the intelligence to realize what was not "fun and games." Then again, maybe there was more fun and gratification in expressing appreciation than giving cold shoulders of indifference. Our rewards were many on Nob Hill. The young ladies in their fur coats gave support to our belief that life was good and our sacrifices had not been in vain.

Returning to the barracks at 2:00 in the morning, carrying (internally) an excessive amount of alcohol, my lack of equilibrium and numbed body produced noises not compatible with sleeping marines. While finding my sack in staggering delight, a voice yelled out, "Knock it off." I replied, yelling with distorted voice, "Who the hell are you?" I reached in my pocket, grabbed a nickel, and threw it in the direction of the voice. I yelled, "Here is a nickel! Call me in the morning!" With numbed ears, I could hear the nickel bounding in the squad room. There was no reply as I collapsed on my sack fully clothed.

Morning came too early for my cobwebbed brain, but guess what? The person I threw the nickel at did not need my nickel to call me in the morning. The voice at 2:00 A.M. was the voice of the 1st Sergeant. Standing at attention in front of him, he read a "polite" riot act, probably laughing inside. He saw the 1st Division patch on my shirt sleeve, and I saw his with the greatest respect. I decided not to throw nickels at first sergeants at 2:00 in the morning. I did not need any more assholes.

Time was vanishing. Ladies were embracing our uniformed bodies. Nob Hill, the doctor, and the marine base had given me a new lease on life.

My day had come to be discharged from the marines. I had fulfilled a dream. I had challenged an impossible task, and I had succeeded. The chance to reenlist and go to China was in front of me. But because of my poor eyesight, I would be treated as a second-class marine with no chance for promotions. Now was the time to go home, find a devoted wife, go to college, become an engineer, have children, and enjoy life. My focus would be on friends, family, and future.

American heroes had made this all possible for me. I would insult their sacrifices if I did anything short of their dreams.

Little did we dream that 88 of our high school chums would not ever come home for a class reunion.

Did we take Prof Cardoff's classroom to the battlefield? Our graduating classes were about 176 per year. Eighty-eight knickered boys in 1938, would not see their 21st birthday. Of the 405,000 killed in World War II, how many never reached their 21st birthday?

Dick Abbott, the Mayor's son, at 16 would have a compartment in a destroyer at the bottom of the Mediterranean as his final resting place. Henessy would die of a heart attack (so the Red Cross said) at 21 while marching on the Batan death march. Art Petinella would die in the Philippines while taking the islands back from the Japs. Eddie Smith would die as a marine on Guadalcanal, bayoneted to death by several Japs. He would receive the Navy Cross for his bravery. Norwood Oper would die of wounds to the head in Africa, while a gunner on a B-26 bomber. He shot down five German planes before sacrificing his life. Jack Dunn, at nineteen, would give up his life on Okinawa.

Another young boy's body would never be found. He was a sailor on an ammunition ship, while I was on Guadalcanal. I heard this deafening explosion in the middle of the night. My mother wrote to me, telling me of the loss. My memory recalled the night, and I fell into temporary grief for realizing the loss of another young schoolmate.

I was home. The war had ended. I was a survivor.

My friends and relatives looked with quizzical stares, wondering where my smiling youth had gone, not knowing I had left it on a Pacific island, hiding in shame and remembered terror.

Their saddened faces would express a "But why?" innocently believing war was not that bad. They all saw the John Wayne movies. But I was a survivor, a product of Prof. Cardoff's and an A+ student, where performance and discipline gave everlasting rewards. Not knowing that surviving could mean the remembering of unwanted happenings, I gave my best with innocent intentions. But I was a survivor for no apparent reason. Maybe there would be a day I could tell unbelievable stories of young boys who died. Maybe I would survive.

16

OKINAWA PLUS FIFTY

Fifty years ago I landed on Blue Beach 2 with the First Marine Division on Okinawa, Japan. Unknown to me, the 9th Division of the Japanese Army had been sent to Formosa, leaving a void in the Okinawa defense. If the 9th Division had stayed, the Battle of Okinawa would have certainly been more bloody and the duration for the final victory may have taken at least another three months. The 9th Division was poised at our landing beaches with strategic locations that would have inflicted loss of life on us that would have weakened our fighting capabilities that were so necessary in assuring a victory against the southern Okinawa Japanese defenses.

The Monday morning quarterback, considering that the 9th Division of the Japanese Army might have remained on Okinawa in its original defensive position, and considering the real amount of manpower that would have needed to gain final victory, would calculate that we were two divisions short. How good God was to us that day April 1, 1945.

Now, 50 years later, I was making another landing on Okinawa. This time not by amphibious tractor, but rather by luxury airliner made possible by the financial support of my son Jim. I was not greeted by bayonet or an exploding shell. Now I was greeted by my grandson, Navy Lt. Matthew Lince.

As we drove from the airport, it was difficult to believe all the prosperity that extended for miles around. "From foxholes to highrises," I kept saying. The journey was a blur of excitement and satisfaction. Tonight I would not have to dig a foxhole to survive, because I would be at the Navy BOQ (Bachelor Officers Quarters) with a complete kitchen, living room, bedroom, luxurious bathroom, TV, stereo music, and maid service. Who said the atom bomb was not necessary to end a war? Or did the atom bomb create a fear in the Japanese that would make them abandon their "code" and their glory of killing as many Americans as possible? The bloodiest victory in the Pacific did not deter the Japanese from their glorious methods of killing. Even though the Japs were defeated, there were no arms raised in surrender. Arms were still throwing grenades and fingers were pulling triggers to the last days.

Now, after 50 years, my grandson and thousands of other young men and women are guaranteeing the peace that was established here 50 years ago. My grandson and I dropped my bags off at the BOQ, then went for pizza and yogurt. Quite a change from C rations and K rations. Then there was Burger

King and MacDonalds. I thought I had never left the USA. But there they were on Okinawa. At MacDonalds, all the employees ran from place to place. Then, on to the commissary that would shame many stores in America. Beautiful paved roads with non-littered streets. Happy people enjoying life. Is this the aftermath of an atom bomb that ended a horrible war? How can any sane thought deny the purpose of the bomb when such a beautiful peaceful life is here today for all to see.

The next day I visited with Kerry Acres at the Kadena USO. She started the ball of recognition rolling and it never stopped. I am so grateful to Kerry.

Retracing my footsteps after 50 years was a satisfying experience. On the Island of Okinawa, there was a living memorial to all of those men and women who sacrificed in their quest for peace. Day by day, hour by hour, I was exalted like a prince of peace. No person or persons asked me how many Japs I had killed, how it felt to be part of a glorious victory, or how it felt to kill a Jap. The personal concentration was how the battle was fought and how we can, as lovers of peace, honor you and show you our appreciation for the sacrifices that were made.

I was not the first American soldier to experience this generosity of spirit on the part of the Japanese. I thought of the example of Charles Byrd, a former navy corpsman form Foley, Alabama. Byrd had been part of a marine patrol from the First Division (to which his platoon was attached) during the action on Okinawa. That patrol discovered a cave full of the bodies of Japanese teenagers, who had blown themselves up with grenades rather than surrender to the Americans. A few survived the explosions and staggered out to meet the patrol, who worked desperately to save them.

Many years later, Charles Byrd initiated some correspondence with officials in Japan in the hope of locating any of those survivors who might still be alive. His efforts resulted in a reunion of six survivors, who wrote the following response to Byrd's letter:

> Fifty years have passed. Thinking of our dear friends, we, at the same time, have been avoiding any recollection of the past. Your highly moral spirit, however, has delivered us the chance to talk about the incident — a long nightmare.
>
> We thank you from our hearts. Now, the burden has finally lessened.
>
> We deeply respect and thank you for giving us your helping hands amid the tragic scene.... It is the greatest relief for us that from now we can pass on to the next generation the importance of peace.

As a remaining survivor of this peace processing event, I prayed that all my happiness could be shared by God's miracle of everlasting life with my fallen buddies and all those that also sacrificed. Their sacrifices should not be ignored by apologizing to the creators of the madness of death and destruction. Only sympathy for their stupidity should be expressed. The atom bomb dropped on Nagasaki and Hiroshima, as well as the fire bombing of Tokyo, was a means to an end to a brutal war. How could we apologize for finding a tool to end the war? Both warring parties should be thankful that the bomb was invented and used. The peaceful life on Okinawa today proves this point without a challenge. Where would Okinawa be today if the Japanese military lifestyle still existed? Still digging holes for glorious battle defense? Still frightening Okinawans into self-destruction?

Among the valuable literature I gathered on this return trip to Okinawa was *An Oral History of the Battle of Okinawa,* a publication of the Okinawan government. This history described the effect of military propaganda on Japanese civilians and its terrible result in Okinawa:

> [The military] hammered the precept of Japan's Military Code of Conduct into the heads of the civilians — that a Japanese should not live to suffer the disgrace of being captured by the enemy. Such indoctrination eventually caused mass suicide by civilians in the battleground, and the military's excessive fears of spies led to the indiscriminate execution of many innocent civilians.
>
> The Battle of Okinawa was the only land warfare involving civilians in Japan during the war. And in such a warfare, defenseless civilians suffer more than the military, as the following figures clearly indicate:

Number of the War-Dead

Japanese Defense Forces	65,908
(regular troops)	
Okinawan conscripts & draftees	29,228
Civilian combat participants	55,246
Other civilians	38,754
Total	122,228

> If the number of those civilians who died from starvation or diseases (mainly from malaria) during and immediately after the battle is added to the civilian deaths cited above, the total is estimated to exceed 150,000, about one fourth of the total population of that time.
>
> Many of those civilians were killed in the southern part of Okinawa, to where remnants of the 23rd Army retreated from the Shuri defense lines....
>
> Although General Mitsuru Ushijima, Commanding General of the 32nd Army, had declared that his forces would make their last stand in Shuri and fight to the last man, he suddenly changed the plan on May 22, ordering the remnants of the units along the Shuri defense lines to retreat to the south.
>
> "We have lost the main strength in the area, but we shall continue to

Okinawan civilians escaping from Okinawa battle. (Courtesy of the Okinawa Prefectural Government.)

fight to the last man with the remaining units assisted by all the able-bodied civilians, as long as there remains a square foot of land unoccupied by the enemy!" he said.

This, in fact, was a declaration that hundreds of thousand[s of] civilians would be killed.

The only purpose of the Japanese forces was to prolong the battle, even for one day, in order to delay the invasion of the mainland, and to give the government enough time to negotiate with the Allied powers for acceptable terms of surrender.

Withdrawal to the south was just a change of positions on the operation map, but, brought about incredible loss of lives of military men and civilians. At the time of the fall of Shuri, the Japanese strength was estimated at some 50,000. The number had been reduced to about 30,000 by the time the troops reached their destinations in the south. Civilians loss was far greater, well exceeding 100,000.[12]

Also in this history were the stories of many civilian survivors, told in

Wounded Okinawan civilian. (Courtesy of the Okinawa Prefectural Government.)

their own words. The sampling that follows only begins to describe the full horror:

Eikichi Shiroma (Male, was 34 at the time of the battle and head of a neighborhood association)

Onaga villagers were hiding in their big family tombs. I asked them if they would let us in, but they said there was no more room and told us to try the next tomb. They said it had probably been reopened only recently to place a new coffin in it.

We decided to do as they had told us to do and opened it. There was new coffin inside as they said, but the body was not in bad condition yet. So we moved the coffin onto an inner altar to make room for us and got inside.

The next day, an old woman about 80 years old came with her three grandchildren. An older boy had a big gash in his shoulder, with worms crawling all over and bloody pus oozing out of it.

They looked really pitiful, so I looked around for a tomb for them to hide in. I found one and opened it. It also had a relatively new coffin. The corpse was only about half-decomposed.

I told them to get inside, but the old lady in turn told two of her grandchildren to get in. She said she had to go back to the cave they had been hiding in before to get some rice and "miso" (bean paste) for soup. She said she would take her granddaughter with her. I said I'd dig up some sweet potatoes for them and told her not to go, but she wouldn't listen and instead asked me to take care of the two children until she came back, then she went away with the girl.

She never came back, even two or three days later. The two kids kept crying in the tomb, calling "Grandma, grandma..."

Koei Kinjo was 14, living at Maehira village during the conflict

I was in this cave about 50 meters east of Maehira. It was only about two tsubo wide (72 sq.ft) inside, but it was packed with 19 people. The place was so crowded and stifling you had to get out now and then to get some fresh air.

One day, an old woman and a younger woman about 35 years old and her two children, one of them about five and the other about three, came near our place. They said they were from Nakagusuku. They'd apparently been forced out of their cave by troops and had no place to go to. They all looked awfully tired. They took refuge under a tall tree near our cave.

Perhaps they were sitting under this tree for two days or so. Then, one day when I got out of the cafe, the two women were dead, perhaps killed by shell fragments. The mother had been hit by a fragment about 20 centimeters in diameter and had a big gash in her ribs. Maybe instantly killed. The old lady had been hit in her temple.

The children were safe. The baby was sucking at her mother's breast, and the older one was leaning against her body. They stayed alive like that for about three days. But when I came out again to relieve myself, I found the kids lying dead beside their mother, soaked in the rain falling all night long. I felt so bad I didn't know what to make of human lives.

Eishun Higa, a man who was 39 living in Nakagusuku village during the battle in 1945.

There was a pond near the road leading to the sugar mill of Itosu village. I saw a woman floating in the water, face down, with her baby on her back. The baby looked about one year old, a girl baby. She was alive, because she was moving her hands and head, though she was not crying. My wife saw this woman and said to me the poor woman was dead. Suddenly, the woman raised herself from the water and said, "I'm not dead, I'm still alive. I was hit by white phosphorus and can't see. Please take my child and adopt her. I'm from Shuri. If you see any friendly troop passing by, ask him to shoot me dead as soon as possible.

I said I couldn't do that and told her to come out of the water and try to survive. But she only said she'd been burnt by white phosphorus and she was in the water because it hurt so much. She said she wanted to die as soon as possible because she had burns all over her body and couldn't even see.

She was saying like that, but then shells started falling everywhere. The bombardment was so intense my wife's younger sister was instantly killed. So we just couldn't take care of that woman. At that time, my children were also exposed to shell blasts. We were all trying desperately to get away... We could do nothing but leave the poor woman behind there....

Toyo Gima, a lady who was 19 and living in Nakagusuku village in 1945.

In Makabe, there was a huge cave called Sennin Go, or One Thousand People Cave (which means it can hold 1,000 people inside). We were hiding in that cave. Only a handful of people there were civilians and the rest were soldiers.

Then Americans attacked the cave with mortar shells. The walls of the entrance were destroyed. The cave was sealed, and we couldn't get out. One of my friends was burned to death there.

So we moved deeper into the cave and lived there for about 20 days. There was enough water to drink there. Many wounded soldiers were staying near the entrance, so they were all killed when the cave was attacked, but other soldiers were safe in the inner part of the cave.

Later, we moved to another cave a little farther away from Sennin Cave. There were many civilians and soldiers in it. It was also a large cave which could house hundreds of people and there were really many people in there. I think there were more civilians than soldiers. It was in this cave that I saw this unbelievable thing.

There was a little boy about four or five years old. He was crying because he couldn't find his mother. The boy was near the entrance of the cave, where there was a hole in the ceiling.

Then, one of the soldiers said if the boy kept crying the enemy would hear him crying and they'd find us. The soldier angrily said someone should take care of the boy and asked if there were his parents in the cave. No one said anything. So they took him deeper into the cave and killed him. There was some light from this hole in the ceiling, so you could see it. They took him inside and tried to strangle him with a triangle bandage, the kind you used for dressing a wound.

I heard one them say the cloth was too thick and they couldn't choke him to death with it. They tore the triangle cloth and made a finer string and strangled him to death with it. All the civilians who saw it were crying. I actually saw them put the string around the boy's neck, but it was so horrible I couldn't watch it to the end....

Touroku Oshiro, a boy then 14, living in Maehira village on Okinawa in 1945.

Only after a certain period of time do we seem to regain genuinely human feeling. Last year, I went there with my children to get Sannin ginger leaves. The sannin plants were in the bush, so I crawled in only by myself. And there I found a pair of leather leggings, the kind the officers wore with their boots. The moment I saw them, I ran away from them. I felt all the more afraid of war, after all those years. In those days, everything was such that you took it as such, for granted. I wanted to tell my children that they should never repeat this thing called "war."[13]

President Harry Truman desperately wanted to end the war soon without another bloodbath like Okinawa. The availability of the atomic bomb gave America a shortcut to victory.

Those of you who believe in apology should go to Okinawa and see what you are apologizing for. To apologize for dropping bombs that stopped death and destruction is insane with shortsighted political rationality.

On Okinawa, there is a lifestyle that maybe is unmatched in any other part of the world: Politeness with honor and respect; horns not blowing in congested traffic; squeezing in and out of traffic with respectful gestures. No blue lights flashing to insult the use of unselfish traffic maneuvers. The way of life seems to control safety practices toward others. There is no need for additional cops to control the insanity of the population. In the family makeup, both civilian and military children are taught family values that last a lifetime. The elderly are valued and happy — not victims of budget-cutting by inconsiderate younger politicians. Centuries of tradition in caring for the elderly and their needs has proven to be the civilized way for a balanced society that does not create the fear of being old. Happiness can be enjoyed to the last days and beyond. Then the Okinawan people take this life-enjoying plan one step further. The sacred care of one's remains after death symbolizes the strong love for one another. Family tradition embraces the remembrance of family members 50 years plus after their death. I was honored to be part of this family tradition in its sacred ritual: A beautiful ceremony in mournful formal dress. The smell of incense, the chant of the priests, the marking of the place to remember, the attention of the media, the presence of dignitaries, the celebration with special foods, the love and respect, with honor given to one another, gave exaltation of a higher form than life to people they intended to never forget.

While all these civilized traditions were taking place, the media in the U.S. found no time to honor the men and women who sacrificed so that we could enjoy the freedom and peace that was given to us.

Even the military did not fly flags at half-mast, nor were there ships at sea honoring those who died so valiantly. Only Major Michael Woodman and I walked the beach that I landed on with many heroes of that day. How much of the national military budget would be needed to have a color guard from every military camp on Okinawa march the length of the landing beaches in honor of those who survived and those who died that day so that many, many millions of people could enjoy peace and freedom?

Where were our minds for remembrance and eyes for focusing on a special day? However void the remembrance day may be, 74 volunteers with no budget were at the Kadena Marina rehearsing for the celebration, a core of dedicated Americans honoring all who died and survived the Okinawa quest for peace. Marine Major Michael Woodman escorted me and drove me up and down, in and out of Okinawa's unmarked streets. With the major's dedication to my emotional desires, we found the actual landing beach I was on 50 years ago this day. Human emotion engulfed my thinking, trying to believe that time did not erase the sound of airplanes overhead, the grinding halt of the amtrac, and the sound of the door opening at the rear of the amphibious tractor. The sound of warships broadside gave a crescendo to one of the greatest battles and to the last battle of World War II. I was there. I was young. I was a marine. My love for home and country ignited my spirit to be victorious on Love Day. Then it was time to go to Burger King and the Marine Museum, magnificently organized and managed by Dave Davenport, a dedicated and appreciative person who was also a veteran from Vietnam. We need more people like Dave to make this world a better place.

Clayton Moore drove me to All Souls Church. Now was the time to pray for the souls of those who departed the days of agony and suffering. At midnight April 1, 1995, the reading of their names would begin. Approximately 243,000 names would be read between April 1, 1995 and June 23, 1995.

All Souls Church of Chatan, Okinawa, would be the scene where Japanese, Okinawans, and Americans would join together in solemn ceremony. The bishop would be an ex-kamikaze pilot. The reverend would be a Japanese-American who was interned with his family in an "enemy" internment camp. His family's property was never regained. After 50 years, differing

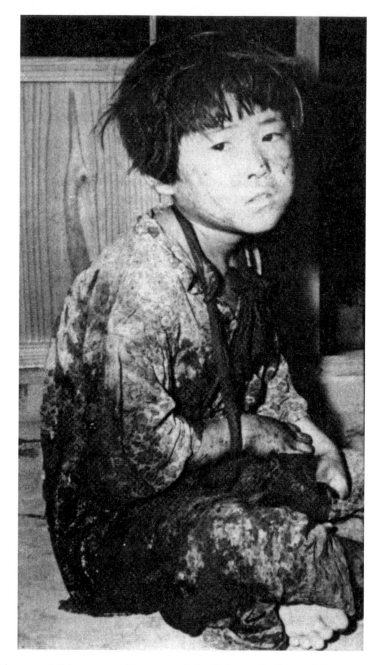

Okinawan child survivor. (Courtesy of the Okinawa Prefectural Government.)

cultures would unite in a common cause of goodness, praying for all those who made the supreme sacrifice so that we and the world would be the bene-factors in the quest for peace. The daily prayers at noon and 7 P.M. would echo throughout the universe and beyond.

They prayed:

> Almighty God who can bring good out of evil and make even human wrath to turn to your praise: We give you heartfelt thanks for blessing us with length of days and the opportunity to observe the Fiftieth Anniver-sary of the Battle of Okinawa. We humbly pray that as we recollect the events of that time, and remember all the souls you will enable us to dis-pose more fully the issues of that war, and become makers of peace. Bring us as peoples of many backgrounds representing many communities of the world into a firmer fellowship for the promotion of your glory and the good of all peoples. We offer this prayer in the love of the God from whom every family in heaven and earth is named, in the grace of God the Savior of the world, and in the fellowship of God the Holy Spirit who leads us into all Truth, now and for ever. Amen.[14]

I prayed, and thought about the grieving Okinawans and their terrible losses. I thought, too, about the American soldiers. I reflected silently on the words of Lt. Col. William Brown (USMC, retired) in an essay distributed that day:

> They probably appear to you like any ordinary group of old people, mostly retirees now, sitting on porch swings or in rocking chairs or wan-dering around malls. They're ordinary parents and grandparents in all respects, save one.
>
> When they were young, they saved the world. No other generation in the history of the world can make that claim... Not the founders of the American Revolution, not the Ancient Greeks or the Romans, not the Baby Boomers, not even the early Christians.
>
> And who were these valiant warriors who secured the blessings of free-dom and liberty for the world back in those dark days? Supermen, Mil-lions of Davids or King Richards or equally well-known historical figures? Hardly. Certainly, that war had its share of legends. But legends don't win wars. Men and women win wars, ordinary people like my brother, two uncles and five cousins: people like your Uncle Roy: or maybe your mother and father.
>
> We need to take a long, loving look at these people now, while we have the chance. If you know any, give them a hug and say "Thanks." No indi-viduals or group have ever matched their achievements. God willing, no one will ever again have to.

Now it was time for dinner. Time for fellowship. Time for family. Time for recognition.

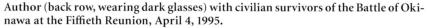

Author (back row, wearing dark glasses) with civilian survivors of the Battle of Okinawa at the Fiffieth Reunion, April 4, 1995.

I felt humbled and honored to be invited to dinners of recognition. It was part of an unknown dream to be so honored. The arrangements were made by Murray Harlan, the spearhead of Okinawa Plus 50 committee with the unending support and interest of Michele Woodman, a mother, a devoted wife, a beautiful lady and a living memorial to the marines who died on Okinawa.

Add to these overwhelming experiences: a Girl Scout meeting with Major Woodman, school play with the Woodman family, family dinners, and more. Then there is enough love and friendship for a lifetime and beyond. My cup runneth over. Maybe this is why D-Day on Okinawa was named Love Day.

The horrifying news to me that over 140,000 Okinawan civilians had perished during the campaign ignited painful memories. I had been involved in accidental civilian casualties and felt strongly about apologizing to the Okinawan people. Fear of the American military generated by the Japanese ignited fear so frightening that the Okinawan civilians destroyed themselves, very often with grenades provided by Japanese soldiers. The Japs were not satisfied with their glory of killing Americans but attempted to create a hatred for the Americans that would last for generations. These methods were not only insanely cruel, but also barbaric in nature. Thousands upon thousands would destroy themselves in caves with a brain-washed terrifying fear. Those who died would never know the true kindness and love of the American soldier. Naming D-Day as Love Day took on a different undeniable meaning. We extended our hands and hearts of love while they hid in frightening terror. What an unmerciful enemy we faced.

I was appalled at hearing the numbers of civilian casualties. I had seen only individual corpses of civilians killed at night by very nervous young marines. Okinawan civilians had come into fields with no fear of our presence. In fact, the only fear I witnessed was when a Jap soldier, disguised as a civilian, started beating the women and children in the field. We instantly removed him as a living peace interrupter. At a nearby village, a marine buddy and I became friends with an elderly man, a young lady with a baby and two children, and another lady. Making three or four trips to their house, we saw no frightened or terrified Okinawan civilians. If they were frightened, it was not apparent. They greeted us when we visited them. What military purpose did the Japanese army gain by brainwashing the Okinawan civilians into destroying themselves? It appears as though the Japanese hated us so much that killing us was not a total satisfaction. The Japanese wanted their hatred of us to continue even after their glorious death. There seems to be no human value. Miwa Saito of the Ryukyu Shimpo Press made my apology possible. She placed my story in her Okinawa newspaper that gave me happiness for a lifetime. I prayed that my personal apology helped soothe the pains of the Okinawan people.

I received my invitation to attend the survivors' ceremony with mixed emotions. I did not know how the Okinawan people would accept me. I was not sure whether to wear my marine hat because it could bring back bad memories. My hat said USMC veteran loud and clear. I felt I should hold my head high with pride, but have humility and sorrow for the Okinawans' tragedy.

As I approached their welcoming tent, I was offered tea. I was choked with emotion. Marine Major Michael Woodman and Michelle, with Miwa Saito and I, started up the grade to the opening of the cave where the ceremony would be held. The line had already formed, so we were about 100 feet from the ceremony. The ceremony began in their language, but the emotion could be felt and the devotion understood.

There I was standing alone among the Okinawans. I tried making eye contact with the men, but they could not look at me. I hoped they did not still have the fear of Americans. Today, we were honoring six survivors and remembering those who had perished in this cave.

Soon Miwa came to me and guided me on a narrow path that led to the prayer ceremony, markers, and priests. Soon we stood before the incense. Three times we picked up the incense and placed it in the burning part of the container. We prayed each time we transferred the incense. I followed Miwa's direction. She was extremely helpful and beautiful. I was so honored that I could not speak. As we returned down the narrowing path, the Okinawans began to bow to me. What a feeling of love to last a lifetime. As I returned their bow, I embraced their hands in great emotion. What a beautiful people they were. I wanted to spend the rest of my life with them. I was hoping I was helping to heal some painful wounds that had lasted for many years. I sat in a chair in mental exhaustion and, as they walked by, they bowed with great dignity. I had to embrace their hands, they were so beautiful. Some of the elderly walked right up to me. I was so honored. Dignitaries from neighboring villages stopped to talk with me. All I could say was that I was very honored to be in their presence. The survivors, dignitaries, and I all stood together while pictures were taken. What a wonderful day this was, all together standing in peace.

As we started to leave, an Okinawan lady gave us all a wrapped assortment of fruit. They were such a kind and loving people; their tragedy 50 years ago was no doubt undeserving. What purpose did their sacrifices provide in the quest for peace? Only God would know.

To cap off my time in Okinawa, I made a trip to Kunishi Ridge and the Peace Park. We made a desperate search for Wana Ridge, Wana Draw, and Dakeshi Ridge. Clayton Moore, my tour guide, had an abundance of energy and a great determination to make my last day a very memorable day. Building and new vegetation hindered our ability to find the exact location of all the important battle scenes that I was at. However, Kunishi Ridge stood out there, forbidding and still revealing the advantage the Japs had in this crucial and bloody battle. I hung my head in silence, thinking of Timothy and Mosher with all the other heroes that defeated the Japs 50 years ago.

This was not only the last battle, but it was the last ridge of World War II. It was appropriate for Clayton Moore to take me to the Peace Park now. Its sprawling beauty of stone, flowers, a tower, and receptive buildings gave notice worldwide that peace was a wonderful environment. The day was dark with clouds, but bright with hope of peace.

Now was the time to leave Okinawa, where peace had been established by young men and women 50 years ago. My grandson took me to the airport, where once again I flew away from Okinawa.

However, this time, as I looked out the airplane's window, I saw no bombing with death and destruction as the act of the day. I left Okinawa not on my way to a naval hospital to be patched up and made ready for the invasion of Japan, but on my way home, to my wife and family. I was going home to peace that was given me 50 years ago by young men and women whom I shall never forget.

APPENDIX A
A MARINE CORPS HISTORY OF THE FIRST MARINE DIVISION ON THE PALAU ISLANDS AND OKINAWA, SEPTEMBER 1944–MAY 1945

BY JOEL D. THACKER, HISTORICAL DIVISION, USMC

On September 15, 1944, the First Division stormed ashore on Peleliu, in the wake of a lengthy Naval and air bombardment. The division met strong opposition from veteran Japanese troops and encountered one of the worst coral reefs since Tarawa. Despite these obstacles, the "First" made a successful landing. Opposition increased as Marines moved inland. The Japs again had taken advantage of every feature of the terrain. They had machine guns concealed in caves, and snipers in the crags and trees. These defensive points inflicted heavy casualties on the advancing Marines.

Japanese mortar shells walked up and down the beach in a bloody procession and enemy artillery churned the water into a dirty, debris-laden froth.

The Japs made three well-organized and determined counter attacks during the afternoon of the first day. The first one hit at the center of Marine lines, then smashed at the left, and finally rallied for one more assault on the center. These attacks were spearheaded by enemy tanks, but most of them were destroyed by U.S. tanks, Bazookas, and anti-tank guns.

At dawn on the second day, Marines began cleaning out enemy caves and pillboxes. They threw bazookas, flame-throwers, mortars, and tanks against the entrenched Japs, but heavy mortar fire, the intense heat, and stiff resistance from concrete fortifications slowed the advance of three Marine regiments.

This second day saw more enemy tanks on the attack. During the morning, seven Jap tanks, attacking a detail of the Division's commissary unit, were knocked out by a Sherman tank and three planes. Shortly after noon, a free-for-all tank battle broke out. Fifteen Jap tanks were knocked out, whereas the Marines lost one of their own.

APPENDIX A

By nightfall, the Peleliu Airfield was in the hands of the First Division. Marines were then in position to assault high ground to the front.

The "First" picked up the attack again on the morning of September 17, lashing out under a cover of Naval gun fire, artillery, and air bombardment.

The day's heavy fighting resulted in the capture of the south part of the island, including the town of Asias and tiny Ngarmoked Island off the southern tip of Peleliu. During the day, the 81st Infantry Division landed on tiny Angaur Island to forestall any move by the Japs to harass the Marines on Peleliu with artillery fire. This landing was supported by Marine heavy artillery placed on Peleliu.

On September 19, at 0700, the "First" again moved to the attack. On the right, the Fifth Regiment advanced rapidly and seized the area of Ngardololok to the northeast, while the first regiment continued its difficult operations against rugged terrain and determined resistance along the west coast.

By September 20, the Fifth Marines had a secure hold on the eastern coast and the First Marines were making slow but steady progress in their sector. During the day, the Seventh Marines moved into position on the right of the First Regiment.

An all out attack by the Fifth Marines completed the seizure of the entire eastern coast on September 21. However, very little progress was made against the ridges along the west coast.

During the afternoon of September 22, advance elements of the 321st Infantry Regiment, 81st Division moved from Angaur to Peleliu to relieve the First Regiment, which had suffered heavy casualties in the bitter fighting on the ridge north of the airfield. After being relieved, the First Marines moved into the area held by the Fifth Regiment. The Fifth was then sent into Division Reserve.

The attack was resumed the morning of September 24, after an intense air and artillery bombardment. The 321st Infantry captured the village of Farekoru and then moved eastward. This advance was slowed by enemy resistance from Kamilianlul Mountain. During the afternoon, a Marine squadron of night-fighting hellcats from the Second Marine Aircraft Wing and a group of transports and patrol planes landed on Peleliu Airfield.

The advance began to roll again on the morning of September 25. The 321st Infantry Regiment reached the ridge line east of Farekoru. Shortly after noon, the First Marines took over the line positions of the Fifth Regiment. The Fifth then passed through the 321st Infantry and launched an attack to the northeast. Then they moved up the west coast of the island and dug in for the night in front of Amiangal Mountain near the northern tip of the island.

By September 26, the Jap defenses on Peleliu had begun to crumble under the terrific pressure applied by our troops. Both the Fifth Marines and the

321st Infantry chalked up new gains. Although the Japs fought desperately, the Fifth Marines captured the hill located about 1,000 yards southwest of Amiangal Mountain and a second height that flanked this mountain on the north.

"Old Glory" was raised in front of the First Marine Division Command Post at 0800 September 27. This was official confirmation of the fact that the situation on Peleliu was "well in hand."

By nightfall, the Fifth Marines had advanced around the northern point of Peleliu, capturing the remainder of the high ground on the northern part of the island. Although the enemy put up a stubborn defense from caves and natural barriers, Marines secured the larger portion of the island, except for a few pockets of resistance that still remained to be wiped out.

On the morning of September 28, the Third Battalion, Fifth Marines, supported by armored LVTS and Sherman tanks, crossed the coral reef along the northern coast of Peleliu and seized Ngesebus Island. Warships, aircraft, and First Division artillery on Peleliu supported the attack. Corsair fighter planes of Marine fighting Squadron 114 covered the landing by strafing the beaches.

Shortly after noon, this small amphibious force had captured the airfield and overcome all enemy resistance on Ngesebus with the exception of one packet on the northwestern tip. Our forces also controlled the adjoining island of Kongauru. A smaller unnamed island nearby was also in our hands. The capture of these islands eliminated the threat of Japanese artillery fire to the Peleliu Airfield.

On September 29, only one pocket of enemy resistance remained — Umurbrogol Mountain (Bloody Nose Ridge). Meanwhile, the Third Battalion, Fifth Marines, completed the mopping up of Ngesebus Island. They were relieved by the 321st Infantry Regiment. Other units of the Fifth Regiment continued blasting the Japs from their last stronghold on the northern tip of Peleliu.

The main assault phase of the Palau Islands operation ended on October 12, 1944, although fanatical Japanese in the remaining pocket of Bloody Nose Ridge continued to offer stubborn resistance. This pocket finally was wiped out on November 27 by elements of the 81st Infantry Division. This Army unit had relieved the First Marine Division during the middle of October. The First Battalion, Seventh Marines, the last unit of the First Division remaining on the lines, was relieved on October 17.

First Marine Division casualties for the period from September 15 to October 14, 1944, were: 842 killed, 4,963 wounded, and 126 missing — a total of 5,931 casualties.

At 0830 on April 1, 1945, the First and Sixth Marine Divisions, Third

Amphibious Corps, and the 24th Army Corps, which made up the newly organized Tenth American Army, began landing on the western coast of Okinawa, largest island of the Ryukyu Island group.

The invasion of Okinawa, the strongest link in the Ryukyu chain that joins Formosa and the Japanese Home Islands, marked the end of the "island hopping" drive against Japan, which had begun at Guadalcanal on August 7, 1942. More than 3,300 miles had been covered and many changes had been made since that memorable date. When the First Division hit the beaches at Guadalcanal, less than 250 planes covered the landing; at Okinawa, more than 1,500 carrier-based aircraft covered the assault.

The Third Amphibious Corps encountered light opposition on the Okinawa landing and even during the early advance inland. The beach area, however, was spotted with strong hill and trench positions.

Within four hours after the landing, the Marines had taken Yontan Airfield and the 24th Army Corps on the right had secured the Kadena Airfield.

The Third Amphibious Corps was commanded by Major General Roy S. Geiger. Major General Pedro A. Del Valle led the First Division and Gen. Shepherd the Sixth Division.

The First Division struck out to the east and, by April 3, had reached the east coast. By the next day, Marines of the Third Amphibious Corps had occupied Katchin Peninsula on the east coast. The Marines stretched their lines across the narrow neck of the island from Yakada on the west coast to Yaka on the east.

After the northern part of Okinawa had been secured by Marines of the Third Amphibious Corps, the First Marine Division (reinforced) was relieved from Tenth Army Reserve and attached to the 24th Army Corps. This came on April 30.

Shortly before daylight on May 2, 1945, 10th Army troops, supported by tanks and flame-throwers, opened a coordinated drive against the fortified positions in Southern Okinawa. The Japs fought back with savage fury.

The Seventh Infantry Division on the east coast bypassed Yonabau Airfield and dropped a deep salient into Jap positions, which extended beyond the southern end of the field. The 77th Infantry Division, reinforced by the First Marine Division, pushed slowly ahead in the central and western sectors, driving toward the island's three major cities, Naha, Shuri, and Yonabaru.

The Japs had massed a tremendous concentration of artillery and mortars. They had installed elaborate machine gun nests in pillboxes, concrete block houses, and reinforced caves. They were prepared for a last-ditch stand.

On May 4, the enemy hurled a vicious counter attack against the American forces. The Japs put into play their tanks, suicide boats, planes, and guided flying bombs.

On the heels of this attack, four amphibious divisions attempted predawn landings behind the American lines. The landings were composed of about 600 men.

Three of these Jap assault units managed to get on the west coast, but were trapped and wiped out.

At dawn, more than 3,000 Jap troops, secured by 20 tanks, attacked Seventh Infantry's positions. The attack came under cover of the enemy's heaviest barrage of the campaign to date. Marine Corps and Army heavy guns smashed the tanks, and Seventh Division Infantrymen blocked the enemy charge in fierce hand-to-hand battles.[15]

As the battle continued the history of the bloodiest battle in the Pacific was etched into the minds of the survivors. Once again the 1st Marine Division played a key role in establishing peace in a world of agony and devastation caused by the Japanese Empire.

From the invisible and eternal halls of honor, young boys and men gave their lives so that the world could live in peace. History, when examined and explored, will expose the might of love, not hate, from these 1st Marine Division heroes.— George Lince

Medal of Honor Men in the First Marine Division

"For conspicuous gallantry and intrepidity at the risk of his life above and beyond the call of duty..."

Major General Alexander A. Vandegrift
Captain Everett P. Pope
Colonel Meritt J. Edson
Major Kenneth D. Bailey
First Lieutenant Carlson R. Rouh
Sergeant Elbert L. Kinser
Sergeant John Basilone
Platoon Sergeant Mitchell Paige
Corporal John P. Fardy
Corporal Louis J. Hauge, Jr.

Corporal Lewis K. Bausell
Private Dale M. Hansen
Private First Class Albert E. Schwab
Private First Class Charles H. Roan
Private First Class Wesley Phelps
Private First Class William A. Foster
Private First Class Richard E. Kraus
Private First Class John D. New
Private First Class (later 2nd Lt.) Arthur J. Jackson

Decorations and Awards

Medal of Honor 19
Navy Cross 71

Distinguished Service Medal 3
Silver Star 395

APPENDIX A

THE SECRETARY OF THE NAVY
WASHINGTON

The President of the United States takes pleasure in presenting the
PRESIDENTIAL UNIT CITATION TO THE

FIRST MARINE DIVISION (REINFORCED)

consisting of FIRST Marine Division; First Amphibian Tractor Battalion, FMF; U.S. Navy Flame Thrower Unit Attached; Sixth Amphibian Tractor Battalion (Provisional), FMF; Third Armored Amphibian Battalion (Provisional), FMF, Detachment Eighth Amphibian Tractor Battalion, FMF; 454 Amphibian Truck Company, U.S. Army; 456th Amphibian Truck Company, U.S. Army; Fourth Joint Assault Signal Company, FMF; Fifth Separate Wire Platoon, FMF; Sixth Separate Wire Platoon, FMF,

for service as set forth in the following

CITATION:

"For extraordinary heroism in action against enemy Japanese forces at Peleliu and Ngesebus from September 15 to 29, 1944. Landing over a treacherous coral reef against hostile mortar and artillery fire, the FIRST Marine Division, Reinforced, seized a narrow, heavily mined beachhead and advanced foot by foot in the face of relentless enfilade fire through rain-forests and mangrove swamps toward the air strip, the key to the enemy defenses of the southern Palaus. Opposed all the way by thoroughly disciplined, veteran Japanese troops heavily entrenched in caves and in reinforced concrete pillboxes which honeycombed the high ground throughout the island, the officers and men of the Division fought with undiminished spirit and courage despite heavy losses, exhausting heat and difficult terrain, seizing and holding a highly strategic air and land base for future operations in the Western Pacific. By their individual acts of heroism, their aggressiveness and their fortitude, the men of the FIRST Marine Division, Reinforced, upheld the highest traditions of the United States Naval Service."

For the President,

Secretary of the Navy

THE SECRETARY OF THE NAVY
WASHINGTON

The President of the United States takes pleasure in presenting the
PRESIDENTIAL UNIT CITATION TO THE

FIRST MARINE DIVISION REINFORCED

consisting of FIRST Marine Division; Fourth Marine War Dog Platoon; Fourth Provisional Rocket Detachment; Fourth Joint Assault Signal Company; Third Amphibian Truck Company; Third Provisional Armored Amphibian Battalion; First Amphibian Tractor Battalion; Eighth Amphibian Tractor Battalion, Detachment, First Platoon, first Bomb Disposal Company; Second Platoon, First Bomb Disposal Company (less First Section); Battery "B," 88th Independent Chemical Mortar Battalion, U.S. Army; Company "B" (less First Platoon), 713th Armored Flame Thrower Battalion, U.S. Army,

for service as set forth in the following

CITATION:

"For the extraordinary heroism in action against enemy Japanese forces during the invasion and capture of Okinawa Shima, Ryukyu Islands, from April 1 to June 21, 1945. Securing its assigned area in the north of Okinawa by a series of lightning advances against stiffening resistance, the FIRST Marine Division, Reinforced, turned southward to drive steadily forward through a formidable system of natural and man-made defenses protecting the main enemy bastion at Shuri Castle. Laying bitter siege to the enemy until the defending garrison was reduced and the elaborate fortifications at Shuri destroyed, these intrepid Marines continued to wage fierce battle as they advanced relentlessly, cutting off the Japanese on Oroku Peninsula and smashing through a series of heavily fortified, mutually supporting ridges extending to the southernmost tip of the island to split the remaining hostile force into two pockets where they annihilated the trapped and savagely resisting enemy. By their valor and tenacity, the officers and men of the FIRST Marine Division, Reinforced, contributed materially to the conquest of Okinawa, and their gallantry in overcoming a fanatic enemy in the face of extraordinary danger and difficulty adds new luster to Marine Corps History and to the traditions of the United State Naval Service."

For the President,

APPENDIX B
DEATHS DURING WORLD WAR II
SERVICE AMONG STUDENTS OF ROME
FREE ACADEMY AND SAINT ALOYSIUS
ACADEMY IN ROME, NEW YORK

I attended Rome Free Academy and had friends and relatives at St. Aloysius, another high school in my hometown.

A note from the Rome, N.Y., Historical Society reads:

> *These American boys attended Rome Free Academy and Saint Aloysis Academy in Rome, New York. Their supreme sacrifice made it possible for all of us to enjoy the freedom that we have today. Let us not forget their honored importance in our lives and to all those who follow their quest for freedom.*

NAME	RANK	BRANCH	DATE WHERE KILLED
Abbott, Richard Paul	Fireman 2nd/C1	US Navy	Tyrrhenian Sea 10/9/43
Abruzzio, Louis James	F/2 C1	US Navy	Pacific 7/23/45
Alder, George J.	Sgt.	Army Tank Destroyer	France 9/3/44
Aiello, Michael A.	PFC	Army	France 1/7/45
Avantini, Carmine	T/Sgt.	USAAF	Sweden 2/9/44
Bates, Clayton E.	Ensign	Navy Flyer	Atlantic Area 1/16/42
Bormann, Lynn G.	T/5	Army	Germany 4/16/45
Brown, C. Naamam (Nin)	PFC	Army	Okinawa 7/30/44
Bryan, William E.	PFC	Army	ParatrooperGermany 3/30/45
Burns, Roger John	S 1/C	Navy	Toyko—No date
Butler, Edward T.	Cpl.	Army	European TO 11/26/43
Buczek, Casimer	PO3	Navy	
Campbell, Norman E.	Pvt.	Army	Germany 12/2/44
Cascarella, Joseph	Pvt.	Army	South Pacific 1/25/43
Catanzaro, Jasper J.	T/Sgt.	Army	Algeria 12/15/43
Cervo, Joseph	Pvt.	Army	European TO 10/1944
Cingranelli, Armand D.	S/Sgt.	USAAF	New Guinea 3/12/44
Crofutt, Eugene	Pvt.	Army	Italy 12/15/43

APPENDIX B

NAME	RANK	BRANCH	DATE WHERE KILLED
Coviello, Michael Joseph	3/C Radioman	Coast Guard	Atlantic 3/9/44
DeLong, Robert G.	PFC	Marines	South Pacific 8/1944
DelVecchio, Orlando F.	2nd Lt.	USAAF	Plane Crash 8/7/44
DeVito, Peter	Pvt.	Army	Germany 3/6/45
Dunn, Jack A.	Pvt.	USMC	Okinawa 6/7/45
Durr, William Joseph	S/1C	Navy	South Pacific 11/10/44
Decristo, Frank J.	S/1C	Navy	Tulagi, Guadalcanal 8/19/42
Edick, Arthur E.	Lt.	USAAF	Pilot Fla. 10/8/43 Plane Crash
Egan, Robert J.	PFC	Army Tank Destroyer	Germany 11/18/44
Ellinger, William Arthur	S/1C	Navy	South Pacific 11/10/44
Enseanat, Gabriel	T/5	Army	Belgium 11/24/44
Espositio, Nicholas	Pvt.	Army Paratrooper	Holland 9/20/44
Eychner, Harley S.	Pvt.	Army	France 10/13/44
Friesz, Arthur R.	Captain	USAAF	Near Troupsburg 11/7/44
Freeman, Clifford	?	?	?
Galluppi, Joseph	Pvt.	Army Quartermaster	European TO 4/28/44
Genovese, Joseph	Pvt.	Army Infantry	Italy 10/7/44
Gorzkowski, Adolph	Gunner's Mate	US Navy	Phil. Navy Yard 4/15/44
Grande, William S.	T/Sgt.	Army Combat Engr.	Cherbourg 6/7/44
Greco, Anthony	S/Sgt.	Army	France 1/24/45
Gruby, Charles H.	Pvt.	Army	Italy 10/10/44
Haggerty, Frances X.	Sgt.	Army	Italy 5/31/44
Hannah, George S.	1st Sgt.	Army	France 8/29/44
Harrington, Donn F.	Lt.	USAAF	Glider Crash — No Date
Holland, Robert E.	Sgt.	USAAF	European TO 2/10/44
Janik, Frank	T/Sgt.	Army	Okinawa 4/29/45
Kraeger, Norbert D.	S/Sgt.	Army	Burma Action 12/8/44
Landers, John J.	PFC	Army	Germany 4/17/45
Long, Harold W.	1st Lt.	USAAF	European TO 5/5 —
Lyke, Ralph	Pvt.	Army	Italy-Truck Accident
Maney, Frederick B.	Pvt.	Army Aircraft Mech.	France 9/23/44
Mannino, John P.	Corporal	Army	Germany 4/9/45
Marsland, John N.	2nd Lt.	USAAF Navy	Atlantic 11/28/43
Megerell, Burton M.	Pvt.	USAAF	Panama — No Date
Miller, Robert Paul	PFC	US Army Infantry	Tupision Campaign 12/24/42
Morat, Darrell W.	PFC	US Army	Italy 1/30/44 — Lee Center

APPENDIX B

NAME	RANK	BRANCH	DATE WHERE KILLED
Mowers, C. Henry	Lt.	USAAF Pilot	Germany 1/24/—
McLean, James G.	2nd Lt.	Army Air Corp.	Pacific Area 3/23/45
Narehood, Joseph L.	Lt.	USAAF Pilot	France — No Date
Orzechowski, Joseph L.	Pvt.	Army	France 12/24/44
Paduch, Theodore	S/Sgt.	USAAF	Germany 8/12/43
Palzer, James D.	Pvt.	Army	France 7/4/44
Pawlowski, Edward	3rd Mate	Navy	At Sea 9/1/42
Pettinelli, Arthur A.	PFC	Army	Luzon 1/15/45
Pinti, Carino Harry	PFC	Army Nat'l Guard	France 9/17/44
Pitts, Hobart E.	S/Sgt.	Army	Germany 3/2/45
Pycior, Frank B.	PFC	Army	France 9/17/44
Rees, William G.	Lt.	USAAF	North Atlantic 2/3/43
Romano, Anthony	Pvt.	Army — Infantry	France 10/21/94
Rossi, Patsy Andrew	S/1C	Navy	Luzon 4/13/45
Szewczyk, Chester C.	PFC	Army	Italy 9/13/43 — Lee Center
Salce, Joseph F.	Pvt.	Army	Germany 3/23/45
Scalero, Tony D.	PFC	Army	Germany 11/18/44
Shacter, Joseph	1st. Lt.	Army	France 7/5/44
Schrider, Karl W.	Pvt.	Army	France 8/31/44
Shepard, Clarence C.	PFC	Army	France 11/17/44
Simons, Leslie James	Pvt.	USMC	Okinawa 6/16/45
Skibitski, Peter B.	Corporal	Army	Holland 10/5/44
Smaldon, James J., Jr.	Corporal	Army	Germany 3/26/45
Smith, Edward L., Jr.	Pvt. 1C	USMC	Solomon Islands 10/9/42
Smith, John Watson	Pvt.	Army	North Africa 8/5/43
Stillman, Myron L. (Mike)	Captain	Army Infantry	Philippines 11/10/44
Swanson, Clarence H.E.	2nd Lt.	USAAF	Denmark 2/20/44
Szur, Stanley A.	Sgt.	Army	Germany 4/8/45
Steczko, Frank J.	Pvt.	Army	12/24/44
Tagliaferri, Vincent J.	Corporal	Army	Marshall Islands 2/20/44
Taylor, Arthur J.	T/Sgt.	Army	Italy 4/15/45
Telesa, Leslie T.	Lt.	Army	Belgium 1/7/45
Thomas, Robert Owen	Sgt.	Army	Germany 4/18/45
Thompson, Murray G.	2nd Lt.	Army	France 11/26/44
Tritsch, F. Arthur	PFC	Army	France 2/1/45
Turner, Kenneth J.	PFC	Army	European TO 12/25/44
Tuthill, Merton C.	Sgt.	USMC	South Pacific 9/14/44
Vertucci, Frank	PFC	Army	Belgium 1/20/45
Vinci, Carl Michael	Mach. Mate 2nd Cl.	Navy	Mediterranean 4/26/44

NAME	RANK	BRANCH	DATE WHERE KILLED
Wales, Leonard H.	Sgt.	Army	Fla. Bus. Accident 9/28/44
Watters, F. Lyle	Captain	USAAF	France 12/9/44
Whitmeyer, Ralph Eugene	F/1C	Navy	Home 5/9/45
Willis, Millard F.	PFC	Army Infantry	Germany 3/2/45
Yaworski, Michael	PFC	Army	North Africa 8/4/43

NOTES

1. Samuel E. Morison, *History of the United States Naval Operations in World War Two, Vol. 3: The Rising Sun in the Pacific* (Boston; Little, Brown, 1948).

2. Frank O. Hough, *The Assault on Pelileu*, Historical Division, Headquarters, United States Marine Corps, 1950.

3. United States Marine Corps, *Victory and Occupation*. United States Marine Corps History.

4. Corporal Andy Poling, United States Marine Corps, *Colonel Ichiki's Last Stand at the Battle of the Tenaru River*.

5. Haruko Taya Cook and Theodore F. Cook, *Japan at War: An Oral History* (New York: New Press, 1992).

6. Hatsuho Naito, *Thunder Gods: The Kamikaze Pilots Tell Their Stories*, trans. by Mayumi Ichikawa (New York: Kodansha, 1989).

7. Henry I. Shaw, *Okinawa, Leatherneck*, April 1995.

8. George C. McMillian, USMC, *The Old Breed*, 1949.

9. Joe Douglas Dogg, "Night Attack on Kunishi Ridge," *Marine Corps Gazette*, April 1985.

10. United States Marine Corps, "The Japs Remember the First Marines,", *Saturday Evening Post*, 1949.

11. Edwin P. Hoyt, *Japan's War: The Great Pacific Conflict* (New York: McGraw-Hill, 1986).

12. *An Oral History of the Battle of Okinawa* (Okinawa: Welfare Department, Okinawa Prefectural Government).

13. *Ibid.*

14. All Souls Episcopal Church, Okinawa.

15. Joel D. Thacker, Historical Division, United States Marine Corps, "The History of the First Marine Division," *Saturday Evening Post*, 1947.

MILITARY HISTORY
OF GEORGE LINCE

Since boyhood George R. Lince had dreamed of serving in the Marine Corps; however, when he turned 17 and attempted to enlist, he was turned down by Marine recruiters because of his poor eyesight. To overcome this hurdle, he registered for the draft, concealing both his true age and his vision problem. Shortly after registering, Lince was assigned to a group of 200 Navy draftees. Before he was inducted into the Navy, however, a Marine officer came to his group asking for volunteers for the Marine Corps. Lince volunteered and was sworn into the Corps.

At boot camp on Parris Island, South Carolina, Lince's poor eyesight was discovered. He was allowed to stay in the Corps but initially was refused combat duty. Instead he was assigned to the Field Music School at Parris Island to become a drummer with the Drum and Bugle Corps.

At his request Lince was eventually transferred to the Infantry. After training at Camp Lejeune, North Carolina, and Camp Pendleton, California, Lince was assigned to the 1st Marine Division in the Solomon Islands. He was an assistant Browning Automatic rifleman with A Company, 1st Battalion, 7th Marines. Over time, and after more training on Guadalcanal, he also took on responsibilities as a flame thrower, bazooka team member, demolitionist and at night, a machine gunner to deter Japanese attacks on the front lines.

In April 1945, Lince participated in the battle of Okinawa. In Central Okinawa he was part of a machine gunner team. During the intensive battle for Southern Okinawa he was a stretcher bearer and carried ammunition, food and water to the front lines.

On June 7 Lince received minor shrapnel wounds. These wounds, coupled with the loss of his eyeglasses, terminated his combat activity. He was sent to naval hospitals on Guam, Hawaii and California and was recovering in Hawaii when World War II ended.

Lince later joined the Marine Active Reserve in Syracuse, New York. In August 1950 he was called to active duty in Korea.

Lince completed his tour of duty at Camp Pendleton, California, and received an honorable discharge from the Marine Corps.

INDEX

INDEX

INDEX

INDEX